Political Inquiry:
The Nature and Uses
of Survey Research

Political Inquiry:

The Nature and Uses

of Survey Research

Herbert McClosky

DEPARTMENT OF POLITICAL SCIENCE AND
SURVEY RESEARCH CENTER
UNIVERSITY OF CALIFORNIA
BERKELEY

The Macmillan Company
Collier-Macmillan Limited, London

To Mitzi

Preface

This volume is directed to readers who wish to learn why, in what way, and to what effect political scientists employ survey research as a method of inquiry. It is not a research manual or "how-to" book and does not aim to convert the novice into a skilled survey investigator. For the reader who wants to acquire technical information about survey sampling, questionnaire construction, scaling, index formation, interviewing, coding, data processing, multivariate analysis, and other ingredients of survey methodology, a number of excellent works are available. Some of these works are included in the bibliography.

Although the present volume touches here and there on questions of survey technology, it primarily seeks to explore the contributions of the survey method to political inquiry, the assumptions underlying its use in the study of politics, and the arguments for and against employing surveys to investigate various political phenomena. Attention is also given to the role of surveys in helping to transform political science from a predominantly documentary, legalistic, and discursive field into a more systematic, empirical discipline.

By way of illustrating the principles, pitfalls, and utility of survey research, a large portion of this volume is devoted to the substantive contributions surveys have made to our understanding of politics. Chapter 1, the primary document of the book, contains a review and evaluation of survey research findings on such topics as public opinion, participation, voting, leadership, extreme belief, political socialization, personality and politics, comparative political institutions, political stability, and internal party politics.

The two chapters that follow—one on foreign-policy attitudes, the other on the social-psychological aspects of anomic belief and alienation—are, in substance, research monographs that grew out of a series of omnibus political surveys on the beliefs and activities of political leaders and voters. These papers are included partly because they illustrate the application of survey methods to problems that could not have been investigated systematically before the development of surveys. I have, in addition, chosen these monographs rather than others we have completed because they nicely illustrate the possibility of using surveys for explanatory and theoretical, as well as descriptive, purposes. Assuming their conclusions are warranted, both demonstrate that surveys need not be confined to mere data collection or superficial description, but can be employed to test theories and to analyze complex belief systems and behaviors. Both testify that survey studies need not be restricted to simple questions and answers, but can draw on the more subtle and sophisticated scaling procedures of clinical psychology to assess the attitudes and personalities of respondents. Indeed, by using a number of scales in a given political survey, we have attained detailed profiles of the attitude and personality as well as the social, political, and personal characteristics of thousands of respondents ranging from the most actively involved to the most apathetic and alienated. Chapters 2 and 3 report some of the findings resulting from a comparison of these profiles and test some theoretical notions about foreign-policy beliefs, feelings of malaise, and other politically relevant attitudes.

The three essays that compose this volume have appeared previously in other publications. Except for a few minor stylistic and bibliographic alterations, they are reproduced here without change. I am extremely grateful to Charles Y. Glock, Orville G. Brim, Jr., and the Russell Sage Foundation for permission to reprint my monograph on "Survey Research in Political Science"; to the *American Sociological Review* and to my coauthor, John H. Schaar, for permission to reprint the paper on "Psychological Dimensions of Anomy"; and to James N. Rosenau, the Princeton Center of International Studies, and The Free Press for permission to reprint my monograph on "Personality and Attitude Correlates of Foreign Policy Orientation."

For my wife, children, and research assistants (Jack Citrin, Eugene Bardach, Paul Sniderman, David Elkins, Shannon Ferguson, and Carol Wallin), who tolerated and assisted my frantic efforts to meet the deadlines set for each of these manuscripts at the time of their original publication, I bear not only gratitude but admiration.

H. McC.

Contents

CHAPTER 1

Survey Research in Political Science

The application of survey methods to the study of politics is approximately as old as the study of political behavior. Although they refer to different things—one is a technique for gathering data while the other is an intellectual orientation toward a field of study—the progress of the one has promoted the advancement of the other. Within two decades the survey method has become the most important research procedure in the "behavioral" study of politics, and is being increasingly adopted by "non-behaviorists" as well.

The growing reliance upon survey analysis in political science is one aspect of a pervasive change that has been transforming the study of politics for the past two decades. Traditionally a discipline concerned mainly with legal, institutional, historical, and normative questions, political science has been shifting its focus toward such phenomena as role, process, group, personality, ideology, elites, political recruitment, socialization, social stratification, mobility, function, political stability, decision-making, and political change. Whereas traditional political science has relied principally upon documentary sources, reportage, anecdotal data, subjective and unsystematic observation, individual interpretations, narrative treatment, and the philosophical examination of analytical and normative statements, the behavioral study of politics has stressed direct observation, objective measurement, systematic data collection, the operationalizing of concepts, quantification, a deliberate search for regularities and variations, and systematic comparison across groups and cultures in an effort to ascertain the limits of generalization. The new political science also differs from the old in being interested in classes of phenomena rather than in individual or unique events and institutions.

Political science journals now contain articles on community power and decision-making; functional analyses of political systems; legislative roll calls and constituency characteristics; mathematical analyses of choice behavior; experiments in leadership, influence, communication, and conformity; clinical studies of the relations between personality and attitudes; applications of game theory to international phenomena; simulation studies of international or organizational processes; psychoanalytic studies of renowned political leaders; and studies of the political impact of the mass media. As these topics suggest, political scientists are drawing on the same research

Reprinted, with permission, from *Survey Research in the Social Sciences,* ed. by C. Y. Glock, Russell Sage Foundation, New York, 1967, 63–143.

techniques employed by the other social sciences: laboratory experiments, surveys, participant observation, clinical and attitude testing, case studies (both of individuals and institutions), content analysis, mathematical models, game theory, systems analysis, macro-studies of the informal and formal features of political communities, simulation studies, and so forth. Not all of these are equally useful to political science, and none of them has so far displaced documentary or institutional studies as the prevailing mode of inquiry; but the proportion is rapidly changing and the trend is unmistakable.

Among the new research techniques employed by political scientists, survey research is perhaps the most common and, up to now, the most useful. Surveys are now being used in almost every branch of political science and, in some areas of inquiry, such as voting, they have become virtually the exclusive method of investigation. Although voting is a form of political behavior that is especially amenable to survey research, survey procedures can be adapted to a wide range and variety of political activities.

In the pages that follow, we first set forth the nature and types of surveys, the different ways in which surveys may be used, variations in the design and purpose of surveys, and the multiple objectives that the survey method can serve. In the second section, we examine the ways in which surveys help to promote the scientific study of politics by forcing improvements in the rigor of research procedures, the quality of measures, and the techniques for certifying facts. The third section reviews the major survey research findings on such topics as public opinion, political participation, voting, political socialization, psychological aspects of politics, political change, and comparative politics. In the fourth section, we consider the potential application of surveys to subjects that have so far been little explored, such as political leadership, internal party affairs, the relation of political belief to action, and historical and trend analysis. In the fifth section, we examine the contribution of surveys to political theory, including the modifications that are being suggested in theories about democracy, parties, and extreme belief and affiliation. Finally, we address some of the limitations and problems that beset the survey method, and some of the criticisms aimed at the use of surveys to study politics.

Nature and Types of Surveys

A survey may be defined as any procedure in which data are systematically collected from a population, or a sample thereof, through some form of direct solicitation, such as face-to-face interviews, telephone interviews, or mail questionnaires. Surveys, of course, are not the only devices political scientists can use to collect systematic data on populations. They can also consult ecological reports for information on consumption, industrialization, and other indices of "modernization"; state and county publications for aggregative data on party registration and voting preferences; or census and other government reports for figures on population changes, income levels, and number and size of voting districts. The utility of these sources, however, is severely limited. Aggregative data, for example, can tell us little about the political attitudes and motivations of the population or its sub-groups; official election returns can furnish only a crude estimate of which groups have voted for whom;[1] and comparisons of gross voting figures in various elections cannot specify which voters have shifted their candidate or party preference from one election to the next. These and scores of similar questions can usually be answered only through surveys. Surveys can, of course, be justified "only when the desired information cannot be obtained more easily and less expensively from other sources."[2]

The survey investigator may be interested in the individuals or groups who compose his "sample" not for themselves but for what they "represent." Usually, in fact, he selects people who collectively possess in miniature the same characteristics as the "universe" of persons he wishes to investigate. That universe may be the adult population of the entire nation or of a smaller unit. It may consist of active party members, political office holders, or some other special group, such as state legislators, judges, or young people attending high school. There is no inherent restriction on either the size or composition of the universe. These are determined by the investigator's interest, and by the questions he wishes to answer. The universe may be small enough to permit the investigator to interview all of its members (this would be the case, for example, if one were doing a survey of national committeemen of the American parties); or it may be so large and geographically far-flung that the sample selected for study will number only a tiny fraction of the whole. Not all samples employed in political studies need to be representative in the sense of being cross-section miniatures of the general population; ordinarily they need only to mirror the characteristics of the particular universe being studied. A cross-section sample of the general population is essential only if one is actually investigating the general population. If one is studying political leaders, it would be wasteful to draw a sample of the general population in order to cull the small number of leaders to be found among them.

The accuracy with which a sample reflects the characteristics of the universe, and the number and type of characteristics represented in the sample, can vary somewhat with the nature of the inquiry. In general, a sample must more perfectly reflect the characteristics of the universe being studied if the investigator wishes to describe that universe than if his main

---

[1] Robinson, W. S., "Ecological Correlation and the Behavior of Individuals," *American Sociological Review*, Vol. 15, June, 1950, pp. 351–357; and Ranney, Austin, "The Utility and Limitations of Aggregate Data in the Study of Electoral Data," in *Essays on the Behavioral Study of Politics*. Edited by Austin Ranney. University of Illinois Press, Urbana, 1962, pp. 91–102, at p. 91.

[2] Campbell, Angus, and George Katona, "The Sample Survey: A Technique for Social Science Research," in *Research Methods in the Behavioral Sciences*. Edited by Leon Festinger and Daniel Katz. Dryden Press, New York, 1953, p. 16.

concern is to discover or test relationships among variables. A scholar seeking to ascertain the number of Democratic voters in the general population will need a sample whose characteristics approximate quite closely those of the general population itself. This requirement becomes still more urgent if he also intends to predict the magnitude of the Democratic vote in an election, for even a small misrepresentation in the sample may lead to an erroneous forecast of the outcome. If, however, he is seeking to discover what the approximate correlation is between, say, belief in democracy and personality characteristics, he may be able to get by with a less perfect sample, for the correlation between these variables is not likely to be severely altered by the over-representation of certain groups—providing, of course, the distortion is not large.

Fulfilling the requirements of representative sampling may in some political studies be hindered by the fact that the characteristics of the universe are not known, and no practicable procedure may be available for ascertaining them. For example, no adequate description of the universe of persons active in politics is presently available, and an investigator who wishes to sample this universe cannot be certain that he has achieved an appropriate likeness. In such cases he may attempt to reduce systematic bias and undesired over-representation by casting a wide net and drawing his sample from many party units at different levels of activity in widely separated localities. Given sufficient funds, he might also employ a procedure known as "double sampling," in which a preliminary survey would first be carried out merely to locate and learn the characteristics of the party actives throughout the nation—merely, in other words, to determine the nature of the universe to be sampled.

The discovery that one can, by scientific sampling, reproduce in miniature and with remarkable accuracy the characteristics of a given universe is the *sine qua non* of the survey procedure, and holds out immense opportunities for the study of politics. Since political science is concerned with institutional and group phenomena involving thousands or even millions of people, procedures are needed for making the observation of such multitudes manageable. Without sampling, the study even of a local election, or of special groups such as Negroes, farmers, and political leaders, would require countless observations of many thousands of people. Through sampling, however, these and dozens of other groups can be reproduced in miniature, reduced to manageable proportions, and studied directly, closely, and in detail. The potential value of this procedure is incalculable, for it has now become possible simultaneously to study one or many political sub-cultures, to collect detailed information on millions of people by sampling only one or two thousand of them, to gather evidence systematically on a large number of questions and hypotheses and, by virtue of these possibilities, to advance the scientific study of politics in a way that could not have been imagined even fifty years ago.

Before the development of survey methods and scientific sampling, the political analysis of mass responses rested upon the observational skills and intuition of the individual investigator. He was often compelled to gather evidence on a hit or miss basis, relying on published articles or books, on such letters or diaries as he could find, and on discussions with persons whose opinions seemed to him worthwhile. Whether the political responses yielded by these sources were truly representative of a larger universe or were opinions unique to the individuals who expressed them was rarely known. Generalizations about slave owners or debtors or Northerners or those who voted for Woodrow Wilson were, as a result, inadequately grounded and lacking in warranty. As retrospective empirical studies of past elections and other political events indicate, many historical inferences formerly regarded as "settled" turn out, in the light of contemporary survey knowledge, to be suspect.[3] They reflect not only the biases of the investigator, but the fortuitous character of his data-gathering procedures.

With the aid of surveys, some of these difficulties can now be mitigated. In principle, we can accurately compare and contrast individuals and groups from every part of the society, occupants of every kind of political role, persons or groups holding every type of political belief, political leaders and followers, Northerners and Southerners, Democrats and Republicans, rich and poor, debtors and creditors, supporters and opponents of various public policies, and every combination of these that interests us. We are thus able to test generalizations that until now have been loosely grounded in impressions gathered from anecdotal and other unsystematic evidence. This potentiality is essential for the development of a scientific understanding of politics.

Survey methods can be used in the comparative study of institutions, nations, and political practices as well as in the study of individuals and groups. One might, for example, discover much about the practices of bureaucratic agencies by surveying samples of their officials. One might learn how their decisions are actually made, whether their procedures differ according to the size of the agency, the degree of "modernization," and the types of training received by their functionaries, how they relate in practice to the legislative branches, and whether executive policies are in fact dominated by permanent civil servants. Comparable studies could be done on the institutional practices of judicial bodies, legislatures, or political parties—all with a degree of scientific refinement rarely possible heretofore.

Just as political surveys differ in the types of universes they investigate, so do they also vary in their design and purpose. The term "survey" usually conjures up the image of an interviewer canvassing house to house, asking direct opinion questions and receiving direct answers. While this is the classic pattern of the public opinion poll, many other kinds of political surveys

---

[3] Truman, D. B., "Research in Political Behavior," *American Political Science Review,* Vol. 46, December, 1952, pp. 1003–1006.

are possible. The primary concern of some surveys has been to describe the beliefs of the general population or certain of its segments, while others have sought to test hypotheses and to investigate the relations among variables. Some have used randomly drawn samples, while others have deliberately over-sampled certain groups in order to study them more closely. Some have merely ascertained surface opinions, while others have probed deeply into the underlying attitude structure and personality characteristics of the respondents. Some have focused upon beliefs and others upon actions, some upon opinion-makers and others upon opinion-consumers. Most surveys have been one-shot affairs, collecting all of their data at a single point in time, but others have employed a "panel" of respondents who are interviewed and reinterviewed at different points in time in order to assess their shifts in opinion and party preference, or their response to changing political events.

The adaptability of the survey method is also illustrated by the range of subjects to which surveys may be addressed. They can, for example, be employed either for omnibus political studies or for studies that are narrowly restricted in subject matter. An investigator may be interested in a single political outcome, such as voting turnout, but if he is to explore adequately even this one variable, he will need information on many different kinds of people. He will require samples of regular voters, occasional voters, and non-voters, and on each of these he will doubtless want information on their group, psychological, political, and intellectual characteristics. He can collect such data in a single survey, and can use the results to explore his respondents' behavior either intensively or extensively. He can use the information yielded by the survey to construct indices and scales that will permit him to examine, from various points of view and with considerable thoroughness and refinement, the relationships in which he is interested. Although a survey utilizing large samples may seem an uneconomical way to collect data on a single dependent variable, it often turns out to be the most efficient and economical method possible. Among the most striking examples of this are the handful of large-scale voting surveys that have in three decades taught us more about the act of voting than was learned in all previous history.[4] These survey studies have shown that even the apparently simple act of voting is in reality the behavioral manifestation of extraordinarily complex forces.

Surveys offer the further advantage of furnishing information simultaneously on more than one set of dependent and independent variables. A survey that is primarily focused on voting can also collect information on a number of related behaviors, any one of which may be treated as a dependent

[4] Lazarsfeld, P. F., B. R. Berelson, and Hazel Gaudet, *The People's Choice:* How the Voter Makes up his Mind in a Presidential Campaign. Duell, Sloan, and Pearce, New York, 1944; Berelson, B. R., P. F. Lazarsfeld, and W. W. McPhee, *Voting:* A Study of Opinion Formation in a Presidential Campaign. Chicago University Press, Chicago, 1954; Campbell, Angus, *et al., The American Voter.* John Wiley & Sons, New York, 1960.

variable and explored in its own right. Party affiliation, level of political participation, and political ideology may, in relation to voting, be considered as independent variables; but from other perspectives they can obviously be treated as dependent variables. A large-scale survey that measures and collects data on many dimensions at once permits the investigator an extraordinary measure of flexibility not only in the manipulation of variables but in the selection of hypotheses he may wish to test. He can observe the same dimension from different perspectives and he can control or vary particular factors so that their relation to certain behavioral outcomes can be assessed more precisely.

Omnibus surveys also permit the investigator to undertake new lines of inquiry or even new studies that were not expressly provided for in the original design. If certain lines of analysis prove fruitless, the investigator often has on hand the information he needs to shift the direction of the inquiry and to test alternative explanations. Every survey of any magnitude contains far more data than the original investigator is likely to use. Indeed, recent scholarship has shown that survey data can often be exploited by investigators who had nothing to do with the original study but who find that it contains information they can readily adapt to their own inquiries. Secondary analysis of the data accumulated by opinion polls has often provided more significant results than were yielded by the initial analysis.

The impression is common, though erroneous, that political surveys have been used almost exclusively to assess public opinion. Although political surveys began as opinion polls, public opinion is only one of many subjects to which they are now addressed. Surveys are being adapted to almost every area of political study and to many different types of problems. They have been used to skim off the opinions of respondents and to interview them in depth, focusing intensively on certain aspects of behavior or on complex systems of belief. While surveys, of course, cannot usually investigate these matters as thoroughly as they can be explored in repeated psychiatric interviews, they can employ clinical personality keys, attitude scales, and other sophisticated measuring devices to achieve a fairly detailed profile of the personality and attitude characteristics of respondents.

Flexibility is also possible in the design of the survey questionnaire and procedure. The questionnaire may be open-ended or focused, loosely or highly structured, intensive or extensive, probing or concerned with surface responses, addressed to a single question or to many questions. It may, in its level of language and conceptualization, be fashioned either for particular classes of people or for people of many different kinds. The procedure may consist entirely of face-to-face interviews, telephone interviews, mail questionnaires, questionnaires delivered by interviewers that are self-administered by respondents and then returned by mail (or alternatively picked up, when completed, by interviewers), or some combination of these. Each method has its advantages and disadvantages.

Survey Methods and the Science of Politics

Reliance upon surveys in political science roughly coincides with the emergence of the behavioral emphasis and the growing desire to make the study of politics more scientific. By tradition a documentary, discursive, and intuitive discipline, political science has compiled vast amounts of information on political institutions and practices and has furnished legal, moral, and philosophical criticism of great value to statecraft. Inspired by the examples of the major political philosophers—Aristotle, Plato, Hobbes, Locke, Machiavelli, Rousseau, *et al.*—students of politics have produced instructive essays on such philosophic and speculative subjects as the nature of political obligation, the optimal balance between order and political freedom, the moral presuppositions of democracy, and the relation of the state to human nature.

Nevertheless, political scientists have characteristically neglected certain practices that distinguish scientific enquiry from other forms of observation, particularly the effort to accrete and link up data in a way that will yield a unified body of principles. A science aims to fashion a coherent structure of knowledge, in which each empirical proposition is systematically and consistently connected with the rest, and all facts can in principle be "explained." It approaches phenomena not as idiosyncratic events but as instances of a class whose regularities and variations can in principle be mapped and assessed. To accomplish this, it must employ rigorous methods for verifying the status of "facts" and for testing the validity of its explanations. It must develop procedures for discovering and correcting its own errors, and it must be prepared to abandon theories or explanations, no matter how cherished, that conflict with the evidence. A science grows by a cumulative process in which certain observations can be regarded as "settled" and new efforts can be devoted to studies at the margins of what is already "known." The value of achieving a cumulative discipline can scarcely be overestimated. In contrast to the discursive forms of inquiry, it promotes an economy of effort, for the same problems do not need in each instance to be restudied or approached as though for the first time. Instead, they can be understood as aspects of familiar problems whose nature has in part already been fathomed. An investigator can proceed step by step, from the known to the unknown, linking each new finding to the body of established knowledge. In this way, the progress of a discipline can be greatly accelerated, for the potential acquisition of new knowledge expands exponentially as the perimeters of what has been established grow continually larger. This accelerating capacity is one of the most remarkable features of the natural sciences, and lies at the heart of the modern scientific and industrial "explosion." The comparative backwardness of the social and humanistic disciplines can in part be traced to their slowness in adopting methods for systematic, cumulative research.

The attainment of a scientific form of social inquiry partly depends on the desire to achieve it; but it also depends on the "state of the art," on the availability of appropriate techniques and opportunities for conducting rigorous empirical research. One needs not only reliable and valid measures for appraising potentially relevant factors, but also analytic and statistical devices for observing, manipulating, and testing the influence of variables. One likewise requires procedures for expressing data in quantitative form so that they may be handled statistically. Failing these, one is compelled to fall back upon inexact descriptions and comparisons ("more than," "less than," "for the most part," " in most instances"), and one can assess only vaguely the impact of a given factor on a given outcome.

The scientific study of politics is designed to uncover, observe, and explain certain regularities and variations in political phenomena. To do this well, an investigator must aim to achieve maximum objectivity and precision. He is obliged to reveal his assumptions, to state his hypotheses explicitly, and to employ his data in a manner that will most rigorously test his claims. He must also make his constructs "operational" so that he can assess their validity (i.e., their ability to measure what he says they are measuring) and ascertain their effects precisely. Failure to operationalize concepts tempts the investigator to substitute metaphorical for exact language, to claim objective warranty for what are only subjective impressions, and to perpetuate errors that, under more rigorous definitions, might quickly be flushed out and corrected. Scholars who seek to build upon work done by scientific procedures know what has and has not been confirmed, and are less likely to be diverted into blind alleys and wasted efforts by the false information, misleading claims, or unwarranted inferences of their predecessors. Behavioral scientists therefore place great emphasis on the methods employed to verify explanations. By their standards, it is no longer sufficient for a theory or explanation to be persuasive, elegant, aesthetic, interesting, or brilliant; it must also be valid. An explanation is accepted or rejected depending upon its ability to account for the evidence and to meet the most critical statistical tests. Unlike the intuitive scholar who argues his thesis in persuasive essays, the behavioral scientist takes special pains to erect barriers against his own biases and convictions. He conducts his research in a conscious, deliberate manner that reveals rather than obscures the structure of the research design, the nature of the procedures employed, and the strength and consistency of the findings. His ultimate aim is to achieve a body of systematic theory adequate to explain political phenomena of the broadest possible range and variety.[5]

[5] Dahl, R. A., "The Behavioral Approach in Political Science: Epitaph for a Monument to a Successful Protest," *American Political Science Review,* Vol. 55, December, 1961, pp. 763–772; Kirkpatrick, E. M., "The impact of the Behavioral Approach on Traditional Political Science," in *Essays on the Behavioral Study of Politics.* Edited by Austin Ranney, *op. cit.,* pp. 24–25; and Alpert, Harry, "Public Opinion Research as Science," *Public Opinion Quarterly,* Vol. 20, Fall, 1956, pp. 493–500, at pp. 495–497.

Among the procedures so far available for achieving a science of politics, the survey has been the most useful. The magnitude of its contribution can be gleaned from a summary of the ways in which it serves the several important requirements of science.

Establishing the Facts

The initial function of a political survey is to collect and certify the facts. What do voters believe about the candidates? What are their opinions of issues? Do individuals at different levels of the society differ in their political attitudes? Before surveys came into use, even such simple questions often could not be answered accurately, or the accuracy of the answer could not be certified by reference to an objective procedure.

The ability to establish the facts is, of course, a *sine qua non* of any scholarly field of inquiry. Yet traditional political and historical studies have tended to pay less attention than they should to the task of certifying the evidence needed to confirm their conclusions. Many of their claims, therefore, are intuitive or conjectural rather than factual—the products of partial, anecdotal, and haphazard observation. They are given, for example, to infer a nation's climate of opinion from a relatively small number of books, articles, speeches, editorials, or legislative acts. They are likely to take isolated events—a demonstration, a violent incident, a sharp conflict, a protest by a vociferous group—as signifying major trends in political belief and preference. When one observes political phenomena anecdotally, one's eye is drawn to whatever is dramatic and exciting, which means, often, to whatever is idiosyncratic and atypical. The tendency to overstress the unusual and to ignore the everyday occurrence or the modal opinion is characteristic not only of journalists but also of scholars who fail to adopt rigorous research techniques.

The habit of generalizing from mere impressions or isolated instances may still be observed in current social and political analysis. Contemporary writing, for example, is ridden with assertions that modern man is alienated, conformist, escaping from freedom, frustrated about his status, other-directed, psychologically disoriented by reason of rapid social mobility, class conscious, hungry for meaning, overwhelmed by a debilitating sense of aimlessness and drift, bothered by conflicting norms and frantic for guidance, separated from meaningful work, oppressed by mechanization, and de-humanized by the anonymities of mass society. I cite these not to contest their validity but only to observe that the facts they allege have not been adequately established and that the magnitude and pervasiveness of the conditions they profess to find have rarely been investigated by their proponents in the thorough, empirical, systematic manner they deserve. Yet many of the facts needed to assess the warranty of such allegations are accessible through survey methods. One can use surveys to map a range and variety of responses bearing on these matters. In place of sweeping generalizations about modern man's anxiety or aimlessness or conformity, one might substitute fairly precise estimates of the frequency and extent of these states. Exactly what proportion of men and women feel this way? Do the old exhibit these responses more than the young? The uneducated more than the educated? Workers more than managers? Rural residents more than urban residents? Non-believers more than those who attend church? Persons in conflicting status roles more than those in congruent roles? One can, if one chooses, also ascertain through cross-cultural comparisons of survey results the essential facts concerning the relation of these attitude states to the level of industrialization and state of political culture.

While surveys are not the only procedures for searching out vital political and social facts, they can often furnish information that is both more precise and more varied than the information supplied by other sources. Surveys, for example, can substantially augment aggregative types of data such as election statistics. Official voting returns can tell us who won an election, which districts voted for which candidates, and whether the turnout was large or small. But they cannot tell us what motivated the voters, why they divided as they did, how much they knew about issues, and whether they were significantly affected by the personalities of the candidates. A careful assessment of the facts on these questions requires a survey of some type. Even if a shrewd observer could, by intuitive observation, correctly divine the answers to such questions, a survey would still be needed to confirm his conclusions since, inevitably, an equally shrewd observer will have been led by *his* intuitive observation to a very different set of conclusions. Even if surveys were employed solely to confirm "what everybody knows" (a widely repeated charge that is patently false), they would still be essential. As it turns out, "what everybody knows" is almost invariably contradicted by an opposing and equally "well-known" conclusion. Unless we can verify which of the two "well-known" claims is correct, we can never resolve the conflict and separate truth from error.

It has become fashionable in some intellectual circles to deplore "fact-grubbing" and to exalt "theory." But the polarity implied by this distinction is spurious. While theory, of course, is vital to scientific advancement, facts are the building blocks of every science, essential both to the construction and testing of theory. Their verification, therefore, is essential to the progress of a science. In the study of politics, survey methods are often indispensable for this purpose.

Increasing the Range and Amount of Information

Surveys also make it possible to collect in a single effort vast amounts of information on large numbers of people. Their potentiality in this regard is probably greater than that of any alternative method. Studies using aggregative data, for example, may supply information on many people, but the range of the information is usually narrow and little or nothing can be learned about any individual. Laboratory or field experiments are in some respects superior to surveys in their power to confirm or disconfirm hypotheses, but they are generally compelled for reasons of cost, manpower, and the nature of the research design, to limit themselves to a small number of subjects and a severely restricted set of variables. Documentary studies of political phenomena can encompass many people and many topics, but are deficient in the ability to portray those phenomena accurately in all their range and variety. They can, furthermore, supply detailed personal information only on the few individuals on whom biographical data are available. Anthropological studies of communities come closest to surveys in their capacity for collecting large amounts and varieties of detailed data on large numbers of people. Many of these studies, however, are in reality crude surveys, less systematic and quantitative than the standard survey, but superior in their ability to observe how men act, how they relate to each other, and how they are affected by institutional practices.

In a single political survey that utilizes a one- or two-hour interview of a sample of, say, 1500 persons, skilled interviewers can collect vast amounts of data on personal and social background factors (e.g., age, sex, education, religion, income, occupation, residence, marital status, organizational memberships) and on such political matters as party preference, political interest and participation, nature and frequency of political discussions, family political background, opinions on issues, attitudes on conservatism, internationalism, equalitarianism, and democratic beliefs and practices. Even psychological information can be collected by using personality scales, questions about primary group involvement, measures of behavioral conformity and non-conformity, and the like. Much can also be learned about the reaction of individuals and groups to current political developments, their response to conflicting political choices, and their predictions about political trends.

Even these questions and answers do not exhaust the data-gathering potential of the survey procedure. Various questions (and their answers) can be combined and recombined into indices and scales that will furnish information on entirely new variables. Consider a simple illustration: if we ask a respondent for his own party preference and that of his father, we can, by combining the answers, simultaneously learn whether the respondent has shifted from or remained loyal to his father's party. This datum may be useful in answering a number of questions that interest political scientists. Do people shift their party preference because of changes in economic status, life style, or geographic location? Are they more likely to shift if their families lack cohesiveness or possess conflicting status characteristics? Are there personality differences between shifters and non-shifters? Is the rejection of the parental party preference an aspect of a generalized rebellion against parents? Thus, even this simple example opens the possibility of exploring many questions that were not specifically asked in the initial questionnaire.

Our illustration contains only two variables that were combined into a third, but indices can be constructed that consist of three, four, or even more elements. A questionnaire containing 25 questions, hence, may yield measures several times that number.

The number of findings yielded by a survey can be further augmented by manipulating variables in the course of the analysis so as to vary, in effect, the conditions under which behavior occurs. The sample, for example, can be divided by education and the less educated compared with the more educated. Or college graduates with high incomes can be compared with college graduates of low income. Numerous other combinations involving occupation, religion, age, rural-urban residence, party membership, and so forth, are equally possible. Nor is the survey investigator restricted to an analysis of the so-called marginals, i.e., the figures resulting from the *prima facie* answers of the total sample to the questions used. The marginals reported in public opinion polls, for example, represent only the first approximation of the knowledge uncovered by the survey. Much more can be learned, some of it of great significance and subtlety, by comparing various subgroups of the population.

New knowledge may also result from unexpected findings that are sometimes turned up by surveys. Such findings usually set off a train of questions and conjectures that lead the investigator to redirect his inquiry. How are the unanticipated findings to be explained? Do they appear to be related to some special circumstance, to the unsuspected influence of some variable, or to the interaction effect produced by the joining of two variables? The survey method frequently provides the information needed to explore and to resolve such questions.

Using survey methods to study politics furnishes not only more and better answers to old questions but new answers to new questions as well. It is characteristic of a science that each improvement in research techniques inspires new questions that had either never been thought of before or were dismissed for want of a method for finding the answers. Surveys have encouraged political scientists to ask and to investigate numerous questions they would scarcely have raised a few decades ago, including, for example, questions about the effects of personality on leader preference, the relation of cognitive habits to political attitudes, the group process by which political beliefs are transmitted and sustained, the degree of correspondence between leader and follower opinions, and scores of other problems that involve social and psychological mechanisms. As answers to these questions are found, they inspire, in turn, new questions, and sometimes new research techniques as well. There is thus a continual interplay between advances in research technique and the acquisition of scientific knowledge.[6]

---

[6] Kirkpatrick, *op. cit.,* p. 15.

Adoption of a Scientific Posture

The increasing use of survey methods is one aspect of a many-sided development toward a science of politics. Surveys have contributed to that development not only by the quality and range of data they make possible, but also by their effect on the investigator himself. They compel him, for example, to pay attention to requirements of scientific inquiry that he might otherwise be tempted to ignore. To begin with, he is forced to define his concepts in operational terms. Such political concepts as power, consent, accountability, liberal-conservative, right wing, freedom, and equality have characteristically been employed so imprecisely as to impede the accumulation of knowledge about them. Survey research, like other forms of systematic, empirical inquiry, forces the investigator to decide exactly what he means by these terms and how he intends to measure them. He cannot settle for a nominal definition, but must specify the empirical criteria he will use as indicators of the phenomenon. If he is measuring, say, liberalism-conservatism, he must decide which actions or verbal responses he will employ in classifying one individual as more (or less) conservative than another. He must also consider whether his measure is valid and whether it can be distinguished from other measures that bear different names.

Similar requirements hold for the many terms employed by political science that describe *relationships* such as conformity, deviation, homogeneity, agreement, support, affiliation, defection, and loyalty. The survey analyst soon discovers that even an apparently simple relationship, such as a voter's party affiliation and loyalty, is more complicated than it seems. How often must one support the party's candidates to be classified as a loyal Democrat (or Republican)? Some persons who call themselves Democrats are active in their party's support, attend meetings, proselytize their friends and neighbors, wear campaign buttons, and contribute money, while others profess partisanship but scarcely bother to vote. Are both Democrats, and should both be classified in precisely the same way?

A more complicated illustration is presented by the notion of "conformity," a fashionable concept, widely discussed (and as widely deplored) by social theorists and lay commentators. One would, however, have difficulty finding in the outpouring of discursive writing on the subject a genuine operational definition that would permit one consistently to classify certain behavioral instances as conformist or deviant. Obviously, every one of us conforms to some standards and not to others, to some groups and subcultures and not to others. A member of the Communist party deviates from certain of the norms of American society but conforms rigidly to the norms of his party. A member of the radical right glorifies conformity to the "American way" but tends, in fact, to deviate sharply (as survey research has shown) from the explicit values contained in the Bill of Rights. One man's conformity may be another man's deviation, depending upon the reference groups and value systems to which they respectively respond. The point can further be illustrated by the differences in outlook between the political influentials and the general public. By the standards of the Constitution and the implicit "rules of the game," the political influentials are more conformist than the masses, for they embrace these standards with greater frequency, firmness, and understanding. The general public, though greatly outnumbering the influentials, are by these criteria more deviant. But which is the "true" norm—that which is described in the nation's official documents or that which is expressed by the majority? Clearly, the concepts of conformity and deviation are much too uncertain and potentially misleading to be allowed to stand as mere literary terms. A survey analyst who wishes to employ them cannot afford such vagueness. He must define the concepts so as to reveal precisely the forms of conformity and deviation he has in mind, who the criterion groups are, and what indicators he has devised for classifying individuals on these dimensions.

I am not suggesting that survey research will inevitably yield better definitions than other approaches will. A survey investigator, like any other scholar, may select a definition that is weak, confused, historically inaccurate, or biased. Nevertheless, once he has chosen a definition he must specify the objective and measurable criteria by which respondents may be classified or ranked with respect to it. If, for example, he is concerned with conservatism, he will first have to decide whether he is talking about classical conservatism, economic and social welfare conservatism, conservatism in the matter of individual rights and duties, extreme conservatism of the radical right variety, or some combination of these. He will then have to select the questions or scale items or opinions that relate to his concept and that afford him an appropriate measure of it. He will further have to decide the form of his measure—whether it should be a scale, a single question, an index composed of several questions, an adjective check list, or a semantic differential. He will need to consider whether the measure should be based primarily on verbal responses or on actions, whether it should directly reflect the values embodied in the concept or utilize instead some secondary indicator such as liberal or conservative group membership. Although he may, despite these speculations, end up with a poor measure, he will have significantly reduced the risk. In addition, by operationalizing his terms, he will have made available to other scholars a clear description of what he has done so that they can check his work, repeat the study on other samples, confirm or refute the findings, and ascertain the limits to which the finding can be generalized.

The demands on a survey investigator are further increased if he elects to employ attitude or personality "scales" as his principal measures. If the items he has chosen reflect disparate elements or have been thrown together carelessly, his measure will not "scale," i.e., the items will not fall together in predictable ways and will not clearly differentiate persons who possess the trait in varying degrees. In constructing his scale, he may need to take account of how others perceive the dimension. He may do this by consulting authoritative works on the subject, or by pooling the judgments of a panel of expert "raters." He may also wish to test the internal consistency or unidimensionality of the scale items or to ascertain how known populations actually respond to the items. All these are efforts to establish the validity of the scale. He may also introduce procedures to estimate the "reliability" of the scale, i.e., its ability to yield the same score on repeated trials and to present itself in the same way to different persons. These procedures are costly and time-consuming, but the results they make possible are likely to be more precise and accurate than are those produced by more intuitive methods.

Just as survey methods compel a student of politics to clarify and make operational his major constructs, so do they also encourage him to organize, arrange, and classify political phenomena according to their relative magnitude, their similarities and differences, and their statistical or analytic unities. The survey procedure promotes quantification and the statistical handling of data which in turn make possible the explicit formulation and testing of hypotheses. Thus, from the drawing of the sample to the analysis of the results, surveys are geared to the processing of research in a conscious, precise, systematic, quantitative, and objective manner.[7]

The survey method also promotes the scientific study of politics by offering unusual opportunities to acquire parallel sets of data. The systematic interview permits the same questions to be asked of people who function in different roles, contexts, or locations. Unlike comparisons in the more discursive forms of inquiry, which are often loose, impressionistic, and cast in metaphorical language, the comparisons made possible by surveys can be controlled and explicit, removing much doubt about what is being compared and what conclusions may properly be drawn. Through appropriate statistical tests, one can describe and assess precisely the magnitude of the differences turned up by the comparisons one has made, and one can further estimate the likelihood that these differences might have occurred by chance variation alone.[8]

The comparative analysis of survey data can also be extended to the weighing of variables across time, place, and situation. A given social force does not exert the same influence in all circumstances, but varies in its influence as conditions change or as the total configuration of forces change. This confronts social science with one of its most formidable difficulties, for

[7] Merton, R. K., *Social Theory and Social Structure* (revised and enlarged edition). Free Press, Glencoe, Ill., 1957: introduction to Part III, "The Sociology of Knowledge and Mass Communications."

[8] Eulau, Heinz, "Segments of Political Science Most Susceptible to Behavioristic Treatment," in *The Limits of Behavioralism in Political Science*. Edited by J. C. Charlesworth. American Academy of Political and Social Science, Philadelphia, 1962, pp. 26–48, at pp. 39–40.

one can never be certain that a given variable will beget the same results from one context to another. Surveys can assist by helping to correct the grand, reductivist theories which seek to explain all political events by reference to class, economics, religion, nationalism, geopolitics, ideology, or some other allegedly ineluctable force. By comparing survey results one can observe the varying impact of these factors as conditions change and as other influences vary. Surveys make it possible to estimate what part of an individual's voting preference can be ascribed to class, issues, religion, or party; to observe the differential influence of ideology on different classes of people; and to discern the shifting influence of social class from one political context to another. Given time, resources, and a sufficient number of research probes, we will eventually learn what to expect from each independent variable in each context, and we should be able to predict with considerable accuracy the consequences of putting together any given configuration of social forces.

The potential contribution of the survey method to the advancement of a science of politics has been greatly enhanced by the invention of the modern computer and the development of computer programs that are applicable to social science problems. With its astonishing capacity for storing and retrieving information on many variables at once, for performing numerous statistical calculations almost instantaneously, and for ordering, analyzing, and testing quantities of data, the computer is an ideal tool for the processing of survey data. The political scientist need no longer be overwhelmed by the formidable array of variables involved in explaining even the simplest act. The computer has made it feasible for him to relate each of these variables to its underlying dimension, to group variables into their appropriate clusters, to ascertain the precise contribution each of them makes to the total variance, and to discover uniformities and variations in large masses of data whose sheer bulk would previously have defeated him. Computer programs now permit him to carry out such statistical operations as factor analyses, cluster analyses, multiple regression analyses, and other procedures that were once too costly, time-consuming, and tedious to be practicable. Programs for partial and multiple correlations, multiple regressions, and other statistical operations permit the analyst to handle many different variables at once, to control for certain of them while permitting others to vary, to demonstrate the effects of combining them, and to rank them according to their contribution to the total variance. Computers also help to increase the sophistication of survey analysis by improving the quality of measures on which the political scientist can draw. Programs are being designed to construct indices and scales, to compute coefficients of reproducibility or other measures of validity, to produce item intercorrelations, and to provide tests for significance of differences. The formidable task of making survey data manageable, in short, is on the way to being solved.

The Substantive Contributions of Surveys

Although the survey has been a tool of political analysis for only three decades, it has become one of the most widely used research procedures in the field. The number and types of political surveys have multiplied so rapidly that we cannot possibly enumerate them all in a brief review. Even a summary, however, will illustrate the many ways in which surveys have been used in political studies and will document the value and richness of the findings yielded by this method.

The early political surveys were mainly concerned with public opinion and voting. As Angus Campbell has observed, they were dominated by concepts familiar to "aggregative analysis," such as age, residence, occupation, income, and other demographic characteristics on which official records were available.[9] Like any new tool, they tended at first to be focused on familiar questions and constructs. Political scientists still collect demographic information, of course, but the typical political survey has been broadened to include such dimensions as personality, role, motivation, attitude, cognition, reference groups, and status.[10] Surveys are still being used to study public opinion and voting, but they are also being turned to studies of political parties, ideology, political belief and affiliation, stability and change, political socialization, legislative processes, constituency representation, judicial behavior, comparative politics, foreign policy formation and opinion, and community power structure. These changes have been accompanied by an increase in the sophistication of the questions being asked. Whereas the early users of political surveys collected evidence on a variable like social class in order to observe its relation to, say, voting preference, a contemporary scholar is more likely to want to know whether a respondent shifts his political point of view as he moves downward or upward in social class; whether he suffers conflicts of status and hence is politically alienated; whether he holds or rejects the modal values of his class; and whether class and its concomitants affect his perceptions, motivations, values, and capacity for adopting the norms of the larger community. The contemporary scholar who uses survey methods often wants to go behind such concepts as class, age, education, residence, or religion in order to learn what they consist of and what gives them their power to influence political behavior. This tendency to translate crude categoric variables into more refined and dynamic ones, and to improve their explanatory power thereby, typifies the changes in intellectual posture that are taking place in almost every substantive area of political inquiry. The nature and scope of these changes will become more evident from the review that follows.

[9] Campbell, Angus, "Recent Developments in Survey Studies of Political Behavior," in *Essays on the Behavioral Study of Politics.* Edited by Austin Ranney, *op. cit.,* pp. 31–46, at p. 32.
[10] Alpert, *op. cit.,* p. 498.

Public Opinion

The use of surveys to sound mass opinion remains one of their important functions, although they are not the only means by which public opinions can be divined. One may also consult journalistic and other published materials, private letters and diaries, the policies of public organizations, and the speeches of influential persons; but none of these can furnish an adequate portrait of the variety, range, and intensity of opinions held by the electorate. All are susceptible to the play of fortuitous factors, and are therefore bound to be distorted—biased by idiosyncracies in the selection procedure, by errors in reporting or self-representation, or by the preconceptions of the investigator. Often the opinions of those who are most visible or vociferous are mistakenly considered to be the opinions of all.

Public opinion studies are being carried out by commercial and government polls as well as by scholars. While polls are less concerned than academic surveys with explorations in depth and hypotheses-testing, the information they provide is important to scholars. Political scientists consult polls for information on party and candidate preferences, shifts in presidential popularity, public orientation toward issues, the level of public information on various political questions, popular responses to the behavior of the President, Congress, or the Supreme Court, the public's perception of impending legislation, and similar matters. Polls also enable scholars to relate public opinion to certain forms of overt political behavior, such as elections, organizational activities, congressional votes, and executive decisions. Some of these questions are being explored in comparative studies using data from commercial polls abroad.

The value of opinion polls to the political investigator, however, lies not only in the information they publish but also in the vast amounts of politically relevant data they collect but rarely bother to report. Almost every public opinion poll gathers information that may have been incidental to the initial survey but that is a potentially rich repository of materials for scholars. Until recently, most of this information was never used, but was simply stored on punch cards or left uncoded. The polling organizations, having skimmed off the relatively few items they were concerned to report, had little interest in the rest. Now, however, they are making their old data available to scholars for secondary analysis.

One or two examples will illustrate the opportunities for secondary analysis that have now been opened. The American Institute of Public Opinion (Gallup Poll) has for many years included in its national surveys questions that assess presidential popularity. As Gallup has reported in newspaper releases, the public's approval of the president rises and falls throughout his tenure. Poll information on the course of these shifts has proven invaluable to scholars who have wondered whether they are related to political events in some systematic, predictable way. They have asked, for example, whether presidential popularity rises rather than falls with the onset of international crises, and they have found that it does.[11] By exploring the poll archives, they can learn whether disaffection with the president occurs most frequently among the educated or non-educated; whether support for the president is related to presidential policies; whether and in what ways his popularity is affected by economic crises, personal style, congressional quarrels, shifts in opinion on issues, respondents' feelings of well-being, growing or declining affluence, and sense of economic opportunity. They can also investigate the relation between presidential popularity and subsequent voting behavior, and relate popular approval of the president to the support enjoyed by his party. Since these poll samples are characteristically miniatures of national or state electorates, the political scientist can explore these questions for every sub-stratum or "public" he thinks appropriate—Northerners or Southerners, young or old, rich or poor, urban or rural, Democratic or Republican, liberals or conservatives, or any combination of these. Secondary analysis of poll data has also been used with considerable benefit in studies of American political values,[12] foreign policy attitudes,[13] stratification and political orientation,[14] and popular responses to "McCarthyism."[15] Polls are proving useful even for cross-cultural political studies. Where they have asked parallel questions in more than one country, they have made possible comparative studies on such political subjects as voting preferences, response to leaders, the impact of left and right ideologies, the relation of mobility to political belief, and response to the party system.

The retrieval and analysis of commercial poll data is a relatively inexpensive way to conduct studies of mass political opinion. An investigator who can afford it, however, will usually prefer to design and execute a survey tailored to his own purposes, one that will yield answers to the exact questions he has in mind. A custom-made survey enables him to probe more deeply, to over-sample and investigate intensively the groups that especially interest him, and to explore the variables that seem on theoretical grounds to explain the political opinion he is studying. Since the political scientist is interested in the relation of opinions to certain political variables, he is often compelled to undertake his own survey in order to achieve the range and variety of responses required for his analysis.

So much is being learned about political opinions through the use of

[11] Polsby, N. W., *Congress and the Presidency.* Prentice-Hall, Englewood Cliffs, N. J., 1964, pp. 25–26.

[12] Hyman, H. H., and P. B. Sheatsley, "The Current Status of American Public Opinion," in *Public Opinion and Propaganda.* Edited by Daniel Katz, *et al.* Ryerson Press, New York, 1954, pp. 33–48.

[13] Almond, G. A., *The American People and Foreign Policy.* Harcourt, Brace, New York, 1950.

[14] Lipset, S. M., *Political Man:* The Social Bases of Politics. Doubleday, Garden City, N.Y., 1960, pp. 97–130 and pp. 285–309.

[15] Polsby, N. W., "Toward an Explanation of McCarthyism," *Political Studies,* Vol. 8, October, 1960, pp. 250–271.

surveys that we can only illustrate their contribution. Surveys have confirmed that there is indeed more than one public and that political issues are often salient for one group and irrelevant for another. They have shown that popular opinions on political questions are frequently labile and that this instability especially characterizes the opinions expressed by the less informed members of the society.[16] They have made it increasingly clear that only a small proportion of the electorate can plausibly be described as "ideologically sophisticated," and that the number of persons who hold consistent and coherent political philosophies is very small.[17]

We have also begun to learn from surveys that not all persons holding the same manifest opinions mean the same thing by them. Unsophisticated voters, for example, often express opinions favoring political freedom largely because those opinions reflect familiar, honorific values. As a result, they frequently endorse these opinions in the abstract but reject them when they are applied to the concrete exercise of freedom. This discrepancy between the general and particular expressions of a principle is less likely to occur among the more articulate segments of the society. Their opinions are more firmly grounded in a coherent point of view and are applied with greater consistency. They are more likely to choose reference groups, candidates, and parties that are consonant with their underlying political beliefs. Articulate Republicans and Democrats, for example, differ more sharply on issues than do inarticulate Republicans and Democrats.[18]

Survey procedures have shown, however, that even educated people exhibit less consistency in their political views than one might suppose. It is not unusual, for example, to find well-informed people holding opinions that intermingle liberal and conservative values—conservatives who respond more favorably to left wing opinions than many liberals do, and persons who are liberal on economic issues but conservative on such matters as procedural rights, traditionalism, and social change. There is even a small, though predominantly inarticulate, segment of the population who simultaneously hold extreme right-wing and left-wing values. Such findings suggest that we may in the past have overstressed the role of ideas in the politics of modern democratic societies. A similar conclusion is suggested by the survey data bearing upon the presumed need for "consensus" as a precondition for democracy. The American electorate, for example, is found to be divided on some important political values and even on the so-called rules of the game, yet the society remains viable.[19]

[16] Converse, Philip E., "The Nature of Belief Systems in Mass Publics," in *Ideology and Discontent.* Edited by D. E. Apter. Free Press, Glencoe, Ill., 1964, pp. 206–261.

[17] Campbell, Angus, *et al., The American Voter, op. cit.,* chap. 10.

[18] McClosky, Herbert, "Consensus and Ideology in American Politics," *American Political Science Review,* Vol. 58, June, 1964, pp. 361–382.

[19] Prothro, J. W., and C. M. Grigg, "Fundamental Principles of Democracy: Bases of Agreement and Disagreement," *Journal of Politics,* Vol. 22, May, 1960, pp. 276–294; Key, V. O., Jr., *Public Opinion and American Democracy.* Knopf, New York, 1961, chap. 2; Dahl, R. A., *Who Governs?:* Democracy and Power in an American City. Yale University Press, New

Survey evidence suggests that certain opinions deserve to be taken more seriously than others because more thought has gone into their adoption. Some opinions are embraced thoughtlessly and casually, while others are derived from strongly held political philosophies. Some merely reflect the current political mood, while others are deeply rooted in the value system. Some are stable and others are labile. Some express the innermost beliefs or interests of their holders, while others merely echo commonplace opinions or familiar phrases. Although *vox populi, vox Dei* has for centuries been proclaimed a literal truth, it is obvious from an enormous amount of survey data that the people speak with more than one voice and that some of their opinions are misguided, contradictory, and repeated without reflection.

Surveys of public opinion have also shown that members of the same class may differ sharply in their opinions, and that class or other demographic categories are but crude classifications that often exert only a modest influence on the formation of political beliefs. Being a Catholic or Protestant, for example, influences what one thinks about church-related questions such as support for parochial schools, but has little direct bearing on the opinions one holds about, say, government intervention in the economy, social welfare legislation, foreign policy, urban redevelopment, or civil rights.[20] In a modern, urban, pluralistic society—in which men are no longer confined to the company of a single group but mingle with persons from many groups and in which, despite differences in their origins, they often attend the same schools and receive the same communications from the same mass media—opinions on public questions are rarely controlled by a single categoric group.[21] Among the general electorate, and especially among the poorly educated, even party affiliation exerts only a modest influence on political opinions.[22] Although a voter's outlook on issues is sometimes correlated with his choice of candidates,[23] the *causal* connection between the electorate's opinions on these issues and their voting decision is by no means established. In the 1952 presidential election, in which Eisenhower voters favored his views on such issues as corruption in government more often than Stevenson voters did, there is reason to believe that many voters who had already decided to support Eisenhower embraced his views on these issues only after he began to stress them in his campaign.

Haven, 1961, chap. 28; Stouffer, S. A., *Communism Conformity, and Civil Liberties:* A Cross Section of the Nation Speaks its Mind. Doubleday, New York, 1955; and McClosky, "Consensus and Ideology. . . ," *op. cit.*

[20] Allinsmith, Wesley, and Beverly Allinsmith, "Religious Affiliation and Politico-Economic Attitude: A Study of Eight Major U.S. Religious Groups," *Public Opinion Quarterly,* Vol. 12, Fall, 1948, pp. 377–389.

[21] Centers, Richard, "Attitude and Belief in Relation to Occupational Stratification," *Journal of Social Psychology,* Vol. 27, May, 1948, pp. 159–185.

[22] McClosky, Herbert, *et al.,* "Issue Conflict and Consensus Among Party Leaders and Followers," *American Political Science Review,* Vol. 54, June, 1960, pp. 406–427.

[23] Campbell, Angus, Gerald Gurin and W. E. Miller, *The Voter Decides.* Row, Peterson, Evanston, Ill., 1954, 145 ff.

Surveys are also helping us to understand the complex interplay between popular opinion and government decisions. We are, for example, now able to assess whether elected officials respond frequently to the opinions of the voters, whether they respond to some voters more than others, whether they listen to the "voice of the people" on some questions but not on others, and whether they relinquish their own strongly held convictions in favor of what they perceive to be voter sentiment.[24] Questions that have long been debated but never resolved—for example, whether popular opinion is heeded in matters of foreign policy—can now be examined with greater assurance that answers will be forthcoming.

In recent years, a few studies have tried to combine surveys of the electorate with surveys of political officials. Such studies enable us to compare the beliefs of the two samples, to estimate the response of political leaders to the wishes of the electorate, and to acquire vitally needed facts about the realities of representative government. They are helping us to discover when a political leader can be expected to follow his own conscience, when he will respond to the opinions of the voters, and to what degree representation is affected by the intensity of party competition. They also make it possible to learn whether popular opinion prevails on domestic matters more than on foreign affairs, on bread and butter issues more than on symbolic or "style" issues, on simple, easily grasped issues more than on complex issues, on questions that touch the moral convictions of the people more than on questions that reflect practical considerations.

Survey methods are beginning to be used to investigate systematically the differences between the private convictions of political officials and their manifest conduct. Political ritual and necessity control so large a part of an officeholder's behavior that it is often difficult to know when he is following his own conscience and when he is concealing his beliefs in deference to political exigency. A properly designed survey that protects the anonymity of the leader-respondent may reveal what part of his behavior is backed by personal conviction and what part is political accommodation. By measuring the disparity between what is believed and what is manifestly said or done, one can assess the impact of other forces that play upon political actors and propel them in certain directions. Since private beliefs influence conduct even when their effects are not visible, ferreting them out is important to a full understanding of political behavior. It is also essential to a more adequate appreciation of the relation between attitudes and opinions on the one hand and overt behavior on the other. As yet, little is systematically known about this relation, or about the manner in which beliefs combine with various situational forces to evoke overt behavior. What part of our overt political behavior is a function of our values, and what part reflects group memberships, personal interest, and other external forces

---

[24] Miller, W. E., and Donald Stokes, "Constituency Influence in Congress," *American Political Science Review,* Vol. 57, March, 1963, pp. 45–56.

with which those beliefs interact? For the investigation of these matters, survey analysis is likely to be indispensable.

Although surveys have become vital to the efficient study of public opinion, their employment for this purpose is not without risk. There are, for example, problems associated with the interpretation of the answers that respondents give to survey questions. We have already observed that some people reply thoughtlessly or express contradictory opinions. Others give answers that do not accurately reflect the way they would behave if they were required to act on their beliefs. Much may depend on the way a question is put. For example, a review of survey opinions in the *Public Opinion Quarterly* reports that two-thirds of the respondents in a general population sample stated (in answer to a question put to them in 1950) that they believed people were "happier and more contented" thirty years ago than they are today.[25] But when asked if they would rather be living during the earlier period than the present one, approximately the same proportion acknowledged that they preferred the present one. An investigator who heeded only the first set of responses might be seriously misled about the public's feelings toward the present society, mistaking a superficial expression of nostalgia for a deeply felt conviction. Dangers of this type, however, can be minimized by using properly validated questions, skilled interviewing, or sophisticated attitude testing. With sufficient resources, care, and ingenuity, an investigator can in fact acquire a comprehensive, complex, and accurate portrait of the public mind on many of the questions that interest political scientists.

Participation

While information on such matters as voting turnout and participation in party work has been available through official or organizational records, most of the interesting questions about political participation could not be effectively investigated prior to the development of the survey method. Surveys have proven invaluable in assessing the influence on participation of such factors as demography, sense of political effectiveness, party loyalty, partisanship, ideological conviction, and perception of candidates. They have also made it possible to explore systematically such matters as political recruitment and participation in party work.

A great deal has been learned through surveys about the demographic correlates of participation.[26] To what extent do demographic forces help to

[25] Erskine, H. G., "The Polls: Textbook Knowledge," *Public Opinion Quarterly,* Vol. 27, Spring, 1963, pp. 133–141.

[26] Berelson, Lazarsfeld, and McPhee, *Voting, op. cit.;* Campbell, *et al., The American Voter, op. cit.,* pp. 291–498; Lipset, S. M., *et al.,* "The Psychology of Voting: An Analysis of Political Behavior," in *Handbook of Social Psychology,* Vol. 2. Edited by Gardner Lindzey. Addison-Wesley, Reading, Mass., 1954, pp. 1124–1175; Almond, G. A. and Sidney Verba, *The Civic Culture.* Princeton University Press, Princeton, 1963, pp. 261–374; Lane, R. E., *Political Life.* Free Press, Glencoe, Ill., 1959, pp. 185–272; and Lipset, *Political Man, op. cit.,* chap. 6.

fashion individuals into participants or, alternatively, into non-voters? Although a given demographic factor may not register exactly the same impact in every context, similar patterns of influence have been discerned from one country to another. Surveys have shown, for example, that voting and other forms of participation are more frequent among the better educated than the less educated, among men more than women, the culturally advantaged more than the disadvantaged, urban dwellers more than rural residents, the middle aged more than the very young or the very old, persons settled in the community more than transients, and individuals who participate in other forms of social and community activity more than those who do not. The underlying factors that govern these correlations appear to be social awareness, sophistication, and the ability to influence one's environment. Political apathy, on the other hand, is in great measure a function of parochialism, ignorance, and feelings of political ineptitude and futility. Role perception may also contribute, as in the case of the lesser participation of women. In general, anything that exposes an individual to the political culture or enlarges his opportunity to learn about politics will stimulate him to acquire habits of political activity; apathy, in contrast, is induced by anything that separates him from the mainstreams of the society, isolates him from the articulate culture, removes him from the sources of political communication, or otherwise causes public events to seem remote, bewildering, or without consequence for his personal affairs.

Data collected from numerous surveys have shown that political participation is not a "natural" concomitant of citizenship, but has to be learned. A sense of civic duty tends to be correlated with participation, but is not its sufficient cause. It appears, rather, to be a concomitant or epiphenomenon of the same configuration of forces that induces participation itself. Hence, hortatory appeals to morality and conscience have little effect on voting turnout or active party involvement. Some people in the society are so far removed from the articulate culture that they never hear the appeals, while others, finding politics remote, impalpable, or irrelevant to their daily lives, turn a deaf ear. Interest in politics is subject to the same kinds of influence that govern interest and participation in other forms of human activity: one must be exposed, perceive politics as salient, understand in some measure what is going on, believe that one's participation matters (if only to oneself), and derive some type of reinforcement or "reward" from the activity. The reward may be the pleasure of competition, the approval and support of friends, the fulfillment of a sense of responsibility, the satisfaction of victory (realized or anticipated), or the promise of something concretely to be gained. A substantial proportion of the population fails, for one reason or another, to find such rewards in political activity, and hence do not even bother to vote.

Participation is a function not so much of demographic influences as such but of the "dynamic" forces they embody and can unleash. The effect of a demographic factor, in other words, is not permanent, but is specific to time and circumstance. Thus, the less frequent participation of women will eventually be overcome as changes occur in their role and as they gain equality with men in such things as education. Similarly, the relatively greater apathy of Negroes in the United States will gradually be corrected as they achieve higher status and education, and become more accustomed to urban life. Farmers will doubtless vote as often as city dwellers when the impact of the mass media and the improvements in transportation further erase the communication distinctions between the city and the farm.

Survey methods have provided a far more accurate and comprehensive description than was previously available of the nature and incidence of political participation in various countries. Reliable information is being collected on voting, on the frequency of discussions and reading about politics, participation in election campaigns, attendance at meetings, and so forth. Surveys have documented with considerable accuracy what has long been suspected, namely, that the number of people who belong to the "political class" is fairly small (depending on how rigorously one defines the criteria, probably fewer than 10 per cent), while a larger group, but still a minority, participates to the extent of attending an occasional meeting, contributing money to a campaign, writing a letter to an elected official, or engaging in political discussions. By observing who does and does not engage in these activities, and by ascertaining their social, intellectual, and psychological characteristics, surveys have begun to shed much light on the sources and correlates of political activity.

Although few surveys have so far been conducted on "party actives," the American data indicate that, compared with other groups in the population, the actives are more ideological, more partisan, more responsive to their party's doctrine, and more inclined to hold a coherent and internally consistent set of political beliefs. This is not to say that they are "ideologically" oriented to the same degree that the active members of the small European parties have been, but only that they are far more developed in their political ideas than are most members of the American electorate. Survey data also show that the actives possess a firmer grasp of the constitutional principles and "rules of the game" on which the political system is founded. As a "class," they are among the most important repositories of the values that define the political culture. The survey evidence also suggests that the competition between parties takes place principally between their active members rather than between their rank-and-file supporters. Democratic and Republican actives, for example, are much further apart in their stands on issues than are their followers. Prior to the investigation of these matters through surveys, the contrary was often assumed.[27]

Until recently, most studies of political participation were confined to

[27] McClosky, *et al.,* "Issue Conflict. . . ," *op. cit.*

individual countries. Now, however, efforts are being made to investigate the subject across cultures. These studies aim to assess the influence of particular variables in different contexts and to determine how existing political institutions and the "political culture" itself affect political involvement. While some light has been thrown on this matter by comparing the results of surveys conducted separately in different countries, the new comparative studies use parallel surveys that ask similar questions and draw on comparable samples. The most notable example of this is the study of participation and civic involvement in five countries done by Gabriel Almond and Sidney Verba.[28] This study suggests that the sense and quality of civic competence varies according to the type of political culture, and this, in turn, is related to the level of education, industrialization, and urbanization. Political participation and sense of civic responsibility are more developed in the United States than in Italy or Mexico. Similarly, the sense of civic competence, i.e., the individual's feeling that he can affect the course of public policy, is significantly stronger in the United States and Great Britain than it is in Germany, Italy, and Mexico. In general, the forces that increase political involvement and participation in one country, e.g., education, also tend to increase them elsewhere.

Survey evidence shows that participation also varies with the "visibility" of the candidate, the character of the campaign, and the dramatic significance of the issues. Well-known candidates inspire a larger turnout than little-known candidates. Campaigns that feature a dramatic issue or highlight a national crisis bring some people to the polls who would otherwise not have turned out. Surveys, of course, are not the only means by which these facts might be learned, but they are needed in order to document in detail the degree to which candidates are "well-known," the sense of felt crises among different groups of voters, the manner in which presumably dramatic issues are in fact perceived, and the attributes of the candidates that inspire (or discourage) voter participation. Surveys likewise may be used to assess the popular response to changing political situations and events. It is difficult at best to discover the impact of a given event on the behavior of citizens, but without some type of survey analysis, it is often impossible.

Voting

No area of political inquiry has profited more bountifully from the development of the survey method than that of voting behavior. Whereas our knowledge of this phenomenon was formerly impressionistic and pervaded with subjective and frequently erroneous beliefs, we now have available a large body of "hard" data of a type that has been repeatedly confirmed in studies of elections in various countries. We can, as a result, elaborate the explanatory model of voting well beyond what was once possible.

---

[28] Almond and Verba, *op. cit.*

Before the development of survey methods, most systematic research on elections drew primarily on official aggregative data. By comparing the voting outcome with the social characteristics of the election district, one could make crude appraisals of the influence of ethnic, religious, economic, or other categoric group memberships. One could also identify voting trends in, say, rural and urban areas, certain districts and states, and even among particular ethnic groups. One could classify voting constituencies according to the closeness of the party vote, and one could relate this information to such other variables as the behavior of a constituency's representatives.

Aggregative data, however, not only reveal but conceal vital information, for, while they make available gross figures about certain categories of voters, they do not tell us how individuals or subgroups in those categories actually behave or what influences them.[29] There are dangers in attributing to any individual the behavioral characteristics of the groups he belongs to—he may be a worker living in a working class district, but he is also Catholic or Protestant, white or Negro, white collar or blue collar, educated or uneducated, Republican or Democrat, participant or apathetic. He is also differentiated from others in the group by personality, attitudes, motivations, and habits of mind that diverge in subtle and complex ways from the modal pattern. Since similar variations mark all other individuals in the constituency, an investigator will miss much essential information about the configuration of forces that govern their respective voting decisions if he consults aggregative data alone. He would, for example, be unable to explain shifts in the voting preferences of a given constituency that has experienced no changes in its social composition.

The uncertainties surrounding the interpretation of aggregative election statistics are apparent in the widely divergent interpretations offered by politicians and commentators about the meaning of a given election. There is a long-standing myth that practicing politicians understand these matters better than other observers do. But one need only consult their post-election interpretations to have the myth quickly dispelled; like most other people, they tend to color their interpretations by their subjective readings and by their desires and fears. It is not uncommon for political opponents to claim that a given election outcome signifies support for or against the expansion of civil rights, for or against decentralization of national power, for or against a more militant foreign policy, for or against tax reform, for or against medical care for the aged—for or against, in short, whatever point of view they happen to value.[30] The interpretations of professional politicians are further warped by their almost unrelieved association with members of their own party and their overexposure to the party's communications. Partly for these reasons, they are notoriously inclined to predict victory for their party's candidate and to discover a popular mandate for its program.

[29] Robinson, *op. cit.*
[30] Campbell, "Recent Developments in Survey Studies," *op. cit.*, p. 38.

Survey studies of elections make it possible to supply many needed details and to achieve a more realistic appraisal of the forces that decide the outcome. They have demonstrated, for example, that party affiliation—the single most compelling factor affecting the voting decision—is shaped and sustained by the family, and that some three-fourths of the adult voters retain the party preference of their parents. Party affiliation is further reinforced by congruent peer and other reference group attachments. Social or geographic mobility, however, including entrance into a "conflicting" economic or religious category, weakens the family's hold on the voter's party preference and leads him to waver in his party support or to switch parties entirely.

Election surveys have also documented the role played by such factors as religion and occupational status in fixing party preference. In the United States at least, the former is less important than the latter. Indeed when socio-economic status is controlled, the influence of religious denomination over party preference tends to decline sharply. Occupational status remains among the most important of the demographic influences on party and voting preference, with the low status occupations tending to support the economically more liberal party, and the high status occupations leaning toward the more conservative party. Occupation, however, has only a modest effect on one's orientation toward the values that define the political culture; attitudes toward freedom, equality, private property, and the profit system are in large measure shared by people in all socio-economic levels, especially if education is held constant.

Election surveys have also confirmed that occupational status and other "class" indicators do not exert a uniform influence on every election. In 1948, with neither presidential candidate able to register a strong personal appeal, the vote closely followed occupational status lines. But in the elections of 1952 and 1956, large numbers of lower income and working class voters shifted their support to Eisenhower, largely because of his popularity as a military figure. Again, in the 1964 election, the survey data so far available suggest that large defections from the Republican candidate occurred even among persons of upper economic status. These findings illustrate that surveys can enlighten us about a particular election, about the impact of the forces that affect election outcomes in general, and about the influence of any one of those forces in a particular election.[31]

As election survey techniques have developed, the handling of categoric factors has become more sophisticated. Investigators have sought to probe beyond the mere ecological categories into such matters as the strength of

[31] Converse, P. E., *et al.,* "Stability and Change in 1960: A Reinstating Election," *American Political Science Review,* Vol. 55, June, 1961, pp. 269–280; Lazarsfeld, *et al., The People's Choice, op. cit.;* Wildavsky, Aaron, "The Intelligent Citizen's Guide to the Abuse of Statistics: The Kennedy Document and the Catholic Vote," in *Politics and Social Life.* Edited by N. W. Polsby, *et al.,* Houghton-Mifflin, Boston, 1964, pp. 825–844.

group identification, the cohesiveness of the groups to which voters belong, and the reference group configurations from which they derive their norms, opinions, and perceptions. They have explored the sources of conformity and deviation relative to a group's values and the location and role within the group of those who most fervently embrace its doctrines. They are no longer satisfied merely to discover that older voters tend to be more conservative and Republican than younger voters, but are now asking why this happens, and they are turning to surveys, in the main, to learn whether these correlations are generational in origin or a function of the aging process itself.

Numerous American and foreign surveys suggest that party affiliation is not only the single most powerful influence on voting, but that it may also be the most important force in inculcating and sustaining political beliefs. There is mounting evidence that parties are not merely the spokesmen of demographic or interest groups but are important reference groups in their own right, capable of inspiring, sustaining, and promoting the political doctrines to which voters respond. This observation holds especially for the active members and articulate supporters of the parties—the groups that are ideologically most highly developed and partisan. Inarticulate voters are more likely to refrain from voting or to shift their preferences from one election to another; articulate voters remain more strongly and consistently loyal to their party in both their beliefs and voting habits. While some articulate voters describe themselves as "independent," survey findings suggest that the classical portrait of the independent as a highly politicized, informed, objective, and conscientious voter is exaggerated; independency, in fact, is more likely to be associated with political indifference and a low level of political information.[32]

Although little systematic research has been done on the candidates' contributions to the outcome of elections, surveys have begun to make some inroads on this question also. We have observed, in the cases of Eisenhower and Goldwater, that a candidate may be so well-known and trusted—or, alternatively, so feared—that his candidacy will cause a large number of voters to shift from their habitual party preference. These instances, however, are atypical, for the candidates in a party election are often rather evenly matched in the degree to which they are known, and tend to be perceived by the voters as possessing similar qualities.[33] Most voters, in short, are unlikely to shift from the party they usually support unless there is a marked difference in the popularity and reputation of the candidates. Despite their protestation that they prefer to vote "for the man rather than for the party," they are likely in practice to reverse this order of preference.

[32] Campbell, *et al., The Voter Decides, op. cit.,* pp. 97–111; Berelson, *et al., Voting, op. cit.,* pp. 25–28; for a contrary view, see Agger, R. E., "Independents and Party Identifiers: Characteristics and Behavior in 1952," in *American Voting Behavior.* Edited by E. L. Burdick and A. J. Brodbeck. Free Press, Glencoe, Ill., 1959, pp. 308–339.

[33] Pool, I. de Sola, "TV: A New Dimension in Politics," in *American Voting Behavior.* Edited by E. L. Burdick and A. J. Brodbeck, *op. cit.,* pp. 236–261.

The survey procedure has also been invaluable for the study of the campaign—a feature of modern elections that has generated much mythology and many misperceptions. Prior to the studies inspired by Paul Lazarsfeld, little was known about the effects of the mass media, the contribution of the candidates, the influence of the campaign in shifting or stabilizing voter preferences, the effectiveness of various campaign techniques, and the processes by which campaign information is disseminated.[34] Our knowledge of these phenomena, regrettably, is still rather thin, but such hard data as we have managed to acquire has come largely through surveys.

The study of the campaign is best approached through the use of the panel survey. By reinterviewing respondents as the campaign progresses, an investigator can trace shifts in voter preferences, observe the process by which decisions are formed, and assess the impact on the voting decision of speeches, campaign activities, and political events. Unless the decision process is followed in this way, the observer of a campaign will find himself confronted by a bewildering assortment of simultaneously occurring forces and events that are difficult to distinguish from one another.

The data now available from surveys suggest that the influence attributed to campaigns by politicians, journalists and other "intuitive" observers is greatly exaggerated. Most voters have decided how they will vote even before the campaign begins—in fact, before the candidates are chosen. The campaign serves largely to reinforce this decision. Voters who at the beginning claim to be undecided usually decide in favor of the party they habitually support. The effect of the campaign, in short, is largely to polarize existing predispositions rather than to produce shifts from one party to the other. Issues may be stressed by the candidates, but, with rare exceptions, they play a much smaller role in forming voting preferences than is commonly supposed. Only a small proportion of voters take them seriously enough to reflect upon them deeply or to be moved by them to shift their voting intention. More likely, voters either ignore issues that conflict with their voting intention or adopt the stands taken by their party or candidate. Of course, if the competing parties are closely matched, any of a number of factors—issues, candidates, or style of campaigning—may shift a sufficient number of votes to win or lose the election. Shifts of large magnitude, however, are likely to occur only if the election reflects, or generates, an unusually severe sense of crisis or malaise.

The role of communication and the mass media in elections has also been explored through surveys. Most voters, it appears, consult the media largely to strengthen the voting intention they have already formed. They tend to avoid communications that conflict with their voting decision, or to reinterpret them in a favorable light. They are, in the course of a campaign, bombarded by so many communications from so many sources on so many subjects that they can easily select whatever they wish to hear and reject

[34] Lazarsfeld, *et al., The People's Choice, op. cit.;* and Berelson, *et al., Voting, op. cit.*

whatever they wish to avoid. Since many of the events they are asked to judge are highly ambiguous, they are prone to accept the interpretations placed upon those events by their party's spokesmen. Many of the communications addressed to the voter during the campaign, therefore, either do not reach him at all, are reinterpreted by him to make them congruent with what he intends to do anyway, or are dismissed as inaccurate and biased. While this describes the typical pattern, there are of course exceptions. If a candidate is not well known, extensive newspaper or television coverage may increase his popularity sufficiently to put him over the mark; or a personally prepossessing candidate may succeed in using his television appearances to win over the conflicted voters or even to shift a few voters who initially supported his opponent. In unusual circumstances, the mass media may help to dramatize certain issues in a way that will benefit one candidate and harm the other.

Survey research by Lazarsfeld and others has also shown that communications via the mass media are most likely to be received by the educated and articulate segments of the population—by those voters who are already best informed about public affairs and most likely, therefore, to have arrived at a firm voting decision. The undecided voters, those whom the candidates most want to reach, are usually the least accessible. Similarly, the campaign more often engages the attention of the partisan than the uncommitted voters. A similar principle determines the selection of voters who are visited by party campaign workers, or who receive literature and phone calls from campaign headquarters. Obviously, these tendencies further diminish the impact that the campaign can register on the outcome of an election. The campaign does, however, bring out the party workers and inspire them to more enthusiastic efforts.

The politically informed also serve as intermediaries between the mass media and the ordinary voter. As survey research has shown, the media exert at least an indirect influence on the ordinary voter through a "two step flow of communication," in which the more informed members of the electorate receive information from the media and transmit it to ordinary voters.[35] Those who transmit information in this way have sometimes been described as "secondary leaders," whose role in conveying basic information from the campaign headquarters to the rank-and-file voters is an essential ingredient of the campaign.[36]

Surveys have enriched our understanding of the individual voting decision

[35] Katz, Elihu, and P. F. Lazarsfeld, *Personal Influence*. Free Press, Glencoe, Ill., 1955.

[36] Berelson, *et al., Voting, op. cit.;* Lazarsfeld, *et al., The People's Choice op. cit.;* Campbell, *et al., The American Voter, op. cit.,* p. 92, p. 271; Simon, H. A., and Frederick Stern, "Effect of Television upon Voting Behavior in Iowa in the 1952 Presidential Election," *American Political Science Review,* Vol. 49, June, 1955, pp. 470–477; Cutright, Phillips, and P. H. Rossi, "Grass Roots Politicians and the Vote," *American Sociological Review,* Vol. 23, April, 1958, pp. 171–179; Rokkan, Stein, and Henry Valen, "A Survey of the 1957 Norwegian Elections," *Revue Français de Science Politique,* Vol. 8, 1958, pp. 73–94; Matthews, D. R., and J. W. Prothro, "Social and Economic Factors and Negro Voter Registration in the South," *American Political Science Review,* Vol. 57, March, 1963, pp. 24–44; "Political Factors and Negro Voter

and have helped us to comprehend the nature and meaning of the election itself. From observing the motivations of individual voters, one survey research group has classified elections into three basic types—maintaining, deviating, and realigning—according to whether they closely reflect the prevailing party division, depart from it momentarily in response to some issue or candidate, or engender a lasting shift in the electorate's party preferences. A fourth type—in which the voters return to their traditional voting patterns after having "deviated" in the previous election—has been added to the classification and is known as a "reinstating election."[37] By making possible such classifications, surveys can help us to learn whether a given election foreshadows changes in the underlying patterns of party affiliation, whether certain questions or stands are likely to become an enduring source of party differentiation, whether the election signifies only a temporary deviation from the "normal" electoral division, and whether the majority's shift to a given candidate or party reflects changes in its doctrinal views.

By comparing the political opinions of voters with their actual voting habits, we can ascertain in what measure elections accurately convey the electorate's beliefs on various political questions. Surveys also enable us to inquire into the validity of such explanatory notions as the "bandwagon effect" and the "coattails effect," to learn whether they occur at all, and under what circumstances. Findings already available on these matters show that the correspondence between party preference and voter opinions on issues is frequently weak: Republican voters, for example, favor the opinions of Democratic leaders more than they do the opinions of Republican leaders. The large popular vote received by Eisenhower in 1952 and 1956 did not, as some have supposed, signify a trend toward economic conservatism or a renewed desire to reduce government participation in social and economic affairs. Taking the election returns at their face value, therefore, would have been extremely misleading.

Election surveys have also proved exceedingly useful in studying the voting practices of particular groups or communities. Two of the most important pioneering election surveys, for example, were conducted in local communities, Sandusky, Ohio, and Elmira, New York.[38] Others have focused mainly on certain subgroups, such as Negroes[39] and Jews,[40] or on certain geographic regions, such as the South. As suggested earlier, the nature of the sample should be geared to the objectives of the inquiry. Much of the controversy over the appropriateness of a national versus a community

Registration in the South," *American Political Science Review,* Vol. 57, June, 1963, pp. 355–367; and Eulau, Heinz, *Class and Party in the Eisenhower Years:* Class Roles and Perspectives in the 1952 and 1956 Elections. Free Press, Glencoe, Ill., 1962.

[37] Key, V. O., Jr., "Theory of Critical Elections," *Journal of Politics,* Vol. 17, February, 1955, pp. 3–18; Campbell, *et al., op. cit.*

[38] Berelson, *et al., Voting, op. cit.*

[39] Matthews and Prothro, "Political Factors . . . ," *op. cit.*

[40] Fuchs, L. H., *The Political Behavior of American Jews.* Free Press, Glencoe, Ill., 1956.

sample for a study of voting is without point, for they serve somewhat different purposes, and each has advantages and disadvantages. A national voting study can accurately describe the motivations and voting decisions of the national electorate and of its major subgroups, divided geographically, ethnically, economically, and educationally. It is invaluable in helping to interpret the meaning of a particular election and makes possible comparisons of different regions and localities. A wide range of factors that affect the election outcome can be represented in appropriate frequency and strength. It is, of course, superior for predicting the election outcome or assessing the influences that have determined the results.

Studies of a national election conducted in local communities, however, also offer advantages. They permit an investigator to take account of such factors as local party organization, the presence of certain local candidates on the ballot, the community's traditions and history, and the role of local influence groups such as trade unions and business associations. As these suggest, surveys of individual communities lend themselves especially to studies in depth. If one is primarily interested in discovering relationships between or among variables, rather than in describing the national election itself, a survey of a single "average" community can for many purposes be as useful as a national survey. One can use the local community, for example, to assess the correlation between education and level of political interest, the influence of personality on voting choice, or the degree to which party affiliation is rooted in family and other peer group memberships. To be sure, one has to use caution in deciding whether a local finding can or cannot be generalized to the nation as a whole; one would scarcely use data gathered on voters in Jackson, Mississippi, to form generalizations about the role of civil rights issues for the rest of the nation. Many phenomena, however, are neither local nor idiosyncratic in nature, and one can safely assume that they yield a similar relationship in most or all communities within the same political culture. Ultimately, of course, all such assumptions—whether employed in a national or community survey—must be checked empirically.

Even this brief review suggests the considerable achievements and potentialities of survey methods for the study of elections. They have furnished solid information on the interaction of such socio-psychological factors as group membership, status, ideology, communication processes, personality, and demographic affiliations; and they have also supplied important information on "political" influences, e.g., party, issues, campaign techniques, partisanship, and candidates. There is, thus, little necessity for the fear, expressed by V. O. Key and others, that behavioral surveys of elections may focus so heavily on non-political variables as to neglect political influences. There is nothing inherent in the survey method to prevent one from taking account of party organization and activity, campaign propaganda, the role of the candidates, institutional influences on voter turnout, or dozens of other political factors. Furthermore, by knowing in a more exact way how much influence has been exerted by group memberships, personality, ideology, reference groups, or the mass media, one can more correctly assess the role played by the more strictly political influences.

Political Elites and Leadership

Although the survey method has so far been used chiefly for studies of mass responses, it is no less valuable for the investigation of political elites. Two difficulties, however, are likely to be encountered in elite studies. The first is that the universe is often more difficult to define, and the sampling procedures may, therefore, present special problems. It is, for example, difficult to decide precisely which groups comprise the universe of "party actives," or the "business elite," or the "foreign policy decision-makers." Second, certain elite groups such as Supreme Court judges or members of the White House staff are likely to be somewhat inaccessible to a survey interviewer. Neither of these difficulties is insurmountable, and they will be increasingly overcome as experience with elite studies is accumulated. Even now, the former of these difficulties does not apply to *all* political elites. There is little problem in defining the universe of state legislators, judges, or county committeemen. The members of these groups, furthermore, have been surprisingly willing to cooperate with survey investigators and, when properly approached, have submitted to lengthy and probing interviews on their political background, experience, and opinions.[41] Others, under the protection of anonymity, have cooperated in great numbers by completing lengthy, searching, self-administered attitude and personality questionnaires involving the most intimate opinions.

Studies of elites are of particular importance for political science. Politics, after all, is less the province of the electorate as a whole than of a small minority of office holders, party professionals, and amateur activists who contest for power, make decisions, and enforce policies. The central questions of political science concern are, "Who governs, how they gain power, how they exercise power, why men obey it, how they are controlled, to what ends they use power, and how its use relates to the values, aspirations, hopes, and fears of those who live under it. . . ."[42] We cannot hope to answer these questions without directly consulting the political elite, and for this the survey method is indispensable.[43] Obvious though this observation may seem, it has achieved currency only within the last decade or two, and only

---

[41] Marvick, Dwaine, ed., *Political Decision-Makers*. Free Press, Glencoe, Ill., 1961. Seligman, L. G., "Political Recruitment and Party Structure: A Case Study," *American Political Science Review*, Vol. 55, March, 1961, pp. 77–86; Wahlke, J. C., *et al., The Legislative System*. John Wiley & Sons, New York, 1962, especially pp. 69–143. For a documentary study, see Matthews, D. R., *The Social Background of Political Decision-Makers*. Doubleday, Garden City, N.Y., 1954. The most valuable summary of the research literature on political socialization is Hyman, H. H., *Political Socialization*. Free Press, Glencoe, Ill., 1959.

[42] Kirkpatrick, *op. cit.,* p. 27.

[43] Heard, Alexander, "Interviewing Southern Politicians," *American Political Science Review*, Vol. 44, December, 1950, pp. 886–896, at p. 894.

within certain quarters of the political science profession. Students of politics have traditionally observed political actors only from afar, studying them through their writings and speeches, or through such aggregative and anecdotal data as they could find. One may learn something about *individual* politicians through their autobiographies or biographies, their public statements, and their observed actions; but these sources cannot furnish the comprehensive portrait of motives, opinions, perceived interests, and ambitions needed for a scientific understanding of their behavior.

We have learned from surveys that political elites are disproportionately drawn from the more advantaged segments of the population—from those who enjoy higher ethnic, social, economic, or religious status. The typical member of the American political elite, for example, is a member of the middle or upper-middle class, college educated, a white Protestant from one of the "upper status" denominations, an urban resident, male, and above average age. He is likely to belong to a greater number of organizations than the average citizen and to participate more in community affairs generally. He has more opinions on public questions, and is ideologically more sophisticated. He displays greater consistency in his opinions, preferences, and political affiliations. He is more tolerant of those who express divergent opinions, and supports with greater understanding and conviction the procedural rights implicit in our democratic constitution.

Survey research has shown that, in the United States at least, the effect of political competition does not produce Tweedledee and Tweedledum parties: the forces that lead the parties to converge are counteracted by other forces that drive them apart. Nor does the support enjoyed by a party elite depend strongly on the particular opinions it expresses.[44] Nevertheless, party representatives and political office holders tend to respond to what they believe to be the desires of their constituents, although this tendency is not so strong as to exclude the expression of their own personal convictions.[45] Our present information also suggests that, contrary to the familiar opinion, the political class is less cynical about politics than are ordinary citizens, less willing to tolerate moral or political delinquency in other politicians, and more likely to embody the community conscience. The available data furnish little support for the widespread portrait of the politician as a callous, cynical, self-serving, purely opportunistic person who believes only in his own success, cares little for ideas, and would readily sacrifice the demands of conscience for the gains of political expediency. Obviously there are exceptions to these generalizations: survey research has identified political actors who are politically unaware, hold inconsistent opinions, or belong to a party but do not share its values. Some politicians have a poor grasp of the rules of the democratic game; some are cynical; and some are extremely confused ideologically. These sub-types have been identified, and something is being learned of their back-

[44] McClosky, *et al.,* "Issue Conflict . . . ," *op. cit.*
[45] Miller and Donald Stokes, "Constituency Influence . . . ," *op. cit.*

grounds, attitudes, personality traits, demographic characteristics, and group affiliations.

Surveys have also helped us to examine special classes of political actors, such as legislators and judges.[46] They have been used to investigate groups that bear a secondary or special relationship to politics, such as lawyers,[47] doctors,[48] military men,[49] business elites,[50] Negro elites,[51] and foreign policy elites.[52] They are also proving invaluable in the study of "community power" and community leaders. These studies have usually sought to identify the "political influentials" in particular communities—to discover the range of their powers and the subjects over which they have effective decision-making authority. Most of these studies have tried to assess the degree to which a community's political actors are the agents of interest groups or an independent force in their own right. Some surveys have identified and compared competing local elites, such as business elites, party elites, political office holders, and trade union elites. As more of these studies accumulate and comparison of their respective findings becomes possible, we will have gained important new insights into the nature, source, and manifestations of elite power in the primary communities in which men live.[53]

Political Ideology and Extreme Belief

Although political scientists have long been interested in the study of liberalism-conservatism, isolationism, fascism, communism, pacifism, populism, and socialism, they have only recently begun to explore systematically the sources and correlates of such doctrines. What kinds of people embrace them, and how do they differ from those who reject them? What inspires and sustains such views? Are they related to economic status, social mobility, political change, personality characteristics, a sense of alienation? Are indi-

[46] Matthews, D. R., *U.S. Senators and Their World.* University of North Carolina Press, Chapel Hill, North Carolina, 1960; Wahlke, *et al., op. cit.,* pp. 29–39; Sorauf, F. J., *Party and Representation.* Atherton, New York, 1963; Patterson, S. C., "Patterns of Interpersonal Relations in a State Legislative Group: The Wisconsin Assembly," *Public Opinion Quarterly,* Vol. 23, Spring, 1959, pp. 101–109; Hirschfield, R. S., *et al.,* "Profile of Political Activists in Manhattan," *Western Political Quarterly,* Vol. 15, September, 1962, pp. 489–506; Truman, D. B., *The Congressional Party:* A Case Study. John Wiley & Sons, New York, 1959.

[47] Eulau, Heinz, and J. D. Sprague, *Lawyers in Politics:* A Study in Professional Convergence. Bobbs-Merrill, Indianapolis, 1964.

[48] Glaser, W. A., "Doctors and Politics," *American Journal of Sociology,* Vol. 66, November, 1960, pp. 230–245.

[49] Janowitz, Morris, *The Professional Soldier,* Free Press, Glencoe, Ill., 1960.

[50] Bauer, R. A., *et al., American Business and Public Policy.* Atherton, New York, 1963.

[51] Wilson, James, *Negro Politics.* Free Press, Glencoe, Ill., 1960.

[52] Rosenau, James, *Public Opinion and Foreign Policy.* Random House, New York, 1961.

[53] Dahl, *Who Governs? op. cit.;* Agger, R. E., and Daniel Goldrich, "Community Power Structures and Partisanship," *American Sociological Review,* Vol. 23, August, 1958, pp. 383–392; Wildavsky, Aaron, *Leadership in a Small Town.* Bedminster Press, Totowa, N.J., 1964; Presthus, Robert, *Men at the Top.* Oxford University Press, New York, 1964; Hunter, Floyd, *Community Power Structure.* Doubleday, Garden City, N.Y., 1963; Vidich, A. J., and Joseph Bensman, *Small Town in Mass Society.* Princeton University Press, Princeton, 1958.

viduals of certain cognitive styles and capacities predisposed to accept or repudiate them? Do those who hold extremely deviant or conformist beliefs in one substantive area tend to deviate or conform in other areas as well?

Students of politics have increasingly turned to surveys to explore these questions. Surveys, for example, have confirmed the popular belief that liberalism—defined by reference to economic or social welfare attitudes—is most likely to prevail in the cities, among the young, the lower socioeconomic groups, minority ethnic groups, and Democrats. But the same pattern of correlations does not hold for other types of liberalism-conservatism—e.g., those expressing attitudes toward change, veneration of the past, or the right of individuals "to think and act for themselves." On these dimensions, the upper status and upper educated groups tend to be more liberal than the working class, the poor, and the uneducated. Young people and urban dwellers, however, are more liberal on these values as well. The articulate members of the society, it seems, have been more exposed to the liberal norms that prevail in the United States on non-economic matters; persons of lower education and status are often poorly situated to learn the value of procedural rights, tolerance of diversity, and social experimentation and change. Among the general population, therefore, the correlation is small between economic and non-economic liberalism-conservatism, whereas among the political influentials it is positive and significant. This reflects not only the greater exposure of political influentials to the prevailing norms, but also their greater ideological sophistication and inclination to adopt attitudes that are consistent with one another.

Surveys have also shown that liberalism-conservatism, especially of the classical or non-economic type, is markedly related to personality factors. Those psychological elements that lead to a pessimistic and suspicious view of human nature, to a punishing attitude toward human frailty, to misanthropy, or to inflexible and intolerant judgments about human diversity, are likely to be positively correlated with support for conservatism.[54] Similar personality characteristics turn up for those who hold extreme beliefs of either the right wing or left wing variety, or for those who score high on such measures as authoritarianism and totalitarianism. Such views are more frequently held by the inarticulate segments of the society (who are less able to discriminate them and to recognize their deviation from American democratic norms), and are also disproportionately expressed by individuals of misanthropic and inflexible personality dispositions who distrust mankind, who desire to control, regulate, and punish departures from approved standards, and who fear variety, contingency, and the "open" society. The embracing of these "radical" doctrines is associated with a tendency toward dogmatism and

[54] McClosky, Herbert, "Conservatism and Personality," *American Political Science Review,* Vol. 52, December, 1958, pp. 27–45; Lipset, *Political Man, op. cit.,* pp. 97–176, pp. 220–263; Campbell, *et al., The American Voter, op. cit.*

intolerance; and these traits, in turn, are related to intolerance of ambiguity and other marks of an inflexible personality.[55]

Comparable studies carried out on extreme isolationists show that they differ from non-isolationists in many of the ways that liberals differ from conservatives. They are intellectually less sophisticated, more parochial in outlook, and likely to lead more narrowly circumscribed lives. They are strongly given to dichotomous, and especially to we-they types of distinctions; and they are unusually intolerant of whatever is different or unfamiliar. The typical isolationist displays a strong element of misanthropy, a lack of sympathy for the misfortunes of others, and a fear and dislike of outsiders that amount almost to a ritualistic form of caste rejection. At the present stage of American history, isolationism is typically more xenophobic and belligerent than pacific: its proponents appear to be less concerned with the well-being of other nations than with shutting them out and refusing responsibility for them.[56]

Survey methods have also been used to investigate particular kinds of extreme groups. Almond, for example, has employed a modified type of survey technique to interview former members of the Communist party from four different countries in an effort to discover, among other things, what motivated them to join the Communist party and what types of appeals were most effective in inducing individuals from different strata of the society to support the party. Something was also learned about the internal nature of the movement and about the intellectual differences between the members of the organization's *apparatus* and those who compose its rank and file.[57] Other surveys have probed the sources of support for various movements of the radical right, including the Christian Anti-Communist Crusade,[58] the Coughlin movement, and the John Birch Society.[59] Several studies of McCarthy supporters, drawing on survey materials, have shown that those

---

[55] Rokeach, Milton, *et al.*, *The Open and Closed Mind.* Basic Books, New York, 1960; Adorno, T. W., *et al.*, *The Authoritarian Personality.* Harper & Bros., New York, 1950; Dicks, H. V., "Personality Traits and National Socialist Ideology," *Human Relations,* Vol. 3, August, 1950, pp. 111–154.

[56] McClosky, Herbert, "Attitude and Personality Correlates of Foreign Policy Orientation," in *Domestic Sources of Foreign Policy.* Edited by James Rosenau. The Free Press, New York, 1967. Reprinted below, chap. 2.

[57] Almond, G. A., *et al.*, *The Appeals of Communism.* Princeton University Press, Princeton, 1954; Micaud, C. A., *Communism and the French Left.* Praeger, New York, 1963; Ernst, M. L., and D. G. Loth, *Report on the American Communist.* Henry Holt, New York, 1952; Cantril, Hadley, *The Politics of Despair.* Basic Books, New York, 1958.

[58] Wolfinger, Raymond E., *et al.*, "America's Radical Right; Ideology and Politics," in *Ideology and Discontent:* The Concept of Ideology in the Light of Contemporary Social and Political Change. Edited by D. E. Apter. Free Press, Glencoe, Ill., 1964; and "The Clientele of the Christian Anti-Communism Crusade," paper delivered at American Political Science Association meeting, September, 1963.

[59] Lipset, S. M., "Three Decades of the Radical Right: Coughlinites, McCarthyites, and Birchers," in *The Radical Right.* Edited by Daniel Bell. Anchor Edition. Doubleday, Garden City, N.Y., 1964, pp. 313–377.

who supported the senator did not disproportionately favor the reckless, bullying, and undemocratic policies with which he was identified.[60]

Political Socialization, Stability, and Change

How are political beliefs and behavior patterns formed and maintained? Once established, how are they changed? Interest in such questions is currently strong and surveys are among the methods most frequently used to find the answers.

The research literature on political socialization prior to 1959 has been codified and reviewed by Herbert Hyman.[61] Merely to enumerate some of the topics covered by Hyman will suggest the range of survey (and other) research addressed to this subject. They include the sources of political participation, the ideals that inspire political involvement, the types of public heroes who serve as ego-ideals for youngsters, differences in political interest between boys and girls, the developmental stages at which voting preferences are firmly established, socio-economic influences on the formation of party preference, family sources of political belief, affiliation, and authoritarian or democratic tendencies, and the origins of tolerant and intolerant attitudes.[62] Survey research since 1959 has deepened and expanded the study of political socialization to include such topics as children's images of political authority, the degree of political awareness at different ages and under different class conditions, the relation between stability of political preference and strength of family indoctrination, the recruitment of state legislators, and the effects of personality on the learning of political responses.[63] Some of these studies have directly surveyed young people, while others have interviewed adults about their early political experiences and development.

[60] Trow, M. A., "Small Businessmen, Political Tolerance, and Support for McCarthy," *American Journal of Sociology,* Vol. 64, November, 1958, pp. 270–281; Lipset, "Three Decades . . .," *op. cit.,* pp. 313–377; Polsby, "Towards an Explanation . . .," *op. cit.;* McClosky, Herbert, "McCarthyism: The Myth and the Reality," paper delivered at the American Psychological Association meeting, New York, September, 1957; Fenton, J. M., *In Your Opinion.* Little-Brown, Boston, 1960, pp. 135–144.

[61] Hyman, *Political Socialization, op. cit.*

[62] *Ibid.,* chap. 2.

[63] Hess, R. D., and David Easton, "The Child's Changing Image of the President," *Public Opinion Quarterly,* Vol. 24, Winter, 1960, pp. 632–644; Easton, David, and R. D. Hess, "The Child's Political World," *Midwestern Journal of Political Science,* Vol. 6, August, 1962, pp. 229–246; McClosky, Herbert, and H. E. Dahlgren, "Primary Group Influence on Party Loyalty," *American Political Science Review,* Vol. 53, September, 1959, pp. 757–776; Eulau, Heinz, *et al.,* "The Political Socialization of American State Legislators," *Midwestern Journal of Political Science,* Vol. 3, May, 1959, pp. 188–206; Greenstein, F. I., "The Benevolent Leader—Children's Images of Political Authority," *American Political Science Review,* Vol. 54, December, 1960, pp. 934–943; "Sex-related Political Differences in Childhood," *Journal of Politics,* Vol. 23, May, 1961, pp. 353–371; "More on Children's Images of the President," *Public Opinion Quarterly,* Vol. 25, Winter, 1961, pp. 648–654; "Children and Politics," in *Yale Studies in Political Science,* Vol. 13. Yale University Press, New Haven, 1965; Maccoby, E. E., *et al.,* "Youth and Political Change," *Public Opinion Quarterly,* Vol. 18, No. 1, 1954, pp. 23–29; Verba, Sidney, *Small Groups and Political Behavior.* Princeton University Press, Princeton, 1961, pp. 17–60; Berelson, *et al., Voting, op. cit.,* pp. 54–117. Hess, R. D., and J. V. Torney, *The Development of Political Attitudes in Children,* Aldine, Chicago, 1967.

As already mentioned, surveys show that the habits of political participation and party preference are mainly implanted by the family and remain with the progeny long after they have left the family homestead. If the family's political interest is strong, and if no major changes in life-style are encountered, an individual is likely to retain these early habits throughout his lifetime. This prospect is reinforced by one's inclination to select friends and associates who share one's own political orientations, and by the tendency to remain in the life style inherited from one's parents. Shifts in political orientations and values do, of course, occur, in response to changing socio-economic status and peer group associations, new political experiences and standards, and the unfolding of political events. Conflicting primary group affiliations may prevent an individual from aligning himself strongly with any one political persuasion, and may lead him to political independency or to an unstable party attachment. The effectiveness of the competing influences will in part depend upon the strength of the family's initial indoctrination, the degree to which the family is attractive to him, and the frequency with which he continues to see them.

Even without "rebelling" against parents, each generation in a modern society is bound to differ somewhat from its predecessor; the offspring resemble the parents, but are not identical with them. Political change arises in part from the distance that invariably develops between generations. While their parents are transmitting one set of political values, the offspring are simultaneously acquiring a slightly different set from their peer culture and from the macro-society. Evidence from surveys conducted at different points in time, or on samples of different ages, plainly shows the extent of these shifts.

But the differences between parents and children on such doctrines as liberalism-conservatism do not result solely from generational changes; they are to some extent a function of the aging process itself, i.e., of experiences accumulated over time together with changes in physical and mental capacities. Generational differences, of course, may be further widened by the political experiences to which the youth have been exposed: war, depression, the election to the presidency of a powerful charismatic personality such as a Franklin Roosevelt, or the emergence of a compelling, overarching issue like civil rights may affect the lives of a generation so pervasively as to alter its views on many social questions. It appears, however, that shifts in political belief tend to be small and gradual rather than large and abrupt. We have sometimes been misled on this matter because of the drama that attends the conversion of an individual from one political extreme to another—from membership in the Communist party, for example, to affiliation with an extreme right-wing group. But such conversions are atypical; the more characteristic pattern is one in which the shifts are small, and proceed by slow stages and by gradual accommodation. Although no panel survey has so far addressed the issue of conversion directly, it would be an excellent device for observing political changes over time, and for uncovering the influences that induce those changes.

Psychology and Politics

The most important spur to research on this subject was the publication in 1950 of *The Authoritarian Personality*.[64] This work and the many research efforts it inspired demonstrate that the adoption of certain political orientations—e.g., the extreme left orientations already discussed—is in part a function of personality characteristics. Hostile, paranoid, or "authoritarian" personality patterns are found with particular frequency among persons who are oriented toward fascism, communism, and other political doctrines that are intemperate, angry, and grandiose in their claims and ambitions. Persons who advocate "extreme" beliefs, whether of the left or right, are on the average more dogmatic, closed-minded, and psychologically inflexible than are those who hold moderate and democratic beliefs.[65] Similarly, those who strongly support doctrines that exclude certain groups or that magnify differences between themselves and others—e.g., isolationism, ethnocentrism, chauvinism, xenophobia—frequently also display the familiar symptoms of paranoia: excessive anxiety, the projection of hostility, grandiose self-inflation, unrealistic fear and depreciation of "outsiders" coupled with a tendency to ascribe mysterious and exaggerated powers to them, and so forth.[66] But while personality dispositions are most often engaged by "extreme" political doctrines, they may also, as we have seen, affect the holding of more moderate beliefs, such as conservatism and liberalism.[67]

The relation of group membership to the establishment and retention of norms is another area of interest to political psychology. The research literature on this subject is so vast and well-known that there is no point in reviewing it here. Suffice it to say that the mechanisms by which primary and other reference groups succeed in indoctrinating their members are in great measure "psychological." Such groups not only set norms which serve their members as psychological anchoring points, but they also have the power to reward and punish, to give or withhold affection, to structure reality, and to determine the individual's self-image. Affiliation with a group, of course, may also be socially or economically instrumental. Whatever the reason for the attachment, survey and other data confirm that members of the same groups tend to hold similar political views, value similar objects and goals, affiliate with the same parties, and have common perspectives on the political process. The more palpable the group, the greater its in-

[64] Adorno, *et al., op. cit.;* Dicks, *op. cit.*

[65] Rokeach, *et al., op. cit.,* pp. 109–131.

[66] Adorno, *et al., op. cit.;* McClosky, "Attitude and Personality Correlates . . . ," *op. cit.;* Perlmutter, H. V., "Correlates of Two Types of Xenophilic Orientation," *Journal of Abnormal Social Psychology,* Vol. 52, January, 1956, pp. 130–135; "Some Characteristics of the Xenophobic Personality," *Journal of Psychology,* Vol. 38, October, 1954, pp. 291–300.

[67] McClosky, "Conservatism and Personality," *op. cit.*

fluence: a peer group, for example, has more psychological weapons than a large and amorphous categoric group, and its capacity for instilling political habits and standards in its members will ordinarily be greater.[68]

Psychological approaches also figure prominently in the study of leadership. Though most of the work on the psychology of leadership has been done through laboratory studies of small groups, some beginnings have been made in applying survey methods to this subject. A few surveys have explored the relation of personality factors to one's choice of leaders and one's image of the qualities of leadership.[69] Several others have sought to learn whether political leaders are distinguished from non-leaders by their personality traits and whether leadership can in itself be considered a "trait" or combination of traits.[70]

Surveys are also beginning to be used to explore the psychological correlates of political conformity and deviation. This subject, too, has mainly been studied through laboratory experiments. Surveys, however, can be useful in locating those who conform to or deviate from the modal political values of their sub-culture or of society. They can be used to observe the relationship between personality and the tendency to conform or deviate. Survey data now under analysis at the Survey Research Center, University of California, Berkeley, strongly suggest, for example, that certain forms of political "deviancy"—including deviancy from the norms of one's party and the embracing of extreme doctrines—are related to an individual's learning capacity and to the psychological needs and motivations that affect that capacity.

Political Institutions and Systems

The manner of applying surveys to the study of politics has been criticized in some quarters for an alleged tendency to ignore "politics" and political institutions in favor of social, psychological, and intellectual characteristics of individuals in the mass public. As Key observed, "Ultimately the concern of the student of politics must center on the operation of the state apparatus in one way or another. Both the characteristics of the survey instrument and the curiosities of those with a mastery of survey technique have tended to encourage a focus of attention on microscopic political phenomena more or less in isolation from the total political process."[71] Studies of primary groups, reference groups, or cross pressures, he complained, do not tell us

[68] Verba, *op. cit.*

[69] Cantril, Hadley, *The Psychology of Social Movements.* John Wiley & Sons, New York, 1941, pp. 233–238; Sanford, F. H., *Authoritarianism and Leadership.* Stephenson Bros., Philadelphia, 1950.

[70] McConaughy, J. B., "Certain Personality Factors of State Legislators in North Carolina," *American Political Science Review,* Vol. 44, December, 1950, pp. 897–903; Gibb, C. A., "Leadership" in *Handbook of Social Psychology.* Edited by Gardner Lindzey, *op. cit.,* pp. 233–238.

[71] Key, V. O., Jr. "The Politically Relevant in Surveys," *Public Opinion Quarterly,* Vol. 24, Spring, 1960, pp. 54–61, at p. 55.

much about the political order, and a bridge is needed "from observation of atoms of the political system to the system itself. . . ."

It must be admitted that political surveys have until now paid less attention to the institutional and systemic aspects of politics than to the forces which induce individual political behavior. This tendency can in part be traced to their ancestry. Having derived from the public opinion poll, academic political surveys continue to be regarded (even by some of their users) primarily as instruments for the assessment of opinion. There are, in addition, some inherent limitations on the utility of surveys for the study of political systems. Surveys, for example, would scarcely be the recommended procedure for observing rapidly changing behavior or institutional practices that involve many interactions occurring in different contexts over long periods of time. Some political processes can more appropriately be observed through participant observation or through reports of journalists and other chroniclers of political events. The formal structure and procedures of a political system can more economically be ascertained by consulting its constitutional and statutory documents than by conducting elaborate surveys.

There are, nevertheless, many institutional and systemic questions that can usefully be approached through surveys. Studies of the actual organization and procedures of a legislature or party would be cases in point. Political institutions, after all, are more than the formal structures prescribed in constitutional documents, statutes, or executive orders. They are agencies or instrumentalities that discuss, respond, decide, and act—which means that they can for some purposes be conceptualized as aggregates of people standing in a certain relationship to each other. One way to understand an institution is to survey the people who occupy its roles and help to carry out its functions. Through appropriate sampling procedures and a well-designed questionnaire, one can learn much about the forces that play upon an institution, how it resolves its internal conflicts, how it arrives at decisions, what it does to put those decisions into practice, how it interacts with other institutions in the system, and how it perceives its constituency. Some of these questions cannot adequately be answered except by consulting the men and women who act for the organization.

Although gathered through interviews with individuals, survey findings have great potential value for the macroscopic understanding of political systems and institutions. For example, a survey of voters in a single election will tell us about that particular election or the individuals who participated in it; but a comparison of many election studies conducted in different places, at different times, under different circumstances, with different parties and issues can teach us something about competitive party systems, the role of ideas and consensus in the viability of democratic governments, and the realities of political representation under modern mass democracy. Election surveys have thrown light on the relation between political belief and party divergence, on the relative influence of two-party and multi-party systems in "balkanizing" the electorate,[72] and on the connection between sense of party responsibility and degree of ideological cleavage between parties. A survey of trade union members has furnished insights into the question of how oligarchical domination has been avoided and a competitive party system maintained in at least one trade union organization.[73] Voting surveys have shown how the form of the ballot affects straight or split-ticket voting, and which voters are most likely to be influenced.[74] They have also furnished new and better information on the ways in which voting laws affect turnout,[75] and on the forces that give rise to party realignment.[76] Similarly, comparative surveys have not only added to our knowledge of political participation, but have also told us something about political modernization and the impact of political cultures on a sense of civic competence.

Surveys are also being used to study "community power." By sampling political elites and voters, these surveys have significantly enlarged our understanding of local political institutions. They have supplied detailed information on the interplay between citizens, elected officials, administrative agencies, the business community, labor organizations, and other urban groups.[77]

The survey method has likewise increased the possibility of understanding the legislature as an institution. While furnishing information on individual legislators—e.g., their social backgrounds, training, motivations, self-images, opinions, partisanship—they simultaneously tell us something about the nature of the legislature itself. Recent surveys, moreover, have directly addressed the question of the legislature as an institution by examining lawmakers in their legislative roles. They have, for example, asked to what extent a legislator's behavior is a response to his legislative party, to the intensity of interparty competition within his constituency, to pressures from the executive agencies, and to his own view of the "representative" function.

[72] Campbell, Angus, and Henry Valen, "Party Identification in Norway and the United States," *Public Opinion Quarterly,* Vol. 25, Winter, 1961, pp. 505-525.

[73] Lipset, S. M., M. A. Trow, and J. S. Coleman, *Union Democracy.* Free Press, Glencoe, Ill., 1956.

[74] Campbell, Angus, and W. E. Miller, "The Motivational Basis of Straight and Split-Ticket Voting," *American Political Science Review,* Vol. 51, June, 1957, pp. 293-312.

[75] Campbell, "Recent Developments . . . ," *op. cit.,* p. 34.

[76] Matthews, D. R., and J. W. Prothro, "Southern Images of Political Parties: An Analysis of White and Negro Attitudes," *Journal of Politics,* Vol. 26, February, 1964, pp. 82-111.

[77] Dahl, *Who Governs? op. cit.;* Agger and Goldrich, "Community Power Structures . . . ," *op. cit.,* pp. 383-392; Greer, S. A., "Mass Society and the Parapolitical Structure," *American Sociological Review,* Vol. 27, October, 1962, pp. 634-646; "Urbanism Reconsidered: A Comparative Study of Local Areas in a Metropolis," *American Sociological Review,* Vol. 21, February, 1956, pp. 19-25; *Metropolitics: A Study of Political Culture.* John Wiley & Sons, New York, 1963; *Governing the Metropolis.* John Wiley & Sons, New York, 1962; Banfield, E. C., *Political Influence.* Free Press, Glencoe, Ill., 1961; A. B. Wildavsky, *Leadership in a Small Town,* Bedminster Press, Totowa, N.J., 1964; Robert Presthus, *Men at the Top,* Oxford University Press, New York, 1964.

They have asked how legislators perceive the norms of the institution, how they define their own role within the body, and what role they assign to the legislature in the political system as a whole. They have further sought to learn in what measure the legislative process depends upon its formal rules and organization and in what measure upon its informal structure—its cliques and factions, its party blocs and conflicts, and its response to lobbies and to reference groups outside the legislature. Some of these matters have been studied by consulting roll-call tabulations, official journals, aggregative data on constituency characteristics, and other documentary sources. Valuable as such sources are, they cannot furnish the detailed information on legislators' roles, perceptions, and responses needed for an adequate understanding of the legislature as an institution.[78]

Survey research on the executive and judicial branches of government has lagged behind the research on the representative bodies, although unsystematic interview studies of executive agencies have, of course, been attempted for some time. Behavioral research on the courts has for the most part drawn on documentary sources, such as biographies of judges or the official reports of their decisions. Various mathematical and scaling procedures have been developed to uncover the central tendency of a judge's decisions or to identify the colleagues with whom he habitually aligns himself. A few survey attempts have been made to relate the political attitudes of judges to their decisions and verdicts, but large-scale surveys of judges, comparable to those now available on legislators, party leaders, or voters, have not yet been undertaken. The empirical study of the judiciary, however, is developing rapidly and surveys of greater scope and depth are bound to be forthcoming before long.[79]

Comparative and International Studies

Although interest in cross-cultural political surveys has been growing rapidly, the number of completed surveys that are genuinely comparative

---

[78] Eulau, *et al.,* "The Political Socialization of American State Legislators," *op. cit.;* Wahlke, J. C., *et al., The Legislative System, op. cit.;* Sorauf, *op. cit.;* Miller, W. E., and Donald Stokes, *Congress and Constituency* (forthcoming); Silverman, Corrine, "The Legislators' View of the Legislative Process," *Public Opinion Quarterly,* Vol. 18, Summer, 1954, pp. 180–190; Patterson, *op. cit.;* Truman, *The Congressional Party, op. cit.;* MacRae, Duncan, Jr., *The Dimensions of Congressional Voting.* University of California Press, Berkeley, 1958. Reviews of the research on legislative bodies may be found in Meller, Norman, "Legislative Behavior Research," *Western Political Quarterly,* Vol. 13, March, 1960, pp. 131–153; and Wahlke, J. C., "Behavioral Analyses of Representative Bodies," in *Essays on the Behavioral Study of Politics.* Edited by Austin Ranney, *op. cit.,* pp. 173–190.

[79] An excellent summary of the behavioral work on the judiciary is presented in Schubert, G. L., ed., *Judicial Decision-Making.* Free Press, Glencoe, Ill., 1963. See also Nagel, S. S., "Off-the-Bench Judicial Attitudes," in *ibid,* pp. 29–53; "Ethnic Affiliation and Judicial Propensities," *Journal of Politics,* Vol. 24, February, 1962, pp. 92–100; "Political Party Affiliation and Judges' Decisions," *American Political Science Review,* Vol. 55, December, 1961, pp. 843–850; Spaeth, H. J., "An Approach to the Study of Attitudinal Differences as an Aspect of Judicial Behavior," *Midwestern Journal of Political Science,* Vol. 5, 1961, pp. 165–180.

is still fairly small. Cross-cultural studies, of course, are likely to be expensive and to involve numerous technical problems arising out of the translation of terms, the framing of cognate concepts, and the validation of measures on different populations. Nor are there adequately trained field staffs in all countries or foreign communities in which one might wish to conduct a survey.

If these difficulties can be overcome, comparative surveys hold out many advantages. Employed, for example, in studies of modernization, surveys can be used to trace the actual changes in the values and behavior of individuals located at different points of the society. They can be used to supplement aggregative ecological data or to collect it when reliable ecological records are not available. By asking the same questions in different countries, an investigator can make precise comparisons, determine whether certain findings are unique or universal, observe variations in the political norms and practices, and assess the impact of different types of "political culture" on behavior. He might even be able to test the influence of certain institutional or systemic differences on behavior. How do different political settings affect political behavior and practices, such as voting, participation, political socialization, political recruitment, and intensity of party competition? Generalizations about so-called "national character" might also be checked out, e.g., are the French really more ideological than other people? Are the Germans authoritarian, the British politically pragmatic, the Italians politically romantic?

Although answers to such questions lie in the future, some beginnings have been made. Almond and Verba, as we noted, have carried out a five-nation comparative survey of political socialization, citizenship, and participation.[80] Almond has also conducted a four-nation study of former members of the Communist party, in an effort to compare the nature and effectiveness of the party's appeals.[81] This study has inspired similar studies in other parts of the world.[82] In an ambitious effort to assess the forces of modernization in underdeveloped countries, Columbia University's Bureau of Applied Social Research undertook a cross-cultural survey of seven Near-Eastern and Mediterranean nations.[83] This inquiry examined the effects of communication on the modernization process, and explored such variables as geographic mobility, exposure to media, the broadening of personal horizons, capacity for "empathy," demographic characteristics, sense of personal well-being and effectiveness, and the role of ideologies.

[80] Almond and Verba, *op. cit.*

[81] Almond, *The Appeals . . . , op. cit.;* and Cantril, *The Politics . . . , op. cit.*

[82] Pye, L. W., *Guerilla Communism in Malaya:* Its Social and Political Meaning. Princeton University Press, Princeton, 1956.

[83] Lerner, Daniel, and Lucille Pevsner, *The Passing of Traditional Society:* Modernizing the Middle East. Free Press, Glencoe, Ill., 1958; Mosel, James, "Communication Patterns and Political Socialization in Traditional Thailand," in *Communications and Political Development.* Edited by L. W. Pye. Princeton University Press, Princeton, 1963, pp. 184–228.

Survey studies on a smaller scale have also been carried out by Campbell and Valen on party affiliation in Norway and the United States,[84] by Converse and Dupeux on political socialization in the United States and France,[85] and by Rokkan on comparative aspects of political participation and voting behavior.[86]

New Applications for Survey Research

It is plain from the foregoing that survey research has penetrated many areas of political science and has become an indispensable tool of political inquiry. It is equally plain, however, that the potential of political surveys has only begun to be explored and that many important questions have not yet been addressed. We cannot list all the questions that might fruitfully be investigated by surveys but we can at least suggest their potential by considering their application to four areas of political study: leadership, internal party affairs, the relation of political belief to action, and the analysis of political events and trends.

Political Leadership

Although leadership is an everyday feature of political life, far less is scientifically known about it than is commonly supposed. Most of what is known has been learned from laboratory studies of small groups, with little having been done on political leadership as such.

Scholars interested in leadership have been unable to agree on its nature or source. Is it a "trait," a composite of traits, a relationship among people similar to other types of relationships (such as friendship), the product of a given environment and circumstance, or a combination of these? Although the trait theory presently enjoys little support among scholars, neither this nor any theory of leadership has been systematically explored and tested in the field of politics. This is, however, an area to which surveys could contribute immensely, especially if they were to be combined with procedures for assessing personality. By comparing political leaders with non-leaders, or with leaders from other elite groups, one might simultaneously test the trait theory of leadership, observe the influence of social background and "situation" on the recruitment and ascendancy of leaders, and learn

---

[84] Campbell and Valen, op. cit.

[85] Converse, P. E., and Georges Dupeux, "Politicization of the Electorate in France and the United States," Public Opinion Quarterly, Vol. 26, Spring, 1962, pp. 1–33.

[86] Rokkan, Stein, "Party Preferences and Opinion Patterns in Western Europe: A Comparative Analysis," International Social Science Bulletin, Vol. 7, 1955, pp. 575–576. For reviews of comparative research, particularly on voting and participation, see Rokkan, Stein and Henry Valen, "Parties, Elections and Political Behavior in the Northern Countries: A Review of Recent Research," in Politische Forschung. Edited by Otto Stammer. Westdeutscher Verlag, Koeln-Opladen, 1960; and Rokkan, Stein, "The Comparative Study of Political Participation: Notes Toward a Perspective on Current Research," in Essays on the Behavioral Study of Politics. Edited by Austin Ranney, op. cit., pp. 47–90; and other works by Rokkan.

something in the process about the relational-situational type of explanation.

Surveys might help us to answer some elementary questions about which, at present, we can only conjecture. To what extent does leadership depend upon a correspondence of views between leader and followers? Are would-be leaders who possess certain outlooks, temperaments, or capacities more likely to be selected under one set of circumstances (say, for example, military exigency) than others? By what criteria or signs do the active members of a political party "select" certain individuals as party leaders or candidates? Do the leaders selected differ in appearance, background, style, personality, or other traits from other party members or from the members of other elites? Are the attributes actually possessed by leaders discernible to the voters or even to the active party members who helped to choose them? Although surveys are now being addressed to some of these questions, we are a long way from having the hard data we need to deal with them adequately.

The nature of the politician, as distinguished from other social types, has long fascinated political observers, and has inspired numerous discursive essays.[87] Few systematic research efforts, however, have been addressed to this question, and we have little established knowledge on which to draw. It has often been thought, for example, that politicians differ markedly from, say, bureaucrats in their adaptability to change, their willingness to indulge human frailty and variety, their empathy and capacity for warm personal relations, and their flexibility in the enforcement of rules. The vocational politician is considered by some observers to have a dislike of theory and idealism, and to embrace a pragmatic, hard-headed realism bordering on cynicism. Surveys are among the principal devices by which these and related claims can be tested. Carried out in more than one country, they can tell us whether there is a universal political vocation or whether the dominant type varies, in predictable ways, from one political system to another, and from one era to another. Such surveys would also furnish essential information on the leaders' educational, occupational, or religious backgrounds, their previous political experience, their reference groups, and so forth. Comparison of vocational politicians in and out of office, or those serving at different levels or in different branches of government, would also be possible.

Internal Party Affairs

Political scientists have devoted considerable attention to the study of political parties, but systematic information is still lacking on many important questions that bear upon the internal life of the party. Little is known, for example, about the nature and sources of party loyalty and partisanship,

---

[87] Probably the most brilliant of these is Weber, Max, "Politics as a Vocation," in *From Max Weber: Essays in Sociology.* Edited by H. H. Gerth and C. W. Mills. Oxford University Press, New York, 1946, pp. 77–128.

and about the relation of these to attitudes toward party discipline and responsibility. Our own inquiries suggest that the correlation is imperfect and that many loyal party participants are unwilling to impose strong party discipline upon other members. Our evidence also suggests that those with the strongest party loyalty do not always conform to the party's modal outlook, a disparity that is especially apparent among the less informed members of the organization. We know much less than we should about the reasons for defection from traditional membership or withdrawal from active participation. To what extent, for example, do shifts result from changes in party programs, from the impact of significant events (such as depression or war), or from changes in the style and tone imprinted upon a party by its leaders?

We still know little about the nature and sources of factionalism within parties. Do cleavages in the American parties tend to be ideological or personal? Do they characteristically develop around geographic or economic interests, contending leaders, differences on issues, responses to oligarchical domination, or conflicting tactical orientations? Are the members of minority factions more militant or "radical" than those in the dominant faction? How does factionalism in mass parties of the American type differ from factionalism in the smaller, more stringently ideological parties of Europe?

These and dozens of other questions about internal party affairs can be approached with considerable profit through survey procedures. By directly consulting party members, one could ascertain which factions or leaders they identify with, where they stand on party issues, how partisan and loyal they are, how they feel about the organization and management of their party, and, most important, whether they respond to these questions in a patterned way. By surveying members at different levels of the party, one could also test current hypotheses concerning the role of leaders in formulating and transmitting the organization's norms. One might also learn whether the distinction Almond finds between the esoteric and exoteric doctrines of an organization like the Communist party holds to any degree among moderate, non-revolutionary parties. Through repeated surveys, one might also determine whether members change their outlook on certain questions as their party moves in and out of power.

Surveys, of course, are not the only research procedures by which the internal affairs of political parties can be studied. For best results, they should be combined with macro-studies of the parties. Survey findings become far more meaningful if one takes account of the party's official activities, its public stand on issues, its choice of candidates, the pronouncements of its spokesmen, and other marks of the party in action.

Relation of Belief to Action

Surveys are repeatedly used to measure beliefs (political and others), but the relation of those beliefs to action has received little attention. Although beliefs are unquestionably important clues to how people act, they are not perfect indicators of action, and the exact connection between the two must therefore be explored if we are to achieve a more scientific understanding of politics. What, for example, are the "behavioral" consequences of changing people's attitudes? Is the correspondence between belief and action greater among articulates or inarticulates, among persons who hold conventional beliefs or those who hold unconventional ones, among those who lead or those who follow? Under what conditions will persons who embrace totalitarian beliefs act on them in a way that endangers democracy? How far can political loyalties be strained without breaking? At present, we lack basic information on most questions of this kind.

Surveys can help in several ways to assess the relation between political belief and action. They can be used, for example, to select for closer observation under laboratory conditions people who express certain political beliefs. Experiments might be aimed at testing the relation between their beliefs as reported in a survey and their overt behavior in response to certain stimuli. Using a measure like the California F Scale, one might employ a survey to select samples of "authoritarians" and "equalitarians," who might then be compared in their responses to "democratic" and "authoritarian" situations as simulated in the laboratory. Would the low and high scorers differ significantly in the way they behave toward power figures, peers, and subordinates? Would they be rigid in the enforcement of the rules of the game, or tolerant and flexible? How would they behave toward members of minority groups?

Surveys might similarly be used to compare conformity "attitudes" with conformity "behavior." By utilizing a conformity scale in a survey questionnaire, one might easily identify respondents who prize conventionality, demand conformity from others or, alternatively, who express independence and applaud "deviation." If these groups were then subjected to conformity pressures of the type employed by Asch and Crutchfield in their laboratory studies of conformity,[88] how would they behave? Would they succumb to group judgments even when those judgments are patently absurd, or would they stand up to the group in defense of their own judgments? From the interplay of their verbal responses, as elicited in the survey, and their overt responses, as evoked by the experiment, an investigator might learn a great deal about the relation between thought and action in this domain. He might add dimension to the inquiry by simulating in the laboratory a council or legislative body or jury, and by observing the effects of communication and persuasion on persons holding different attitudes. This combination of research methods might also be employed to see whether a respondent who

[88] Asch, S. E., "Effects of Group Pressure upon the Modification and Distortion of Judgment," in *Groups, Leadership, and Men*. Edited by H. S. Guetzkow. Carnegie Press, Pittsburgh, 1951; Crutchfield, R. S., "Personal and Situational Factors in Conformity to Group Pressure," *Acta Psychologica*, Vol. 15, 1959, pp. 386–388.

presents himself on a questionnaire as politically responsible, flexible, and open to negotiation actually behaves this way in an experimental group. One might also compare a respondent's professed belief in civil liberties and procedural rights with his tendency to behave tolerantly or repressively in political or judicial situations simulated in the laboratory. The effect of beliefs on overt behavior can in some instances also be examined in "real-life" situations outside the laboratory; here, the respondents selected by survey procedures might be observed as they participate politically, make choices, respond to political communications, engage in political discussions, and align themselves with one political group or another.

It is also possible to compare political beliefs and actions without going outside the survey method itself. One can, for example, reinterview respondents to see whether they have acted consistently with the opinions they expressed in earlier interviews. Even a one-shot survey may permit the investigators to compare the beliefs a respondent expresses in the interview and the overt behavior he reports about himself. One may find respondents who claim to be politically independent but invariably vote for the same party; others who assert beliefs about democracy, tolerance and party loyalty to which, as their responses show, they fail to adhere in practice. A survey investigator can also make use of the case method, presenting respondents with problem cases to see whether their responses are consistent with the principles they have previously stated. How, for example, would the respondent vote if he were on a jury hearing a case of high treason? Would he intercede with the police to gain protection for a group of civil rights workers threatened by segregationists? A respondent's answers to such questions will not predict perfectly how he would actually behave under the circumstances stated, but they do introduce an action dimension that goes beyond the mere expression of opinions. It is, in any event, clear from these and the foregoing examples that the survey method does not restrict the political scientist to the study of opinions and attitudes. Used imaginatively, it permits him to learn something about overt political behavior as well.

Historical and Trend Analysis

Key, among others, has criticized surveys for being "static," and for providing us "with a reading at one point in time." Even panel studies, he maintains, cover too brief a period to make a correct reading of the "great and really significant political actions . . . [that] take place over comparatively long periods of time."[89]

Although there is some merit in this criticism, the survey method does not need to be time-bound to the degree that Key's comment implies. Since the method is new, we have not yet had an adequate test of its capacity

[89] Key, Jr., "The Politically Relevant . . . ," *op. cit.*

to furnish parallel data collected over long periods of time. It is not necessary to conduct panel studies in order to document trends, for this can also be done by surveys repeated on different samples of the same universe. Surveys conducted in series can reveal important changes in beliefs, practices, life styles, social characteristics, and patterns of response to given stimuli. By accumulating parallel data collected at different points in time, surveys make it possible both to trace changes in the political culture and to ascertain the events that have produced those changes. As survey data accumulate, there will be less need to rely on the familiar secondary indicators upon which historians have had primarily to depend—newspapers, diaries, business invoices, published speeches, etc. These sources should not be depreciated, of course, but they rarely furnish hard and reliable data in as useful a form as can be obtained through parallel surveys conducted over time. Deriving cumulative data from surveys diminishes the selection bias that plagues the historian's efforts, and he is less likely, therefore, to be misled by the writings, speeches, or documents that happen to fall into his hands or that his leanings have led him to search out.

Surveys conducted at different historical stages will help us to ascertain something about changes in the value system and mood of a nation, the people's sense of well-being or malaise, their satisfaction with political institutions, and their attitudes toward government policies. We will be able to learn which aspects of political culture are stable and universal, and which are labile, transitional, or unique to a given time and place. We will also be able to discover which policies increase or diminish political morale, awaken or dampen one's sense of civic responsibility, and incite certain segments of the population to protest and disaffection. Thus, while a single survey may furnish a portrait of political life at a given moment in time, successive surveys on parallel questions become the equivalent of a moving portrait.

Hence, if one is interested in such phenomena as "modernization," one can trace in considerable detail the process by which a political system or nation unfolds, opens itself to experience, casts off old forms, and integrates new ones. One can also discern which influences and events retard or speed up the diffusion of political values.

The quality of trend analyses can be significantly improved through the use of computers to process the mountains of data that are bound to be generated by a series of surveys. Computers can be set to divine trends, to reveal discontinuities, to take notice of deviations from modal patterns, and to search out configurations that have held for a long time. They can show which influences remain constant, despite changing institutions and events, and which vary as conditions change. Their extraordinary capacity for retrieving and processing data will permit us to test numerous hypotheses that until now have been difficult or impossible to test. If, for example, one is interested in the effects of certain types of international events on a nation's attitudes, one can "ask" the computer to select all instances of such events on which survey data are available, tabulate the responses, and compute the statistics needed by the investigator to test his hypotheses.

It is also possible to use surveys—or, more accurately, the findings drawn from surveys—to reanalyze past historical events. By applying survey results retroactively, for example, one can analyze past elections with the more sophisticated concepts and knowledge learned from survey studies of recent elections. A few historians have already begun to conduct such studies, and their efforts have thrown considerable doubt on the standard interpretations of these events.[90] Equally important, an investigator's awareness of survey results may impel him to search out new, systematic, and more trustworthy data on which to test his explanations. An historian who works in this way will no longer be satisfied with impressionistic observations and *ad hoc* explanations, but will attempt to force the historical repositories to relinquish their secrets in more quantifiable and systematic form. He will also be able to avoid assumptions he has reason to believe are unfounded: he is unlikely, considering what is known about the contemporary electorate, to attribute a high level of political awareness and ideological sophistication to the voters of the past, especially when one considers their lower average education and greater removal from the sources of political communication.

The Contribution of Surveys to Theory

Surveys are normally thought of as fact-gathering procedures, and their ability to perform this function, as the foregoing attests, is formidable. Less often appreciated, however, is their potential contribution to the construction and testing of theory.

The value of surveys for political theory lies, to begin with, in the intellectual rigor demanded by their methodology. A survey user must clarify the meaning of his principal terms and decide precisely how they are to be measured. He must try to state his theory in an orderly, coherent form and to derive from it the hypotheses he wishes to examine. He must decide by what evidence and by what logic these hypotheses are to be tested. When his results are in, he must analyze and reason about them, deciding in what measure his theory has been supported and in what ways it must be qualified or changed.

A theory need not be tested to survive, but it is more likely to retain its vitality if its claims can be validated. In the absence of an empirical confrontation, it may be passed on, without challenge, from one generation to another, but it will probably grow limp and cease to have force. Theoretical advances depend not only on the theorist's intuitive brilliance, but on his

[90] Benson, Lee, "Research Problems in American Political Historiography," in *Common Frontiers of the Social Sciences.* Edited by Mirra Komarovsky. Free Press, Glencoe, Ill., 1957, pp. 118–183.

ability to face facts and to furnish meaningful explanations for them. As facts emerge from surveys and other types of empirical inquiry, they compel the investigator to reconsider and adjust his theories so as to account more adequately for the new data. The influence of surveys on political theory can be discerned in virtually every branch of the subject in which they have been employed. We have space, however, only to point to a few examples.

One area that has felt the impact of survey findings most sharply is that of democratic theory. Findings from survey research have forced scholars to revise their views about the nature and practice of democratic government. Although no single or standard definition of democracy has been accepted everywhere and at all times, the model most frequently presented in the textbooks portrays democracy as a system based on the active consent of an alert popular electorate which chooses its rulers only after a careful appraisal of alternatives. The electorate is represented, in effect, as enjoying perfect communication and full knowledge of all competing parties, candidates, and programs. They are presumed to exercise their choice in a perfectly rational manner after having weighed their own best interests and the interests of the nation. Upon observing their would-be rulers, a majority forms, achieves consensus, and selects the men who will represent the people for the period prescribed in the constitution. The majority choice is usually the "correct" one, for the people are supreme not only in law but in wisdom.

Our concern here is not with the utility of this or any other "rational" model of democracy, for such models unquestionably have their uses (much as a rational model of a perfectly competitive economy is useful to the economist). We are obliged, nevertheless, to observe that survey research on voting and other democratic processes shows various elements in the textbook theory to be empirically indefensible and to misrepresent the process by which democratic systems actually function and manage to survive. Moved by this realization, students of democratic politics have begun, here and there, to modify the theory in order to take account of the part actually played by the electorate in the exercise of consent, and to reconsider the role of the parties, candidates, issues, communication processes, etc., in the conduct of elections.[91] They have likewise begun to reconsider the meaning of such concepts as public, public opinion, and majority rule, redefining these terms to reflect their nature and complexity, as revealed by survey research. The role of elites in democracy is being re-evaluated, and their value as repositories of democratic beliefs and as the agencies that enforce the democratic rules of the game is being stressed.[92] Also being questioned are the traditional assumptions about the "natural" democracy of the poor, the ignorant, and the unsophisticated. As a result of survey findings on the divided political beliefs of the American electorate,

---

[91] Berelson, *et al.*, *Voting*, *op. cit.*, chap. 14.
[92] Dahl, *Who Governs? op. cit.*, chap. 28.

suggestions are being made to modify the long-standing assumptions about consensus, i.e., about the alleged need for agreement on constitutional norms as a precondition for democracy.[93]

Survey results are also inspiring changes in our theories about political parties and their role in the political process. The familiar portrait of the parties as mere agencies of interest groups is being reconsidered. The parties, it seems, are principals as well as agents, reference groups in their own right, that formulate policy out of intellectual conviction as well as political accommodation. The data also show that loyalty to a party (in the United States, at least) depends less on agreement with its doctrines than on various non-rational factors, such as primary group attachments. These and numerous other observations derived from surveys are forcing political scientists to re-examine such questions as the nature and role of so-called "brokerage" parties in a two-party system, the alleged differences between these parties and the presumably more ideological parties of multi-party systems, the place of parties in the democratic process, their function in helping to achieve a balance between cleavage and consensus, and so forth.

Survey research is also forcing modifications in our theories about extreme political belief and affiliation. Among other changes, the introduction of social-psychological constructs in the survey analysis of these phenomena has altered and added new theoretical dimensions to our understanding. We now appreciate, for example, that we cannot understand the adoption of extreme right-wing or left-wing beliefs by reference to political or socio-economic factors alone, but must also take account of such personality predispositions as paranoia, psychological inflexibility, dogmatism, and "authoritarian" tendencies.[94] Persons attracted to the radical right and other extreme doctrines can be found in all occupations, educational categories, and communities; what they often have in common are the same personality needs, the same ways of meeting the disappointments and frustrations of the world, the same rages and anxieties.

Similar observations leading to appropriate theoretical adjustments are also being suggested for the explanation of such phenomena as alienation and anomy. The standard theories that relate these responses to industrialism, urbanization, mass society, status frustration, or the decline of ideology appear from survey evidence to be inadequate or questionable; theoretical revisions are required that will take account of the role of personality factors in inducing "anomic" responses, and of the learning and socialization processes which affect the internalization of norms.

We are also discovering from survey data that the *a priori* political categories set out by theorists and publicists frequently do not hold up in practice. The political left and the political right, for example, are not in all respects

---

[93] Key, Jr., *Public Opinion and American Democracy, op. cit.,* chap. 2; McClosky, "Consensus and Ideology . . . ," *op. cit.*

[94] Rokeach, *et al., op. cit.;* Adorno, *et al., op. cit.*

the polarities they are made out to be; indeed, the values of both are sometimes embraced by the same individuals. Respondents are turned up by surveys who score high on both left wing and right wing scales, or who are, by different measures, liberal and conservative at the same time, or who favor the same leaders but diverge in their beliefs. Traditional political theories have tended to oversimplify political attachments and to attribute more order to political thought than is usually manifested in behavior. The research findings, however, are compelling scholars to reconsider the standard assumptions about these matters and to arrive at explanations that more plausibly account for such facts as these: both the radical right and radical left reject existing political institutions, especially parliamentary government, liberal democracy, the open society, freedom of speech and press, and the right of individuals to think and act for themselves; both exhibit strong underlying elements of paranoia, such as conspiratorialism, megalomania, and unfounded fears; both are intemperate and angry, righteous, inflexible, intolerant, dogmatic, and contemptuous of human frailty. These qualities, which show up in survey analyses of extreme groups, can also be observed in the macro-analyses of extreme left or right movements (Nazism, Communism, etc.). The shift that is beginning to take place in our theoretical understanding of these phenomena cannot, of course, be credited to surveys alone; but survey research has added important documentation and thereby reinforced what some scholars working in other ways have long suspected.

Limitations and Problems in the Use of Political Surveys

To recognize that surveys have extraordinary utility for the study of politics is not to deny that there are problems associated with their use. Surveys are not a methodological panacea. They have limitations, some of which are inherent and some of which are by-products of their present stage of development.

One inherent limitation is their high cost for, while they are addressed to only a small proportion of the universe being studied, the expense of questioning even this number is usually fairly large. Another limitation arises from the inaccessibility of certain respondents, either because they occupy eminent and unapproachable roles (e.g. Supreme Court justices), or because they are uneducated, poor, geographically isolated, or for some other reason difficult to communicate with. Some potential respondents simply refuse to be interviewed. Other limitations grow out of the fact that certain problems cannot be studied unless the investigator can manipulate public events to meet the conditions of his hypothesis—a requirement that can rarely be fulfilled. An investigator, for example, has little chance of persuading public officials to adopt certain policies, even temporarily, in order to test their impact on the mass public.

Like other rigorous empirical procedures, surveys may have little value if the constructs one deals with cannot be operationalized, or cannot be presented in a form appropriate to a questionnaire. The attempt to operationalize concepts sometimes leads to their oversimplification; the conversion of a rich, complex, subtle, or multifaceted concept into a measure that can be used on a questionnaire may reduce it to a bloodless, uninteresting, or oversimplified version of the original. Even notions that appear simple are often complex and difficult to capture adequately in a brief interview. Take, for example, party loyalty, which is often measured by asking the respondent how strongly he feels about his party, and by giving him an opportunity to say "very strongly" or "strongly" or "not so strongly." Unfortunately, however, not all groups perceive or respond to party loyalty in the same way. Uneducated people are far more willing to proclaim undying love for their party, though they do not necessarily practice it. Some groups, no matter how attached to a party, like to think of themselves as independent and free of any affiliation that blinds their judgment. Some are intensely loyal to their party so long as it takes political stands they approve of, while others are emotionally or symbolically attached in a way that has nothing to do with the party's program. Some believe themselves to be loyal to a party but defect from it for casual reasons, while others call themselves independent but invariably vote a straight ticket. Party attachment, in short, is not the simple one-dimensional response it seems. To get at it properly, one may need more and subtler questions than one can ordinarily assign to it.

It is also a limitation of the survey method that it cannot easily observe aggregates or institutions. Something can be learned about an institution by studying the individuals who occupy various roles within it, but this will not necessarily provide an overview of the institution as a functioning entity. To achieve the latter, one needs to take account of the formal rules that govern the institution, its power and structure, its relation to other institutions in the system, and so on. One can, in short, learn a great deal about the nature and conduct of the British parliament without interviewing a single member. All this merely underscores what we have intimated earlier, that surveys are not equally appropriate to all forms of social science inquiry, that they have limits, but that they also have great utility—either in their own right or as supplements to other methods.

We have cited the complaint that surveys are in the nature of still photographs that capture responses at a single instant in time, and we have observed, in rejoinder, that by conducting surveys in serial fashion we may achieve something akin to a motion picture. Nevertheless, it must be admitted that surveys are not the optimal procedure for observing change, process, or action. They can enlighten us to some degree about these phenomena and, when used in conjunction with other approaches, they can enhance what is learned. One would not use a survey to follow a bill through the legislature, but one might augment the study of that process by interviewing legislators, lobbyists, interest groups, and citizens who are involved in the passage of the bill. Similarly, surveys would not be the prescribed procedure for studying certain kinds of political *relationships*—for example, the relationship between a leader and his supporters. But one might be wise to employ survey methods in an auxiliary role to gain a fuller understanding of how the governed perceive their leaders, and what forces strengthen or weaken their support. Surveys, in short, are not primarily designed to observe interaction among individuals or groups, for that requires the simultaneous observation of two or more people. This can best be done through laboratory experiment, participant observation, or on-the-scene observation of the type practiced by anthropologists. Each of these, however, can beneficially be combined with the survey method.

While the complaint that surveys characteristically measure political beliefs rather than actions is exaggerated and even a bit "tired," it must, nevertheless, be conceded that surveys have most often centered on verbal behavior, and that they have paid insufficient attention to the institutional forces and political contexts from which verbal responses spring. Few political surveys (except those concerned with voting) have tried to predict the future behavior of respondents or taken into account the consequences of holding certain opinions. One reason for neglecting this task is the obvious difficulty of fulfilling it. The difficulties, however, are not insurmountable and can, with imagination, be overcome, as they eventually will be.

The investigation of beliefs and attitudes is an integral feature of the study of overt "behavior." Beliefs and attitudes represent facets of behavior and both must be assessed if political life is to be understood adequately. The difficulty of assessing them, however, has to do not only with the limitations of the survey method but with the imponderables and contingencies in complex human situations. A person holding a given attitude may be unable to act on it because the conditions in which he finds himself are uncongenial. Conditions may even force him to act in ways that violate his private convictions. A man holding race prejudices may act on them in the South but conceal them in the North, while a man free of such prejudices may in the South be led to discriminate in order to survive in business or be accepted by the community. How a person behaves in an actual situation depends, in short, upon the content and intensity of his attitudes, the strength of the external forces that play upon him, and the conditions in which he must act. Surveys cannot always predict overt behavior because it is difficult to ascertain all these factors in any given case. Similar restrictions hold, however, for other research procedures, and the need to find ways to overcome them is common to all types of inquiry.

There are also a number of technical limitations associated with political surveys. Some have to do with sampling, e.g., the characteristics of the universe are not always known, some persons cannot be reached or refuse to participate, or a carefully designed probability sample may be physically or financially unfeasible. Other limitations have to do with the nature of the questionnaire and the quality and interpretation of the responses. Not only must one's measures be valid and reliable, but they must be appropriate to the groups on which they are being used. A measure useful in surveying, say, intellectuals may be extremely misleading if used on the uneducated. Nor can a respondent's answers always be taken at face value. His responses may be uninformed and even capricious, they may vary with time, or be inconsistent with other beliefs he holds. He may, for reasons of his own, furnish answers that he knows to be false or, if intimidated or "led" by the interviewer, give answers he thinks the interviewer wants. Since politics is for many people a taboo or threatening subject, not to be discussed with strangers, the possibility of such misrepresentation can be serious. Some reporting errors are made innocently, as when a respondent is too uninformed to classify his own political views correctly or cannot accurately recall the candidates he supported in earlier elections. Difficulties of this type can be mitigated somewhat by employing attitude scales and complex measures that do not depend on answers to one or a few questions but contain numerous items that have been carefully tested and validated. Even these, however, may be subject to "response set" and other biases associated with their wording, content, or form. Some respondents, for example, are inclined to agree with statements presented to them, regardless of content; others tend to disagree. Some dissemble, either because they prefer to present themselves in a certain light, or because they are too defensive to perceive realistically their own motivations and behavior. Some respondents do not take the research task seriously and make frivolous responses, while others take it so seriously that they are crippled and unable to answer honestly. We have alluded to other difficulties that arise in cross-cultural surveys where, in addition to the problems just recited, there are difficulties arising from the translation of terms, the posing of cognate questions, and the interpretation of responses elicited in different cultures. All these difficulties are potentially serious but not insurmountable—particularly as the measuring methods and the techniques for assessing opinions, attitudes, personality, and actions are continually being improved.

I have left for last a class of criticisms leveled against survey research—and, for that matter, against all types of behavioral studies—by critics whose persuasion is predominantly humanistic. Survey research, they allege, deprives the study of politics of its "vitality." By collecting verbal responses at a single moment in time, by dealing with component variables rather than with the individual as a whole, by focusing upon isolated instances of behavior rather than upon the total configuration of responses, by seeking to convert man's flesh-and-blood characteristics into quantities that can be dealt with abstractly and statistically, and by neglecting normative and moral questions in favor of empirical ones, the survey analyst (they claim) both outrages and misrepresents man's nature. He debases man's character and motives by reducing him to dimensions that can be measured; and he diminishes man as a political animal by regarding him as a bundle of needs, · motives, group memberships, roles, and statuses.

It is difficult to decide how much of this criticism to take seriously, for much of it is vague and represents feeling rather than reason. To a student of behavioral science, it seems plain that the quantification made possible by surveys adds to rather than detracts from our understanding of political phenomena. The difference between the measurements used in surveys and the observations made by earlier methods lies not in their reliance upon quantification but in the rigor and precision of the quantitative methods employed. Even traditional political studies can scarcely avoid such terms as "many," "most," "usually," "as a rule," a "minority," "more than," and so forth. They describe "the farmers" as resentful, "the workers" as Democrats, or "the businessmen" as opposing social legislation. But how many farmers, or workers, or businessmen, how frequently and with what degree of intensity are they resentful or Democrats or opposed to social legislation? It is impossible, in short, to record meaningful political observations without resorting to statements of magnitude or proportion; one can strive for statements that are either precise and based on careful measurement, or that are vague and based on crude impressions. By electing the former, survey users have enriched rather than narrowed the range and variety of questions on which they can make useful observations.

What of the argument that survey research deprives the study of politics of its vitality by dealing with political man as a conglomeration of abstract "variables" that are examined independently of the individuals who possess them? This claim (it will be recognized) is essentially the "whole man" argument so frequently advanced by humanistic critics of the social sciences. The response to the argument, of course, is that it is impossible to understand any man, much less a group of men, all at once and in his (or their) entirety. Since every man is potentially many things, plays many roles, behaves differently in different contexts, and holds various and often conflicting beliefs, he cannot possibly be understood as a "totality." His behavior cannot be explained by describing everything about him at once, even if it were physically possible to do so. When one asks what "causes" a political actor to behave in a certain way, one expects an answer in terms of some specific force that one has reason to believe is relevant to that particular type of behavior.

When we say that a man is a union member, a Republican, educated, a Southerner, hostile in personality, politically apathetic, or a leader of his party, we neither violate him as a person nor diminish our capacity for understanding him. On the contrary, only by observing him in the ways he can be classified can we hope to understand his behavior. Thus, we observe him as an economic actor, as a member of a social class, as a voter, or as a consumer of mass communications. By the statistical manipulation of these observations, we can learn much about the ways in which these categories affect each other, and our understanding of human behavior will, thereby, be enhanced rather than diminished. A science strives to achieve a set of generalizations, preferably of a highly abstract order, in the hope of being able to explain complex phenomena with the fewest possible number of assumptions and a small number of observations. It is difficult to see why this aim is less defensible when applied to man's behavior than when applied to other natural phenomena.

The argument that politics is a unique domain that cannot be understood except in "political" terms is similar in some ways to the arguments about the "whole man." Politics is hereby invested with a mystique that places it beyond ordinary understanding. But to observe individuals in their group, class, or personality characteristics does not violate what is "political" about man; on the contrary, it adds new and important dimensions to our knowledge of his political behavior.

We come, finally, to the relation of surveys to normative questions. It must, of course, be conceded that surveys cannot be employed to confirm normative statements, for no form of empirical inquiry can do this. Surveys can, however, throw light upon the factual status of many of the empirical claims implicit in normative systems of thought. Although they cannot, for example, decide where sovereignty ought to lie, they can tell us much about the limits of popular participation in government, the ability of the electorate to exercise consent effectively, the extent to which people can be expected to obey certain kinds of laws, the questions that citizens of little education can be expected to understand and judge, and the degree to which voters correctly perceive the beliefs and actions of their leaders. Surveys can, in short, teach us a great deal about how popular sovereignty *works* or can be expected to work under various conditions, and this may help us to decide what types of power ought to be exercised by the people.

For those interested exclusively in normative questions, the empirical findings yielded by surveys are sometimes regarded as trivial. But for those who are also empirically oriented, the question of what is significant and what is trivial becomes difficult to decide. All questions, of course, are not equally significant, but many questions, seemingly inconsequential in themselves, take on significance by their relationship to other, obviously important questions. The topics to which surveys have been addressed, and which we have reviewed, can scarcely be described as inconsequential. They deal with voting, loyalty, conformity, leadership, communication, role perceptions, representation, decision-making, and numerous other topics of major interest to political science. That some survey analysts ask trivial questions and compile insignificant data cannot be denied; survey users are in this respect no different from scholars who use other methods. Every discipline has its share of men who are preoccupied with trivial questions and who turn up insignificant results. It is not only the method that determines the significance of the product but the intellectual force that lies behind the use of the method. A scholar with serious intellectual concerns, a sense of what is important in his field, and a technical mastery of research procedures stands a chance of doing useful work no matter which research technique he employs. A man lacking these traits will probably contribute little even if his methods are the best available.

Bibliography

Adorno, T. W., *et al., The Authoritarian Personality.* Harper & Bros., New York, 1950.

Agger, R. E., "Independents and Party Identifiers: Characteristics and Behavior in 1952," in *American Voting Behavior.* Edited by E. L. Burdick and A. J. Brodbeck. Free Press, Glencoe, Ill., 1959, pp. 308–339.

Agger, R. E., and Daniel Goldrich, "Community Power Structures and Partisanship," *American Sociological Review,* Vol. 23, August, 1958, pp. 383–392.

Allinsmith, Wesley, and Beverly Allinsmith, "Religious Affiliation and Politico-Economic Attitude: A Study of Eight Major U.S. Religious Groups," *Public Opinion Quarterly,* Vol. 12, Fall, 1948, pp. 377–389.

Almond, G. A., *The American People and Foreign Policy.* Harcourt, Brace, New York, 1950.

Almond, G. A., *et al., The Appeals of Communism.* Princeton University Press, Princeton, 1954.

Almond, G. A., and Sidney Verba, *The Civic Culture.* Princeton University Press, Princeton, 1963.

Alpert, Harry, "Public Opinion Research as Science," *Public Opinion Quarterly,* Vol. 20, Fall, 1956, pp. 493–500.

Asch, S. E., "Effects of Group Pressure Upon the Modification and Distortion of Judgment," in *Groups, Leadership, and Men.* Edited by H. S. Guetzkow. Carnegie Press, Pittsburgh, 1951.

Backstrom, Charles H., and Gerald D. Hursh, *Survey Research,* Northwestern University Press, Evanston, Ill., 1963.

Banfield, E. C., *Political Influence.* Free Press, Glencoe, Ill., 1961.

Bauer, R. A., *et al., American Business and Public Policy.* Atherton, New York, 1963.

Benson, Lee, "Research Problems in American Political Historiography," in *Common Frontiers of the Social Sciences.* Edited by Mirra Komarovsky. Free Press, Glencoe, Ill., 1957, pp. 113–183.

Berelson, B. R., P. F. Lazarsfeld and W. W. McPhee, *Voting:* A Study of Opinion Formation in a Presidential Campaign. University of Chicago Press, Chicago, 1954.

Blalock, H. M., Jr., *Causal Inferences in Non-Experimental Research,* University of North Carolina Press, Chapel Hill, 1964.

Campbell, Angus, "Recent Developments in Survey Studies of Political Behavior," in *Essays on the Behavioral Study of Politics.* Edited by Austin Ranney. University of Illinois, Urbana, 1962, pp. 31–46.

Campbell, Angus, Gerald Gurin, and W. E. Miller, *The Voter Decides.* Row, Peterson, Evanston, Ill., 1954.

Campbell, Angus, and George Katona, "The Sample Survey: A Technique for Social Science Research," in *Research Methods in the Behavioral Sciences.* Edited by Leon Festinger and Daniel Katz. Dryden Press, New York, 1953.

Campbell, Angus, and W. E. Miller, "The Motivational Basis of Straight and Split-Ticket Voting," *American Political Science Review,* Vol. 51, June, 1957, pp. 293–312.

Campbell, Angus, and Henry Valen, "Party Identification in Norway and the United States," *Public Opinion Quarterly,* Vol. 25, Winter, 1961, pp. 505–525.

Campbell, Angus, *et al., The American Voter.* John Wiley & Sons, New York, 1960.

Cantril, Hadley, *The Psychology of Social Movements.* John Wiley & Sons, New York, 1941.

Cantril, Hadley, *The Politics of Despair.* Basic Books, New York, 1958.

Centers, Richard, "Attitude and Belief in Relation to Occupational Stratification," *Journal of Social Psychology,* Vol. 27, May, 1948, pp. 159–185.

Converse, P. E., "The Nature of Belief Systems in Mass Publics," in *Ideology and Discontent.* Edited by D. E. Apter Free Press, Glencoe, Ill., 1964, pp. 206–261.

Converse, P. E., and Georges Dupeux, "Politicization of the Electorate in France and the United States," *Public Opinion Quarterly,* Vol. 26, Spring, 1962, pp. 1–23.

Converse, P. E., *et al.,* "Stability and Change in 1960: A Reinstating Election," *American Political Science Review,* Vol. 55, June, 1961, pp. 269–280.

Crutchfield, R. S., "Personal and Situational Factors in Conformity to Group Pressure," *Acta Psychologica,* Vol. 15, 1959, pp. 386–388.

Cutright, Phillips, and P. H. Rossi, "Grass Roots Politicians and the Vote," *American Sociological Review,* Vol. 23, April, 1958, pp. 171–179.

Dahl, R. A., "The Behavioral Approach in Political Science: Epitaph for a Monument to a Successful Protest," *American Political Science Review,* Vol. 55, December, 1961, pp. 763–772.

Dahl, R. A., *Who Governs?:* Democracy and Power in an American City. Yale University Press, New Haven, 1961.

Dicks, H. V., "Personality Traits and National Socialist Ideology," *Human Relations,* Vol. 3, August, 1950, pp. 111–154.

Easton, David, and R. D. Hess, "The Child's Political World," *Midwestern Journal of Political Science,* Vol. 6, August, 1962, pp. 229–246.

Eldersveld, Samuel J., *Political Parties: A Behavioral Analysis,* Rand McNally & Co., Chicago, 1964.

Ernst, M. L., and D. G. Loth, *Report on the American Communist.* Henry Holt, New York, 1952.

Erskine, H. G., "The Polls: Textbook Knowledge," *Public Opinion Quarterly,* Vol. 27, Spring, 1963, pp. 133–141.

Eulau, Heinz, *The Behavioral Persuasion in Politics.* Random House, New York, 1963.

Eulau, Heinz, "Segments of Political Science Most Susceptible to Behavioristic Treatment," in *The Limits of Behavioralism in Political Science.* Edited by J. C. Charlesworth. American Academy of Political and Social Science, Philadelphia, 1962, pp. 26–48.

Eulau, Heinz, *Class and Party in the Eisenhower Years:* Class Roles and Perspectives in the 1952 and 1956 Elections. Free Press, Glencoe, Ill., 1962.

Eulau, Heinz, and J. D. Sprague, *Lawyers in Politics:* A Study in Professional Convergence. Bobbs-Merrill, Indianapolis, 1964.

Eulau, Heinz, *et al.,* "The Political Socialization of American State Legislators," *Midwestern Journal of Political Science,* Vol. 3, May, 1959, pp. 188-206.

Fenton, J. M., *In Your Opinion.* Little-Brown, Boston, 1960.

Festinger L., and Daniel Katz, *Research Methods in the Behavioral Sciences,* Dryden Press, N.Y., 1953.

Fuchs, L. H., *The Political Behavior of American Jews.* Free Press, Glencoe, Ill., 1956.

Gibb, C. A., "Leadership," in *Handbook of Social Psychology,* Vol. 1. Edited by Gardner Lindzey. Addison-Wesley, Reading, Mass., 1954, pp. 233-238.

Glaser, W. A., "Doctors and Politics," *American Journal of Sociology,* Vol. 66, November, 1960, pp. 230-245.

Glock, C. Y. (ed.), *Survey Research in the Social Sciences,* Russell Sage Foundation, New York, 1967.

Greenstein, F. I., "The Benevolent Leader—Children's Images of Political Authority," *American Political Science Review,* Vol. 54, December, 1960, pp. 934-943.

Greenstein, F. I., "Sex-Related Political Differences in Childhood," *Journal of Politics,* Vol. 23, May, 1961, pp. 353-371.

Greenstein, F. I., "More on Children's Images of the President," *Public Opinion Quarterly,* Vol. 25, Winter, 1961, pp. 648-654.

Greenstein, F. I., "Children and Politics," in *Yale Studies in Political Science,* Vol. 13. Yale University Press, New Haven, 1965.

Greer, S. A., "Urbanism Reconsidered: A Comparative Study of Local Areas in a Metropolis," *American Sociological Review,* Vol. 21, February, 1956, pp. 19-25.

Greer, S. A., "The Mass Society and the Parapolitical Structure," *American Sociological Review.* Vol. 27, October, 1962, pp. 634-646.

Greer, S. A., *Governing the Metropolis.* John Wiley & Sons, New York, 1962.

Greer, S. A., *Metropolitics:* A Study of Political Culture. John Wiley & Sons, New York, 1963.

Heard, Alexander, "Interviewing Southern Politicians," *American Political Science Review,* Vol. 44, December, 1950, pp. 886-896.

Hess, R. D., and David Easton, "The Child's Changing Image of the President," *Public Opinion Quarterly,* Vol. 24, Winter, 1960, pp. 632-644.

Hirschfield, R. S., *et al.,* "Profile of Political Activists in Manhattan," *Western Political Quarterly,* Vol. 15, September, 1962, pp. 489-506.

Hunter, Floyd, *Community Power Structure.* Doubleday, Garden City, N.Y., 1963.

Hyman, H. H., *Political Socialization.* Free Press, Glencoe, Ill., 1959.

Hyman, Herbert, *Survey Design and Analysis, The Free Press,* New York, 1955.

Hyman, H. H., and P. B. Sheatsley, "The Current Status of American Public Opinion," in *Public Opinion and Propaganda.* Edited by Daniel Katz, *et al.,* Ryerson Press, New York, 1954, pp. 33-48.

Janowitz, Morris, *The Professional Soldier.* Free Press, Glencoe, Ill., 1960.

Katz, Elihu, and P. F. Lazarsfeld, *Personal Influence.* Free Press, Glencoe, Ill., 1955.

Kendall, P. L., and P. F. Lazarsfeld, "Problems of Survey Analysis," in *Continuities in Survey Research: Studies in the Scope and Method of "The American Soldier,"* ed. by R. K. Merton and P. F. Lazarsfeld, Free Press, Chicago, 1950.

Kendall, P. L., *Conflict and Mood: Factors Affecting Stability of Response,* Free Press, Chicago, 1954.

Key, V. O., Jr., "Theory of Critical Elections," *Journal of Politics,* Vol. 17, February, 1955, pp. 3–18.

Key, V. O., Jr., "The Politically Relevant in Surveys," *Public Opinion Quarterly,* Vol. 24, Spring, 1960, pp. 54–61.

Key, V. O., Jr., *Public Opinion and American Democracy.* Alfred A. Knopf, New York, 1961.

Kirkpatrick, E. M., "The Impact of the Behavioral Approach on Traditional Political Science," in *Essays on the Behavioral Study of Politics.* Edited by Austin Ranney. University of Illinois Press, Urbana, 1962, pp. 1–30.

Kish, Leslie, *Survey Sampling,* John Wiley and Sons, New York, 1965.

Lane, R. E., *Political Life.* Free Press, Glencoe, Ill., 1959.

Lazarsfeld, P. F., B. R. Berelson, and Hazel Gaudet, *The People's Choice:* How the Voter Makes up his Mind in a Presidential Campaign. Duell, Sloan and Pearce, New York, 1944.

Lazarsfeld, P. F., and Morris Rosenberg (eds.), *The Language of Social Research: A Reader in the Methodology of Social Research,* Free Press, Glencoe, Ill., 1955.

Lerner, Daniel, and Lucille Pevsner, *The Passing of Traditional Society:* Modernizing the Middle East. Free Press, Glencoe, Ill., 1958.

Lindzey, Gardner, (ed) *Handbook of Social Psychology, Theory and Method,* Vol. I, Addison-Wesley, Cambridge, Mass., 1954.

Lipset, S. M., *et al.,* "The Psychology of Voting: An Analysis of Political Behavior," in *Handbook of Social Psychology,* Vol. 2. Edited by Gardner Lindzey. Addison-Wesley, Reading, Mass., 1954, pp. 1124–1175.

Lipset, S. M., *Political Man:* The Social Bases of Politics. Doubleday, Garden City, N.Y., 1960.

Lipset, S. M., "Three Decades of the Radical Right: Coughlinites, McCarthyites, and Birchers," in *The Radical Right,* Anchor Edition. Edited by Daniel Bell. Doubleday, Garden City, N.Y. 1964.

Lipset, S. M., M. A. Trow, and J. S. Coleman, *Union Democracy.* Free Press, Glencoe, Ill., 1956.

McClosky, Herbert, "McCarthyism: The Myth and the Reality." Paper delivered at the American Psychological Association meeting, New York, September, 1957.

McClosky, Herbert, "Conservatism and Personality," *American Political Science Review,* Vol. 52, December, 1958, pp. 27–45.

McClosky, Herbert, "Consensus and Ideology in American Politics," *American Political Science Review,* Vol. 58, June, 1964, pp. 361–382.

McClosky, Herbert, "Attitude and Personality Correlates of Foreign Policy Orientation," in *Domestic Sources of Foreign Policy.* Edited by James Rosenau. Free Press, New York, 1967.

McClosky, Herbert, and H. E. Dahlgren, "Primary Group Influence on Party Loyalty," *American Political Science Review,* Vol. 53, September, 1959, pp. 757–776.

McClosky, Herbert, *et al.,* "Issue Conflict and Consensus Among Party Leaders and Followers," *American Political Science Review,* Vol. 54, June, 1960, pp. 406–427.

McConaughy, J. B., "Certain Personality Factors of State Legislators in North Carolina," *American Political Science Review,* Vol. 44, December, 1950, pp. 897–903.

MacRae, Duncan, Jr., *The Dimensions of Congressional Voting.* University of California Press, Berkeley, 1958.

Maccoby, E. E., *et al.,* "Youth and Political Change," *Public Opinion Quarterly,* Vol. 18, No. 1, 1954, pp. 23–29.

Marvick, Dwaine, ed., *Political Decision-Makers.* Free Press, Glencoe, Ill., 1961.

Matthews, D. R., *The Social Background of Political Decision-Makers.* Doubleday, Garden City, N.Y., 1954.

Matthews, D. R., *U.S. Senators and Their World.* University of North Carolina Press, Chapel Hill, 1960.

Matthews, D. R., and J. W. Prothro, "Political Factors and Negro Voter Registration in the South," *American Political Science Review,* Vol. 57, June, 1963, pp. 355–367.

Matthews, D. R., and J. W. Prothro, "Social and Economic Factors and Negro Voter Registration in the South," *American Political Science Review,* Vol. 57, March, 1963, pp. 24–44.

Matthews, D. R., and J. W. Prothro, "Southern Images of Political Parties: An Analysis of White and Negro Attitudes," *Journal of Politics,* Vol. 26, February, 1964, pp. 82–111.

Matthews, D. R., and J. W. Prothro, *Negroes and the New Southern Politics.* Harcourt, Brace and World, New York, 1966.

Meller, Norman, "Legislative Behavior Research," *Western Political Quarterly,* Vol. 13, March, 1960, pp. 131–153.

Merton, R. K., *Social Theory and Social Structure,* Free Press, Glencoe, Ill., 1957.

Micaud, C. A., *Communism and the French Left.* Praeger, New York, 1963.

Miller, W. E., and Donald Stokes, "Constituency Influence in Congress," *American Political Science Review,* Vol. 57, March, 1963, pp. 45–56.

Miller, W. E., and Donald Stokes, *Congress and Constituency,* (forthcoming).

Mosel, James, "Communication Patterns and Political Socialization in Traditional Thailand," in *Communications and Political Development.* Edited by L. W. Pye, Princeton University Press, Princeton, 1963, pp. 184–228.

Mosteller, Frederick, *et. al., The Pre-Election Polls of 1948: Report to the Committee on Analysis of Pre-Election Polls and Forecasts,* Social Science Research Council, New York, 1949.

Nagel, S. S., "Political Party Affiliation and Judges Decisions," *American Political Science Review,* Vol. 55, December, 1961, pp. 843–850.

Nagel, S. S., "Ethnic Affiliation and Judicial Propensities," *Journal of Politics,* Vol. 24, February, 1962, pp. 92–100.

Nagel, S. S., "Off-the-Bench Judicial Attitudes," in *Judicial Decision-Making.* Edited by G. L. Schubert. Free Press, Glencoe, Ill., 1963, pp. 29–53.

Parten, Mildred, *Surveys, Polls, and Samples: Practical Procedures,* Harper & Brothers, New York, 1950.

Patterson, S. C., "Patterns of Interpersonal Relations in a State Legislative Group: The Wisconsin Assembly," *Public Opinion Quarterly,* Vol. 23, Spring, 1959, pp. 101–109.

Perlmutter, H. V., "Some Characteristics of the Xenophobic Personality," *Journal of Psychology,* Vol. 38, October, 1954, pp. 291–300.

Perlmutter, H. V., "Correlates of Two Types of Xenophilic Orientation," *Journal of Abnormal and Social Psychology,* Vol. 52, January, 1956, pp. 130–135.

Polsby, N. W., "Toward an Explanation of McCarthyism," *Political Studies,* Vol. 8, October, 1960, pp. 250–271.

Polsby, N. W., *Congress and the Presidency.* Prentice-Hall, Englewood Cliffs, N.J. 1964.

Pool, I. de Sola, "TV: A New Dimension in Politics," in *American Voting Behavior.* Edited by E. L. Burdick, and A. J. Broadbeck. Free Press, Glencoe, Ill., 1959, pp. 236–261.

Presthus, Robert, *Men at the Top.* Oxford University Press, New York, 1964.

Prothro, J. W., and C. M. Grigg, "Fundamental Principles of Democracy: Bases of Agreement and Disagreement," *Journal of Politics,* Vol. 22, May, 1960, pp. 276–294.

Pye, L. W., *Guerilla Communism in Malaya:* Its Social and Political Meaning. Princeton University Press, Princeton, 1956.

Ranney, Austin, ed., *Essays on the Behavioral Study of Politics.* University of Illinois Press, Urbana, 1962.

Ranney, Austin, "The Utility and Limitations of Aggregate Data in the Study of Electoral Data," in *Essays on the Behavioral Study of Politics.* Edited by Austin Ranney. University of Illinois Press, Urbana, 1962.

Robinson, W. S., "Ecological Correlation and the Behavior of Individuals," *American Sociological Review,* Vol. 15, June, 1950, pp. 351–357.

Rokeach, Milton, *et al., The Open and Closed Mind.* Basic Books, New York, 1960.

Rokkan, Stein, "Party Preferences and Opinion Patterns in Western Europe: A Comparative Analysis," *International Social Science Bulletin,* Vol. 7, 1955, pp. 575–576.

Rokkan, Stein, "The Comparative Study of Political Participation: Notes Toward a Perspective on Current Research," in *Essays on the Behavioral Study of Politics.* Edited by Austin Ranney. University of Illinois Press, Urbana, 1962, pp. 47–90.

Rokkan, Stein, and Henry Valen, "A Survey of the 1957 Norwegian Elections," *Revue Français de Science Politique,* Vol. 8, 1958, pp. 73–94.

Rokkan, Stein, and Henry Valen, "Parties, Elections and Political Behavior in the Northern Countries: A Review of Recent Research," in *Politsche Forschung.* Edited by Otto Stammer. Westdeutscher Verlag, Koeln-Opladen, 1960.

Rosenau, James N. (ed), *Domestic Sources of Foreign Policy,* Princeton Center of International Studies and the Free Press, New York, 1967.

Rosenau, James, *Public Opinion and Foreign Policy.* Random House, New York, 1961.

Sanford, F. H., *Authoritarianism and Leadership.* Stephenson Brothers, Philadelphia, 1950.

Schubert, G. L., ed., *Judicial Decision-Making.* Free Press, Glencoe, Ill., 1963.

Seligman, L. G., "Political Recruitment and Party Structure: A Case Study," *American Political Science Review,* Vol. 55, March, 1961, pp. 77–86.

Selvin, H. C., *The Logic of Survey Analysis,* Monograph 12, Survey Research Center, University of California, Berkeley, 1965.

Silverman, Corrine, "The Legislators' View of the Legislative Process," *Public Opinion Quarterly,* Vol. 18, Summer, 1954, pp. 180–190.

Simon, H. A., and Frederick Stern, "Effect of Television Upon Voting Behavior in Iowa in the 1952 Presidential Election," *American Political Science Review,* Vol. 49, June, 1955, pp. 470–477.

Sorauf, F. J., *Party and Representation*. Atherton, New York, 1963.

Spaeth, H. J., "An Approach to the Study of Attitudinal Differences as an Aspect of Judicial Behavior," *Midwestern Journal of Political Science,* Vol. 5, 1961, pp. 165–180.

Stephan, F. F., and Philip J. McCarthy, *Sampling Opinions: An Analysis of Survey Procedure,* John Wiley & Sons, N.Y., 1958.

Stouffer, S. A., *Communism, Conformity, and Civil Liberties:* A Cross Section of the Nation Speaks Its Mind. Doubleday, New York, 1955.

Stouffer, S. A., *et al., Measurement and Prediction,* John Wiley & Sons, New York, 1950.

Trow, M. A., "Small Businessmen, Political Tolerance, and Support for McCarthy," *American Journal of Sociology,* Vol. 64, November, 1958, pp. 270–281.

Truman, D. B., "Research in Political Behavior," *American Political Science Review,* Vol. 46, December, 1952, pp. 1003–1006.

Truman, D. B., *The Congressional Party:* A Case Study. John Wiley & Sons, New York, 1959.

Verba, Sidney, *Small Groups and Political Behavior.* Princeton University Press, Princeton, 1961.

Vidich, A. J., and Joseph Bensman, *Small Town in Mass Society.* Princeton University Press, Princeton, 1958.

Wahlke, J. C., "Behavioral Analyses of Representative Bodies," in *Essays on the Behavioral Study of Politics.* Edited by Austin Ranney. University of Illinois Press, Urbana, 1962, pp. 173–190.

Wahlke, J. C., *et al., The Legislative System.* John Wiley & Sons, New York, 1962.

Weber, Max, "Politics as a Vocation," in *From Max Weber:* Essays in Sociology. Edited by H. H. Gerth and C. W. Mills. Oxford University Press, New York, 1946, pp. 77–128.

Wildavsky, Aaron, *Dixon-Yates:* A Study in Power Politics. Yale University Press, New Haven, 1962.

Wildavsky, Aaron, "The Intelligent Citizen's Guide to the Abuse of Statistics: The Kennedy Document and The Catholic Vote," in *Politics and Social Life.* Edited by N. W. Polsby, *et al.* Houghton-Mifflin, Boston, 1964, pp. 825–844.

Wildavsky, Aaron, *Leadership in a Small Town.* Bedminster Press, Totowa, N.J., 1964.

Wilson, James, *Negro Politics.* Free Press, Glencoe, Ill., 1960.

Wolfinger, R. E., "The Clientele of the Christian Anti-Communism Crusade," paper delivered at the American Political Science Association meeting, September, 1963.

Wolfinger, R. E., *et al.,* "America's Radical Right: Ideology and Politics," in *Ideology and Discontent:* The Concept of Ideology in the Light of Contemporary Social and Political Change. Edited by D. E. Apter. Free Press, Glencoe, Ill., 1964.

CHAPTER 2

Personality and Attitude Correlates of Foreign Policy Orientation[1]

Students of international politics have traditionally focused upon the analysis of institutions or systems in which the principal actors are nation-states, associations of nation-states, or the decision-making agencies of nation-states. Although they have in recent years devoted more attention to such "exotic" factors as public opinion, political attitudes, and personality, few of them have accorded these variables sustained or systematic scrutiny. To most students of foreign affairs such factors remain novel, uncongenial, and difficult to incorporate into the analytical framework with which they are accustomed to work. Hard data on the influence of psychological variables in foreign policy are, so far, not abundant, and the obstacles to be surmounted in collecting such data are often formidable. In addition, some students of international politics, in a conscious effort to narrow the inquiry and concentrate upon the variables that promise (as they see it) the greatest payoff, exclude attitude or personality factors on the assumption that they will not sufficiently enhance the explanatory power of their model to warrant the additional complication of integrating them into their analysis.[2]

As a non-specialist, I cannot accurately assess the weight of these considerations. I believe, however, that the utility of psychological explanations cannot be decided by *a priori* judgments or even by appraising the rudimentary research so far completed. Whether analytical perspectives employing personality and attitude influences prove feasible and helpful in the study of international politics is an empirical question to be settled only after much more research—presumably of an increasingly sophisticated and systematic nature—has been undertaken. This research may help not only to identify

Reprinted, with permission, from *Domestic Sources of Foreign Policy,* ed. by James N. Rosenau, Princeton Center of International Studies and The Free Press, New York, 1967, 51–109.

[1] This is publication A48 of the Survey Research Center, University of California, Berkeley. Support for the collection and analysis of data reported in this paper has been received from the Social Science Research Council and the Institute of Social Sciences, University of California, Berkeley. This investigation was supported in part by Public Health Research Grant MH–05837 from the National Institute of Health. I am greatly indebted to Paul Sniderman, Fellow at the University of California, for invaluable assistance in the preparation of this chapter.

[2] See in particular S. Verba, "Rationality and Non-Rationality in Models of the International System," in K. Knorr and S. Verba (eds.), *The International System: Theoretical Essays* (Princeton: Princeton University Press, 1961), pp. 93–115.

important relations among variables but also to specify the conditions under which other (nonpsychological) influences are likely to be potentiated or reduced. Then, too, even if we find that psychological influences rarely if ever dominate the course of international affairs, their role at times may nevertheless be decisive: they may, for example, furnish precisely the increment that tips the scales toward one course of action rather than another.

In this paper I shall confine attention to that aspect of the problem that deals with the relation of attitude and personality factors to foreign policy orientations.[3] I shall say little about the influence of these factors on the actual formulation of foreign policy. *A fortiori*, I shall ignore such questions as the influence of psychological variables on the roles played by various publics and policy elites in the decision-making process. These are, of course, important questions, but they are not the questions to which the present research is addressed. It is concerned, rather, to explore on various fronts the utility of psychological constructs for explaining political belief, orientation, and activity. Foreign affairs is one of those fronts.

The major foreign policy orientation on which this chapter centers is that contained in the isolationist-nonisolationist distinction.[4] The persons falling into these categories will for certain purposes be further divided into those with aggressive (or *jingoistic*) international orientations and those with nonaggressive (or *pacific*) orientations. The responses to foreign policy issues that reflect these tendencies will also be examined.

Definitions

Like many terms attended by political controversy, isolationism is a value-loaded concept, bearing honorific connotations in some circles and pejorative ones in others. Inevitably, perhaps, it has borne a variety of competing and conflicting meanings. It has been embraced by pacifists who abhor militarism and by jingoists who celebrate it. It has been favored as the appropriate orientation toward Europe but not Asia; toward Asia but not Europe; toward all continents outside the Western Hemisphere; or toward foreign nations anywhere. Variations are also evident in its focus, which has sometimes been military, sometimes economic, sometimes politi-

---

[3] Two recent works that utilize a psychological focus, although to different degrees, are O. Klineberg, *The Human Dimension in International Relations* (New York: Holt, Rinehart and Winston, 1964) and L. Doob, *Patriotism and Nationalism, Their Psychological Foundations* (New Haven: Yale University Press, 1964). A review and discussion of research on psychology and international affairs is also contained in Herbert C. Kelman (ed.), *International Behavior: A Social-Psychological Analysis* (New York: Holt, Rinehart and Winston 1965).

[4] On the relevance of isolationism for present-day American politics see W. A. Scott and S. Withey, *The United States and the United Nations* (New York: Manhattan, 1958); G. Almond, *The American People and Foreign Policy* (New York: Harcourt, Brace & World, 1950); V. O. Key, Jr., *Public Opinion and American Democracy* (New York: Alfred A. Knopf, 1961); and R. Dahl, *Congress and Foreign Policy* (New York: Harcourt, Brace & World, 1950).

cal, and sometimes all three.[5] Writers commonly find it necessary to discriminate "types" of isolationists: Walter Lippmann, for example, has recently distinguished between the "old isolationists" who regard any military commitment outside the boundaries of the two oceans as contrary to America's vital interest, and the "neo-isolationists" who favor "economic assistance, technical assistance, the Peace Corps [and] cultural exchanges," who approve collective military action to defend vital American interests, but who oppose unilateral military intervention in places like Africa and Asia, where American interests are not "vital."[6] Other writers have distinguished between older types of isolationism that focused on the "decadence" of Europe and the "danger of infection" from abroad and a current type of isolationism that is belligerently anti-Communist, prefers unilateral action, and aims to slash foreign spending.[7]

The literature on isolationism abounds with definitions, variously shaped by the bias of the investigator, by the historical period he is studying, or by the political movements he is describing. Differences are found in emphasis, coloration, and point of view as the doctrine passes from one historical stage to another and from one group of advocates to another. Its origins have ranged from American "nativism," on the one side, to the Marxist conviction on the other, that all American overseas activities are impelled by capitalism's search for markets, raw materials, and opportunities for imperalist domination. Some isolationist manifestations are of long standing, deeply rooted in American populism; others have been of brief, almost momentary duration, e.g., the "isolationism" of the Communist Party during the Stalin-Hitler Pact, or the short-lived support of the America First Committee in the late 1930s by the more pacifist members of the Socialist Party.

Despite variations, certain elements have been common to most public expressions of the isolationist point of view. One of these is a sense of disengagement from other nations, accompanied often by the conviction that American interests differ from and are incompatible with those of the rest of the world. To the traditional isolationist, there is no community of international interests, and Americans have little to gain by participating in international affairs. They have even less reason to be drawn into "entangling alliances," which are bound to be costly, dangerous, and incapacitating. The element of disengagement is the dominant feature of the isolationist persuasion. From it flows the desire to avoid joint action, the emphasis upon

---

[5] For a study of the roots of congressional support of isolationist policies, see L. Rieselbach, "Congressional Isolationist Behavior, 1939–1958," unpublished doctoral dissertation, Yale University, 1963.

[6] Quoted in a news release, March 2, 1965.

[7] See the discussions of A. Schlesinger, Jr., "The New Isolationism," *Atlantic Monthly* (May, 1952), pp. 34–8; F. Klingberg, "The Historical Alternation of Moods in American Foreign Policy," *World Politics,* Vol. 4 (1952), pp. 239–73; and N. A. Graebner, *The New Isolationism: A Study in Politics and Foreign Policy Since 1950* (New York: Ronald Press, 1956).

the unlimited and eternal sovereignty of nation-states,[8] and the reluctance to commit the United States to any policy that would increase its obligations to foreign nations.[9] In its more extreme form, the sense of disengagement passes from mere feelings of nonresponsibility for other nations into a ritualistic fear that sustained intercourse with them is bound to be contaminating. Not only will it diminish our freedom to act but it will debase and demoralize us. The nation's purity and vitality will be overcome by the decadence and corruption of the countries with which it is compelled to mingle. Thus the United States is portrayed, implicitly or explicitly, as innocent, naive, and trusting, a ready victim of unscrupulous foreign powers.

If variety has attended the definition of isolationism, confusion has been the mark of whatever it is that isolationism is not. The difficulty is that there is no single, logical antithesis to the isolationist persuasion. Such terms as internationalism, cosmopolitanism, world-mindedness, interventionism, and even globalism have been employed to characterize the orientation of those who are not isolationists. Each of these terms, in turn, has been variously conceived and defined. Internationalist, for example, has been employed to describe world federalists, pacifists, members of the Peace Corps, supporters of the United Nations, and even war hawks who favor unilateral military action to maintain American hegemony. It would be idle to attempt to untangle these terms and to furnish each of them with an appropriate definition. Nor is it necessary to our research task, for while we will doubtless find it helpful to use these terms—if only for stylistic variety—it should be understood that those who score at the lower end of what we will call the Isolationism scale can properly be designated only as "nonisolationists"; their particular form of nonisolationism cannot in the context of the present research be specified.[10]

Later in the paper we will subdivide isolationists into those who are jingoistic or aggressive and those who are pacific or conciliatory. The terms aggressive or jingoistic refer not to psychological aggressiveness—a trait we will measure separately and treat as one of our independent variables—but rather to a belligerent and bullying posture toward foreign nations. Obviously

---

[8] A. Weinberg, "The Historical Meaning of the American Doctrine of Isolationism," *American Political Science Review,* Vol. 34 (1940), pp. 539–49.

[9] Rieselbach, *op. cit.*

[10] Definitions and operational measures of nonisolationism or internationalism also abound. See, for example, D. Sampson and H. Smith, "A Scale to Measure World-Minded Attitudes," *Journal of Social Psychology,* Vol. 45 (1957), pp. 99–106; W. A. Scott, "International Ideology and Interpersonal Ideology," *Public Opinion Quarterly,* Vol. 24 (1960), pp. 419–35; W. Mackinnon and R. Centers, "Authoritarianism and Internationalism," *Public Opinion Quarterly,* Vol. 20 (Winter, 1956–57), pp. 621–30; D. Levinson, "An Approach to the Theory and Measurement of Ethnocentric Ideology," *Journal of Psychology,* Vol. 28 (1949), pp. 19–39; M. Farber, "The Armageddon Complex: Dynamics of Opinion," *Public Opinion Quarterly,* Vol. 15 (1951), pp. 217–24; and B. Fensterwald, Jr., "The Anatomy of American Isolationism and Expansion," II, *Journal of Conflict Resolution,* Vol. 2 (1958), pp. 111–39.

it is a term highly correlated with chauvinism—i.e., patriotism of an uncritical, zealous, and boastful type—but is not identical with it. The jingoist, as we have conceived him, is given to sabre-rattling, prefers quick and, if necessary, violent action in response to external threats, and seeks to insulate the United States from the rest of the world by sheer superiority of force. A pacific isolationist, by contrast, usually prefers to withdraw from or avoid conflict with other nations. Both typify what might be called the "perimeter" mentality. Both regard the outside world as dangerous and hostile, but one prefers to counter this danger by retreat or withdrawal, the other by a military stance and, if necessary, retaliation.

A word might also be said about the terms *attitude* and *personality,* which figure so prominently in our analysis. By attitude I have in mind the generally accepted definition of the term, excellently stated by Selltiz and Cook "as a disposition to evaluate, or to respond to, an object or class of objects in a given way, this disposition being inferred from consistency of response to the object or members of the object class."[11] By personality I mean a readiness or disposition to respond in a patterned way to stimulus objects of many different types across a range of subject areas. Whereas an attitude disposition is characteristically tied to a particular class of objects, a personality disposition may encompass more than one class of objects or behaviors and these objects need not be manifestly related. Personality is both a more general and more fundamental or genotypic term in the sense that it often underlies attitudes and furnishes the motive force that impels them. When one uses the term personality, one is talking about such things as needs, motives, affect, defense mechanisms, and the like; when one uses the term attitude, one is talking about implicit or explicit beliefs regarding a specified class of objects. One has an attitude toward foreigners, civil rights, political freedom, or international cooperation; but one exhibits a personality disposition when one's responses are marked by stimulus boundedness, a tendency to narrow the number and complexity of stimuli from the phenomenal field, premature closure and the rejection of incompatible material, cognitive restriction, a propensity for dichotomous distinctions, avoidance of trial-and-error behavior, and so forth. These will be recognized as the diagnostic responses of an inflexible personality.

There are, of course, response states that fall on the borderline, reflecting both attitude and personality dispositions so equally that one cannot wholly locate them in either category. A few of the measures considered in later sections of this paper might be classified under either heading, e.g., pessimism, social responsibility, and contempt for weakness. While dimensions of this type obviously contain elements of the personality genotype, they are also unusually dependent upon social learning and exhibit many of the characteristics of the attitude phenotype.

---

[11] C. Selltiz and S. Cook, "Theory and Measurement of Attitudes," mimeograph, p. 2.

Isolationism: Background and Theory

In the mid-nineteenth century, a large number of Americans were undoubtedly isolationists. Many had little reason to be anything else. They were citizens of a vast continental power, safeguarded against military danger by two great oceans, secure against weak neighbors to the north and south, physically and culturally remote from the world's great centers. They lived, for the most part, in small, widely separated, rural communities, where they had little access to information about the rest of the world. Some were immigrants or the children of immigrants for whom Europe was a continent marked by unceasing quarrels, decaying aristocracies, political and religious oppression, rigid class stratification, and narrow opportunities. It was obviously a place to be avoided. The objective realities, as they appeared to many Americans of that day, made the isolationist point of view a "natural" one, easily learned and internalized, and (one assumes) sustained without help from any special psychological forces.

American isolationism grew not only from geographic insularity but also from a sense of having created a unique culture that owed little or nothing to Europe. This feeling, in turn, was related to the colonial struggle for independence, the conquest of the wilderness, and the successful fashioning of a new national state. It was further reinforced by the democratic and radical features of American society. Among populist movements, for example, freedom from domination by "Wall Street" and the Eastern seaboard became identified with freedom from European domination. Not only were they protesting against industrial and commercial capitalism but also against the effete, European type of culture to which (in their eyes) Washington diplomats and the Eastern upper classes aspired. As one writer has observed, they feared "the shape which American society would assume were it to return to a broader trans-Atlantic culture."[12] Their isolationism, thus, expressed both their estrangement from Europe and their anxiety about the forms of American life.

No one can be certain whether the isolationists of the nineteenth century differed from the nonisolationists of that era in the same ways that isolationists and nonisolationists differ today. But one can scarcely ignore the contrast between America's insularity then and its "vulnerability" now. Apart from the fantastic changes in education, travel, communication, and exposure to other cultures, America's place in the international scene has been so drastically transformed as to defy comparison with that of earlier times. The United States has been engaged in wars on almost every continent, and has participated in numerous international organizations and alliances. Millions of Americans have lived or traveled abroad for extended periods of time. The oceans no longer safeguard American territory, and

---

[12] Paul Seabury, "The Irreconcilables" (unpublished). This volume contains an excellent analysis of the historical sources of American isolationism.

the lives of Americans have become interlaced with those of other nationals in countless ways.

One may wonder, then, whether isolationism is any longer a "natural," easily learned and accepted view, and whether the forces that once produced it are the same forces that are generating it now. Is isolationism today a "deviant" orientation, one that has different social and psychological meanings from those associated with it a hundred years ago? If, in light of contemporary realities, it is a less plausible and viable point of view than it once was, is it likely to win support from anyone who is not impelled towards it by strong inner needs? To what extent, in short, must we draw upon psychological explanations to account for the holding of isolationist beliefs in mid-twentieth century America?

That personality can be an important determinant of political attitudes has been too often confirmed by previous research to require extensive discussion here.[13] Research on the relation of personality to foreign policy attitudes is less extensive, but the findings turned up on this question are consistent with those from other types of attitude research.[14] There is, indeed, no reason to expect anything else. Needs, motives, defenses, frailties, and fears color men's judgments about foreign affairs just as they do their evaluation of other matters. In some ways, foreign policy offers an especially rich field for the play of personality variables. Many of the issues confronted have been heavily invested with symbolic meanings. They have, in some instances, occasioned struggle and sacrifice and have been dramatized as rallying points for mankind's hopes and fears. Often they present a highly ambiguous set of stimuli, thereby furnishing special opportunities for the engagement of psychological needs. Since they usually bespeak some type of conflict between nations, they furnish numerous occasions for the mobilization of appropriate affect (anger, anxiety, and the like). Sometimes they are incidents in the clash of rival ideologies, one or more of which may be intemperate in its claims. The prospect they raise is often one of danger

---

[13] There has been considerable research into this question. Among the major works is T. Adorno, E. Frenkel-Brunswik, D. Levinson, and R. N. Sanford, *The Authoritarian Personality* (New York: Harper and Row, 1956). Other relevant articles are R. Stagner, "Studies of Aggressive Social Attitudes: I. Measurement and Interrelation of Selected Attitudes," *Journal of Social Psychology*, Vol. 20 (1944), pp. 109–20; "Studies of Aggressive Social Attitudes: II. Changes From Peace to War," *Journal of Social Psychology*, Vol. 20 (1944), pp. 121–28. More generally, H. Goldhamer, "Public Opinion and Personality," *American Journal of Sociology*, Vol. 55 (1950), pp. 346–54.

[14] See M. B. Smith, J. Bruner, and R. White, *Opinions and Personality* (New York: John Wiley & Sons, 1956); M. B. Smith, "Personal Values as Determinants of a Political Attitude," *Journal of Psychology*, Vol. 28 (1949), pp. 447–86; L. Queener, "The Development of Internationalist Attitudes: I. Hypotheses and Verifications," *Journal of Social Psychology*, Vol. 29 (1949), pp. 221–36; "The Development of Internationalist Attitudes: II. Attitude Cues and Prestige," *Journal of Social Psychology*, Vol. 29 (1949), pp. 237–52; "The Development of International Attitudes: III. The Literature and A Point of View," *Journal of Social Psychology*, Vol. 30 (1949), pp. 105–26. For an excellent review of much of the recent literature see B. Christiansen, *Attitudes Towards Foreign Affairs as a Function of Personality* (Oslo: Oslo University Press, 1959).

to national pride, to independence, to territorial integrity, and even to survival.

There is reason to believe that the isolationist orientation is particularly susceptible to the influence of personality. As we shall see, isolationism offers numerous opportunities for marshalling aversive and appetitive dispositions, for the potentiation or projection of motives, for the activation of defense mechanisms, and for the ready translation of psychological needs (e.g., hostility) into appropriate attitude phenotypes. If it is also, as appears to be the case, a deviant view in contemporary American politics, it will be subject to those psychological factors that affect socialization, cognitive function, and the learning of norms.

It should not be necessary to state again that nothing I shall report here is meant to suggest that foreign policy attitudes are determined solely by personality. Obviously they also result from social learning, indoctrination, reference groups, ratiocination, and other nonpersonality influences. The stands men take on international questions are affected by time, geography, and social circumstance and by the configuration of forces in which personality variables are imbedded. In the present paper, however, the focus has been deliberately restricted and no attempt has been made to deal with the entire range of possible determinants.

Assumptions, Hypotheses, and Procedures

Owing to the profusion of variables employed in this study, the list of hypotheses that could possibly be investigated is unusually lengthy. It would burden the reader to face him at this point with the entire list, especially as some hypotheses will in any event need to be reiterated later in the chapter. Specific hypotheses, therefore, will be presented in subsequent sections, where they can be discussed simultaneously with the relevant findings. It might be helpful, however, to indicate at this time some of the major assumptions, general hypotheses, and theoretical considerations on which the analysis proceeded and on which the findings will, hopefully, throw some light. Principal among these are the following:

- Isolationism is in reality a complex political orientation that can originate in different ways and from diverse motives. It may spring from psychological needs and impulses as well as from social, intellectual, or political elements and it need not serve the same function or possess the same meaning for all persons who embrace it.
- Personality variables are most likely to evoke isolationist responses when the elements of the former are psychologically close to, cognate with, or readily converted into, the components of the latter and when the stimulus objects (say, foreigners) afford adequate opportunity for the mobilization of appropriate affect (say, fear).
- From a psychological standpoint, foreign policy attitudes are in principle no different from other political and social attitudes; they spring, together

with other attitude phenotypes, from common personality genotypes (or from similar cognitive styles); many of these attitudes will often be more usefully (and more correctly) understood as part of a substantively diverse network of attitudes than as a unique stance arising wholly or largely out of elements intrinsic to the domain of international politics.

• Isolationist beliefs will be strongly related to aversive rather than appetitive personality dispositions (i.e., response dispositions that aim to avoid, deny, deflect, shut out, or incapacitate other persons or related stimulus objects rather than to reach out to, embrace, accept, or involve them). This disposition will clearly manifest itself in generalized hostility, suspiciousness, misanthropy, inflexibility, a tendency toward "we-they" distinctions, intolerance of differences, and so forth.

• Isolationism in its traditional form is, at the present stage of American life, a deviant political orientation, possessing many of the same characteristics and correlates that mark other extreme or deviant outlooks; support for isolationism, therefore, represents in part a failure of socialization.

• Whatever interferes with the learning of political norms—ignorance, political apathy, cultural impoverishment, impaired cognitive functioning, restricted interaction, and even personality disorders—will increase the strength and frequency of isolationist sentiment.

• Nonisolationism is an orientation requiring, by comparison with isolationism, a greater element of sophistication and cosmopolitanism (in the intellectual and cultural sense). It will be more frequently represented among those who are, by various criteria, more participant, more informed, more mobile, closer to the articulate mainstream, more worldly—in a word, less parochial.

• Isolationism is more likely to signify a posture of international belligerency than of international pacifism, and has more to do with hostility against foreign nations and disavowal of responsibility for the well-being of others than with the considered assessment of the risks arising from international entanglements; but a subgroup of pacific isolationists can be identified who will more closely reflect, though they will not match, the personality and attitude traits of the nonisolationists.

• Foreign policy attitudes are more likely than specific foreign policy issues to engage other attitude and personality variables, and they will engage them more strongly; opinions on concrete foreign policy questions will be susceptible to social and economic forces and to political exigencies more than to personality influence; but among the political class especially, for whom issues are more salient and more clearly understood, correlations between personality and attitude factors on the one side and concrete issue outlooks on the other will be clearly discernible and significant.

The exploration of these and other notions was carried out through the analysis of data collected from three extensive field surveys during the

middle and late nineteen-fifties. I have described the sample and questionnaire procedures in previous publications and shall refrain, therefore, from
an extended discussion of those matters here.[15]

At least this much might be pointed out, however: the first of the three
surveys was carried out on a cross-section sample of the population of
Minnesota (n = 1,082), with the cooperation of the Minnesota Poll. The
second was a national cross-section survey of 1,484 respondents, administered
with the assistance of the American Institute of Public Opinion (Gallup Poll).
The third, and most important for present purposes, was a mail survey of
3,020 Democratic and Republican leaders, ranging from office holders at
the national levels of party and government to local officials and precinct
workers. All had, two years earlier, served as delegates and alternates to
the 1956 national Democratic and Republican conventions.

The questionnaires employed in the three studies had many similarities.
All contained large batteries of attitude and personality scales of the self-
administering type, together with numerous questions relating to political
experience, personal background, political opinions, and social characteristics. The nature and diversity of these scales will become evident from
their presentation in the next section. Approximately forty-five scales were
utilized in all three studies; others, however, were employed in the Minnesota
(MB) study but not in the national (PAB) studies, while still others appeared
in the national but not in the Minnesota studies. Altogether, data are
available for more tthan 70 separate scales, containing almost 550 individual
items.

Isolationism was one of the scales employed in all three studies. All scales
were subjected to validity and reliability tests, including, variously, empirical
validation by means of criterion groups, face validity assessments by expert
raters, modified Guttman reproducibility checks, and an ongoing construct
validity evaluation that compares our theoretical expectations with the actual
results. The Isolationism scale has been subject to all but the criterion group
procedure, and we are satisfied that it meets the tests of unidimensionality
and other criteria of validity. In addition, the items were initially drawn
from materials published by, and about, active isolationist groups, and they
express the sentiments that appeared most frequently in those writings. Built,
like the other scales, from a much larger initial pool of items, it was reduced
to a nine-item scale after testing and retesting.[16] The items in the Isola-

---

[15] See the discussion of these questions in H. McClosky, "Conservatism and Personality,"
American Political Science Review, Vol. 52 (1958), pp. 27–45; and H. McClosky, P. Hoffman,
and R. O'Hara, "Issue Conflict and Consensus Among Party Leaders and Followers," *American
Political Science Review,* Vol. 54 (1960), pp. 406–27.

[16] Although some of the scales were constructed by McClosky alone, the majority of the
scales in the initial inventory were built in collaboration with Professors Paul E. Meehl and
Kenneth E. Clark, of the Psychology Department, University of Minnesota. They were developed initially in a preliminary survey, for scale construction purposes only, of 1,200 residents
of the Twin Cities, Minnesota.

Table 1
The Isolationism Scale—Items and Item Frequencies

Items	Percentage Agree	
	National Leader Sample (n = 3,020)	General Population Sample (n = 1,484)
The best market for American goods is right here at home.	67%	51%
We almost have to restrict the amount of goods we let into this country because labor is so cheap in most other nations.	66	56
Most of the countries which have gotten economic help from America end up resenting what we have done for them.	61	54
These foreign wars America has been in are just part of the old quarrels Europeans have been having among themselves for centuries.	37	49
The federal government should be prevented from giving away any more of our wealth to foreign governments.	37	82
In spite of all the claims to the contrary, America can defend herself, as she has always done, without the aid of our so-called allies.	24	69
George Washington's advice to stay out of agreements with foreign powers is just as wise now as it was when he was alive.	23	75
By belonging to the UN we are running the danger of losing our constitutional right to control our own affairs.	17	55
Anytime American boys are found fighting on foreign shores, it is doubtful that the war is one that the United States should really be in.	17	30

tionism scale are presented in Table 1, together with their item difficulties for the national leader and general population samples.

In most of the analysis to follow, I have, for convenience of presentation, classified respondents as high, middle, and low on each of the scales. The cutting points for these divisions were set by finding the arithmetic thirds in the distribution for the general population on each particular scale. Thus, those who score from 6 to 9 on the Isolationism scale have been classified as high, or "isolationists"; those scoring from 3 to 5 have been called middle isolationists; and those scoring from 0 to 2 have been designated as low, or nonisolationists.

I will begin by presenting some descriptive data on the distribution of isolationist sentiments among American political leaders and voters today.

I will then consider the data on isolationism as an outgrowth of aversive personality traits, as a function of psychological and cognitive deprivation, and as part of a network of attitudes. This will be followed by an examination of the personality and attitude correlates of foreign policy issue orientations, and this, in turn, by an analysis of the pacific-jingoist distinction.

Findings

For reasons that will become plain, isolationist beliefs are far more common among the general population than they are among the political leaders. (See Table 2 and Figure 1.) Similarly, isolationism is more frequently expressed among the less educated than the more educated. Intellectuals,

Table 2

Mean Scores on Isolationism for Three Levels of Articulateness* Among Party Leaders and Supporters

	Level of Articulateness											
	Democratic Leaders			Republican Leaders			Democratic Followers			Republican Followers		
	H	M	L	H	M	L	H	M	L	H	M	L
Mean Isolationism Score	1.94	3.54	5.21	3.04	4.60	6.14	2.54	4.50	5.92	2.71	4.56	5.94
Number in Sample	638	1,047	103	384	782	66	76	527	222	83	415	125

* High articulates or intellectuals (H) are defined as college graduates who also score high on the Intellectuality scale. Low articulates (L) are persons of grade school education who score low on the Intellectuality scale.

as the mean scores show, are least isolationist of all. By every criterion on which we have data, isolationism increases as political and social awareness decline: It is more common among the unthinking than among the informed segments of the electorate, stronger among the poor, the culturally deprived, and any other groups who have been cut off from the mainstreams of the articulate culture.[17] Some of the reasons for this will be considered at a later point.

[17] On the role of education and information see Almond, *op. cit.,* Key, *op. cit.,* pp. 336–38, for example; K. Garrison, "Worldminded Attitudes of College Students in a Southern Town," *Journal of Social Psychology,* Vol. 54 (1961), pp. 147–54; M. Kriesberg, "Dark Areas of Ignorance," in L. Markel (ed.), *Public Opinion and Foreign Policy* (New York: Harper and Brothers, 1949), pp. 49–64; R. Lane, "Political Personality and Electoral Choice," *American Political Science Review,* Vol. 49 (1955), pp. 173–90. Also A. Hero, *Americans in World Affairs* (Boston: World Peace Foundation, 1959). See, in addition, "Citizen Participation in World Affairs: Problems and Possibilities," a special issue of *Journal of Social Issues,* Vol. 4 (Winter, 1948).

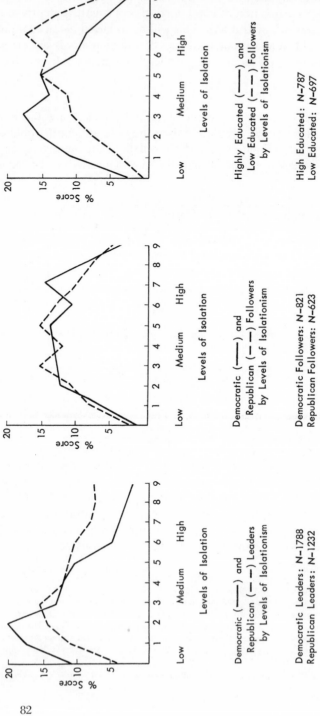

FIGURE 1 Percent Scoring at Each Level of Isolationism[1]: Comparison of Democratic and Republican Leaders and Followers[2].

[1] 0–2 Scorers are low on Isolationism; 3–5 Scorers are middle on Isolationism; 6–9 Scorers are high on Isolationism.
[2] National Samples only.

Isolationism also turns out to be significantly stronger among Republican than among Democratic leaders.[18] The difference is related to the liberal-conservative differences that separate the participating members of the two parties, and will be further explored when those attitudes are discussed. Note, however, that the rank-and-file Democratic and Republican supporters differ scarcely at all on the isolationist dimension, and the small differences that can be discerned are found principally in the comparison of their most articulate members.

Isolationism and Aversive Personality Traits

Need Aggression

Of all the personality states that one might expect, on theoretical grounds, to relate to isolationism, *n Aggression* and its concomitant aversive dispositions should be among the most powerful.[19] The need to punish, reject, avoid, or contain others is very close to being a genotypic parallel of the values contained in the classical expressions of isolationism. Persons of more appetitive disposition are characterized by their openness to experience, their acceptance and trust of others, their tolerance of human foibles, their sympathy, and their desire to relieve human suffering. Clinical studies show that such persons carry less guilt and anxiety, impute less hostility to others, and are more willing to become involved with their fellow men. We expected, then, that persons of strong misanthropic inclinations would turn out substantially more isolationist than persons of more benign persuasion. Since the content of the two dimensions in no way overlap, we anticipated this correlation for dynamic reasons, and not because of any similarity in the substance of the values being correlated. Take, for example, the Misanthropy index. A seventeen-item measure, it contains statements that bear

---

[18] On party differences in foreign policy oreintation—in this case attitudes toward Cuba—see P. Ekman, E. Tufte, K. Archibald, and R. A. Brody, "Coping with Cuba: Divergent Policy Preferences of State Political Leaders," *Journal of Conflict Resolution,* 10 (1966), 180–197, and Key, *op. cit.*

[19] The aggressiveness trait has been paid more attention by researchers than most other personality variables. A review of a wide range of experimental research is given in L. Berkowitz, *Aggression* (New York: McGraw-Hill, 1962). See also D. J. Levinson, "Authoritarian Personality and Foreign Policy," *Journal of Conflict Resolution,* Vol. 1 (1957), pp. 37–47; H. Grace, "Hostility, Communication and International Tension: I, The Hostility Inventory," *Journal of Social Psychology,* Vol. 34 (1951), pp. 31–40; "Hostility, Communication and International Tension: II, Social Group Backgrounds," *Journal of Educational Psychology,* Vol. 41 (1950), pp. 161–72; H. Grace and G. L. Grace, "Hostility, Communication and International Tension: III, The Hostility Factors," *Journal of Educational Psychology,* Vol. 42 (1951), pp. 206–14; R. Stagner, *op. cit.;* B. Christiansen, *op. cit.* In addition, see H. P. Smith and E. Rosen, "Some Psychological Correlates of Worldmindedness and Authoritarianism," *Journal of Personality,* Vol. 26 (1958), pp. 170–83; M. B. Smith, "The Personal Setting of Public Opinions: A Study of Attitudes toward Russia," *Public Opinion Quarterly,* Vol. 11 (1947–48), pp. 507–23; and W. MacKinnon and R. Centers, "Social and Psychological Factors in Public Orientation toward an Outgroup," *American Journal of Sociology,* Vol. 63 (1958), pp. 415–19.

entirely on one's feelings about mankind in general and various kinds of individuals in particular. (Typical items: "You have to be pretty choosy about picking friends." "I distrust people who try to be different from the rest of us." "People ought to be satisfied with what they have.") The other scales in Table 3, such as Hostility and Paranoia, are typical clinical scales designed to assess the genotypic personality states suggested by their names. Nothing in the face content of their items suggests a connection with isolationism either.

The connection is as powerful as we had predicted. As can be seen in Table 3, whereas 37 per cent of the isolationists in the political leader sample score high on the Misanthropy scale, only 2 per cent of the nonisolationists are misanthropic to the same degree. For the general population, the scores range from 65 per cent high to 4 per cent. Differences of comparable magnitude are apparent throughout the entire table for every sample (educated and uneducated) and every measure. Correlations computed on the intellectuals in both the elite and general population samples (not shown in this table) yield essentially the same results. Even for intellectuals—and in some instances especially for intellectuals—the holding of isolationist beliefs is powerfully correlated with the disposition to punish, reject, and diminish other men.

The scores on the Paranoia scale in Table 3 are equally consistent and impressive. Paranoia, of course, is a complex response disposition, but it may be understood in part as a projection of hostility. The paranoid tends to impute to others the impulses and desires to which he is himself prey. When he perceives others with suspicion, and regards them as deceptive, conspiratorial, and diabolical, the paranoid is expressing his fear and aversion of others and his desire either to shut them out or to bring them under control. The wish to dominate and to contain others is one of the elements in the megalomania and grandiosity that so often mark the paranoid personality. No great leap is required to move from these response dispositions to an orientation which holds foreigners and foreign nations to be scheming and dangerous.

The Intolerance of Human Frailty and Contempt for Weakness scales measure other aspects of the aggressive-aversive response. It may be logically inconsistent for an isolationist simultaneously to fear the demonic power of others and to scorn them for their weaknesses. It is not, however, psychologically inconsistent. While he fears their power to harm him, he loathes what he perceives to be their uncertain character, their shabby morals, and their lack of pride in seeking his collaboration and sympathy. Then, too, one who has a strong antagonism toward others is often led to reject them on any ground or pretext that presents itself. The object of the complaint is less telling in many cases than the impulse that gave rise to it.

The data collected in the present study—only a small part of which are being presented here—suggest that the relation between *n Aggression* and

Table 3
Isolationism and Misanthropy
(Percentages Down)

		Isolationism							
		National Leader Sample (n = 3,020)			General Population Sample (n = 1,484)					
					High Education*			Low Education*		
		H	M	L	H	M	L	H	M	L
		(643)	(1,150)	(1,227)	(199)	(359)	(229)	(358)	(260)	(79)
Scales										
Hostility	H	37	22	8	35	22	7	49	27	10
	M	48	48	38	47	42	35	41	50	41
	L	15	29	55	18	36	58	11	23	49
Paranoia	H	34	17	8	51	25	10	70	34	23
	M	36	35	24	32	35	26	21	37	29
	L	29	48	67	17	40	64	9	29	48
Misanthropy	H	37	15	2	45	25	5	67	42	13
	M	46	44	20	43	48	28	28	41	49
	L	17	41	78	12	27	67	4	16	38
F-Authoritarianism	H	38	15	3	43	20	3	67	34	6
	M	48	49	21	48	49	29	30	57	53
	L	15	37	76	9	31	68	3	9	41
Contempt for Weakness	H	36	20	8	31	19	8	47	25	8
	M	51	56	39	50	53	45	42	57	61
	L	13	24	54	19	28	47	11	17	32
Intolerance of Human Frailty	H	41	25	10	50	27	15	62	43	23
	M	47	50	45	44	53	45	31	42	46
	L	13	24	45	6	20	40	6	15	32

		Minnesota Sample Only (n = 1,082)					
		High Education*			Low Education*		
		H	M	L	H	M	L
		(147)	(272)	(224)	(203)	(177)	(51)
Faith in People	H	9	32	48	11	32	27
	M	48	41	33	39	40	53
	L	43	27	19	50	28	20

* On these and subsequent tables High Education respondents are high school graduates and above; Low Education respondents are those who did not graduate from high school.

isolationism is not unique. Persons of hostile disposition, it seems, fasten upon various objects to vent their anger. Foreign nations are only one of many classes of stimuli to which they respond in the same way. This is not to suggest, of course, that persons of aggressive disposition will express their anger in all contexts. A person may be manifestly kindly in his everyday life but fiercely antagonistic in his response to certain public questions. The manner of his response, after all, is a function not only of a general response disposition but of other factors as well, including the saliency of the stimulus object. If he is indifferent to the state of the nation or its place in the world, his hostility may be engaged scarcely at all. How strongly he aggresses also depends on whether it is safe to do so. A man who hesitates to disagree with his wife on any question whatever may not shy at all from expressing his rage toward foreigners, foreign nations, or any other groups outside his immediate household.

Whether hostility is expressed also depends on whether the prevailing conditions are limiting or facilitating, i.e. whether the expression of enmity is "legitimate" in the context. Hatred of Cuba or China is currently legitimate in most subcultures of the United States, and one may assail them with impunity. There are, in addition, internal restraints on the expression of such "antagonistic" attitudes as isolationism. Some individuals are psychologically less free than others to admit, much less to express, their hostility. A highly "defensed" person who cannot admit even to himself the rage that boils within him may be unable to show his anger or may express it only against targets that are safe in the sense that he can attack them without fear of arousing guilt.

Despite these qualifications, our data show plainly that *n Aggression* tends to be generalized across a range of attitudes, and that many objects can serve to satisfy it. But there is no mistaking that psychologically hostile persons will score isolationist far more often than persons who are more compassionate. The willingness to take on international entanglements or obligations plainly reflects not only one's judgment about the utility of such involvements for securing the national safety but also, in many cases, the degree to which one has concern for other people.

Psychological Inflexibility

The parallels between psychological inflexibility and isolationism are not so immediately apparent as were those shown in the case of *n Aggression*. Nevertheless, there are reasons to expect inflexibility and isolationism to be strongly and positively correlated. These reasons will become evident from a description of the inflexible personality configuration.

In a study undertaken elsewhere to explore the nature of psychological inflexibility and its significance for political belief and behavior,[20] we have conceptualized inflexibility as an attribute of the defense mechanisms (e.g., reaction formation, rationalization, projection, denial, and the like). The inflexible person is one whose dependence upon these substitute expressions is extreme. Inflexibility, we believe, is a genotypic source trait, for the most

---

[20] The volume reporting the results of this research is currently in progress, under the joint authorship of McClosky, Paul E. Meehl, and Kenneth E. Clark.

part under aversive rather than appetitive control. Its manifest characteristics include an inclination toward black-white polarization and dichotomous distinctions, premature cognitive closure, stereotypic and automatized thought sequences, stimulus fixation, selective attention, and a narrowing of exposure to exclude unfamiliar persons and other stimulus objects. The inflexible person is also characterized by a strong need for order and autonomy, and is made acutely uncomfortable by ambiguity, uncertainty, contingency, complexity, and unfamiliarity. He tends, characteristically, to oversimplify by narrowing the phenomenal field and by assigning fixed, predictable roles to all the players. He is in a continual struggle against his own impulse life, and is rigidly constrained in the limits he imposes upon himself and others. Partly for these reasons, he is unusually susceptible both to hostility and anxiety. He is impatient with, and even angered by, differences and he accommodates poorly to novelty and change. He is severe in his judgments and intolerant of unconventionality. He is attracted to opinions that are categorical and dogmatic and he tends more than most to exclude incompatible information. Despite his elaborate defenses, he has low self-esteem, for which he often compensates by demeaning the motives and behavior of others. Individuals with this personality pattern often suffer a reduction in their capacity for interaction and an impairment in cognitive function.

Although this portrait is based on considerable evidence from our own research and the research of others, it is, of course, ideal-typical and inevitably overdrawn. Even so, we can easily see why individuals of inflexible personality might be expected to favor isolationist sentiments.[21] The parallel, it seems, is far closer than we originally had reason to think. Isolationism offers its supporters a dichotomous choice, a polarization of forces so clearly etched as to contain little or no ambiguity. The world is made simple, with "them" on one side and "us" on the other. "They"—the nationals of other countries—are irrevocably estranged from "us" by culture, politics, language, manners, skin color, customs, and national character. These variations, which might intrigue some people, merely confound and repel the inflexible. He partitions the world in an effort to make order out of diversity, simplicity out of complexity, clarity out of confusion. He also manages in this way to reduce his anxiety about "strangers" who (as he characteristically sees it) freely gratify their impulses at the expense of character, duty, integrity, and independence. Why become involved with such people? Why rescue them from the misfortunes they have inflected upon themselves?

Since it is important for the inflexible to achieve control and make the world manageable, he resists attachments that deprive him, or his country, of autonomy and initiative. Every treaty, every alliance gives hostages to

---

[21] A study concerned with personality traits related to our notion of psychological inflexibility is M. Farber, "The Anal Character and Political Aggression," *Journal of Abnormal and Social Psychology,* Vol. 51 (1950), pp. 486–89.

disorder and uncertainty and strengthens potential enemies. A nation that looks to its own interests without regard for the demands of others is a nation that commands fate; a nation that allies itself with others becomes fate's pawn. Not only does it lose power over the behavior of other nations, but over its own affairs as well.

The strength of the relationship between isolationism on the one side and psychological inflexibility on the other is clearly evident in Table 4. Among the political influentials, 63 per cent of the isolationists score high on in-tolerance of ambiguity, compared with 24 per cent of the nonisolationists. Differences of comparable magnitude hold for the general population, for Democratic and Republican leaders, and for both the educated and un-educated. The pattern is equally unmistakable when we examine the re-sults on the Rigidity and Obsessiveness scales, and on the Inflexibility Index. Again it should be observed that the items on these scales are free of political content. All refer to comments about one's personal habits, one's feelings about carelessness, disorder, perfection, decisiveness, the manner of organizing one's work, and so forth. Nothing in the items suggests on their face a connection with isolationism.[22]

Anxiety, Ego-Strength, and Feelings of Marginality

Both anxiety and low ego-strength are aspects of the aversive personality, for while they manifestly testify to dissatisfaction with oneself, they also carry heavy loadings of fear and rage and reflect an implicit wish to escape, avoid, or disarm others. The scales we have listed in Table 5 as measures of anxiety (Psychological Disorganization and Manifest Anxiety) refer primarily to constitutional states, such as restlessness, inability to concentrate, and exces-sive worry. So too do Guilt and Need Inviolacy (Table 6) which measure, as their names imply, profound disappointment in oneself and the fear of being found naked and unprotected before the world. The remaining scales included under the ego-strength category in Table 6 report not so much the inner life of the respondent as his ability (or inability) to accomodate to the world and command successfully the life-space in which he functions. All the scales in these tables, however, register in one fashion or another feelings of frustration, fear, disappointment, self-doubt, inadequacy, or failure.

It is, of course, now well established that such psychological states tend— through displacement, the frustration-aggression phenomenon, or the play of other defense mechanisms—to emerge in many of their victims as resent-ment and envy. As we have elsewhere observed,[23] those who strongly harbor

---

[22] In reporting these results, we are not unaware of the controversy that has developed among psychologists concerning the nature and generalizability of so-called rigidity. We are satisfied that that controversy offers no difficulties for the conclusions drawn here. Part of the justification is similar to that offered in the discussion of the generalizability of *n Aggression*. Much more can be said, but this is not the place to say it.

[23] H. McClosky and J. Schaar, "Psychological Dimensions of Anomy," *American Sociological Review*, Vol. 30 (1965), pp. 14–39. Reprinted below, chap. 3.

Table 4
Isolationism and Inflexibility
(Percentages Down)

| | | National Leader Sample (n = 3,020) | | | General Population Sample (n = 1,484) | | | | | |
| | | | | | High Education | | | Low Education | | |
		H (643)	M (1,150)	L (1,227)	H (199)	M (359)	L (229)	H (358)	M (260)	L (79)
Scales										
Intolerance	H	63	42	24	53	23	13	64	43	29
of	M	24	29	26	34	37	30	26	35	25
Ambiguity	L	13	28	50	13	40	57	10	22	46
	H	62	51	35	54	32	25	57	38	18
Obsessive	M	21	22	25	20	29	24	23	27	33
	L	17	26	40	26	40	52	20	35	49
	H	46	32	16	53	30	21	65	48	28
Rigidity	M	28	28	24	26	28	23	22	24	37
	L	26	40	60	22	42	57	14	28	35
	H	30	17	8	27	8	3	43	18	4
Inflexibility	M-H	42	34	26	40	30	21	32	39	24
Index	M-L	21	30	33	22	35	29	19	27	37
	L	7	19	32	11	27	48	6	17	35

Table 5
Isolationism and Anxiety
Minnesota Sample Only
(Percentages Down)
(n = 1,082)

| | | Isolationism | | | | | |
| | | High Education | | | Low Education | | |
		H (147)	M (272)	L (224)	H (203)	M (177)	L (51)
Scales							
Psychological	H	36	31	19	51	37	24
Disorgani-	M	37	39	40	33	34	29
zation	L	27	30	41	16	29	47
Manifest	H	26	22	13	37	22	10
Anxiety	M	53	49	46	47	53	49
	L	21	29	42	15	25	41

Table 6
Isolationism and Ego-Strength
(Percentages Down)

		National Leader Sample (n = 3,020)			General Population Sample (n = 1,484)					
					High Education			Low Education		
		H	M	L	H	M	L	H	M	L
		(643)	(1,150)	(1,227)	(199)	(359)	(229)	(358)	(260)	(79)
Scales										
Dominance	H	68	79	87	40	41	64	19	30	42
	M	23	17	11	31	34	24	30	34	33
	L	9	5	2	29	25	12	51	36	25
Guilt	H	33	22	14	35	22	12	46	29	20
	M	32	33	26	33	32	28	31	35	28
	L	35	45	60	32	46	60	23	36	52
Life Satisfaction	H	58	62	61	25	34	48	21	29	39
	M	27	27	28	35	35	34	32	32	34
	L	15	11	11	40	31	18	47	40	27
Need Inviolacy	H	35	18	9	42	21	12	62	28	13
	M	25	24	16	29	28	19	23	30	29
	L	40	57	75	29	51	69	15	42	58
Social Responsibility	H	23	37	53	18	32	49	8	22	42
	M	46	48	38	39	39	44	32	45	44
	L	30	14	9	43	29	7	60	33	14
Status Frustration	H	16	12	8	20	14	9	35	25	14
	M	35	37	26	48	40	33	41	41	38
	L	49	51	66	32	47	59	25	34	48

		Minnesota Sample Only (n = 1,082)					
		High Education			Low Education		
		H	M	L	H	M	L
		(147)	(272)	(224)	(203)	(177)	(51)
Self-Confidence	H	35	35	45	24	15	22
	M	41	42	37	44	44	41
	L	24	23	19	32	41	37

these feelings "tend to project upon the external world the doubts and fears that dominate their own mental life." They are likely to be disgruntled and suspicious toward the world in general. This includes the international world, which mirrors for them the uncertainty, disorder, drift, and normlessness they are inclined to find everywhere.

On this reasoning, we would expect isolationism to be embraced by some people as a way of handling their own insecurities, doubts, and frustrations. Like ethnocentrism, to which it is closely related psychologically, an isolationist orientation would permit them not only to blame others (including other nations) for the bad fate that life has dealt them, but also to satisfy their impulse to punish, reject, and demean others, partly as retribution and partly as a way of bringing other men down to an even lower, more miserable level than their own. Foreign nations, it should be observed, represent a fairly safe target for such aggression. Not only can one usually assail them with impunity, but by doing so one can simultaneously demonstrate one's patriotism.

Except for Self-Confidence and Life Satisfaction, which do not consistently yield correlations that are statistically significant,[24] the results from the various measures of anxiety and ego-strength presented in Tables 5 and 6 furnish strong, inferential support for these hypotheses. Even among the political leaders—where foreign policy orientations, one assumes, are more rationally calculated in response to objective international realities—the isolationists are, by a ratio of two to one, more likely than the nonisolationists to manifest strong feelings of guilt, and, by a ratio of four to one, to express anxiety about the inviolacy of their inner selves. Isolationists in all samples feel themselves less dominant or in command of themselves, tend to lack self-assurance, and, by comparison with nonisolationists, have accommodated themselves less successfully to their immediate surroundings.

Similar results are found in the data on feelings of marginality presented in Table 7. Here we test more directly the hypothesis that isolationism is one expression, among others, of a general feeling of malaise or of alienation from the world as one finds it. The Alienation scale shown in that table refers primarily to feelings of personal isolation from primary groups and the absence of a nurturant environment. The Anomy scale assesses the degree to which individuals feel that the society is normless and lacking in direction and meaning. The Cruel World scale measures the tendency to regard the world as cold and indifferent, unconcerned with the respondent's fate. The Bewilderment scale, used only in the MB study, testifies to the respondent's feeling that the world is hopelessly complicated and unfathomable.

The response on each of these measures is uniformly in the predicted direction. Isolationists in both the political leader and general population samples register significantly stronger feelings of estrangement, bewilderment, and moral chaos.[25] By an overwhelming margin, they are also disposed to regard the world as a hostile, dangerous, or indifferent place, populated by potential enemies and harboring innumerable threats. Similar findings

---

[24] Unless otherwise noted, all differences reported in these tables are, by chi-square tests, statistically significant at or beyond the .01 level of confidence.

[25] On anomy, see C. Farris, "Selected Attitudes on Foreign Affairs as Correlates of Political Anomie and Authoritarianism," *Journal of Politics,* Vol. 22 (1960), pp. 50–67.

Table 7
Isolationism and Feelings of Marginality
(Percentages Down)

		National Leader Sample (n = 3,020)			General Population Sample (n = 1,484)					
					High Education			Low Education		
		H (643)	M (1,150)	L (1,227)	H (199)	M (359)	L (229)	H (358)	M (260)	L (79)
Scales										
	H	25	17	12	35	26	17	54	33	24
Alienation	M	38	37	31	41	39	28	36	38	37
	L	37	47	57	24	35	55	11	29	39
	H	21	7	1	41	20	5	70	37	13
Anomy	M	48	38	18	46	46	30	25	45	49
	L	32	55	80	13	34	65	5	17	38
Cruel,	H	26	9	2	35	15	2	53	20	6
Indifferent	M	52	44	23	33	49	27	41	52	42
World	L	23	47	77	12	36	70	7	27	52

		Minnesota Sample Only (n = 1,082)					
		High Education (n = 643)			Low Education (n = 431)		
		H (147)	M (272)	L (224)	H (203)	M (177)	L (51)
	H	48	22	10	58	29	12
Bewilderment	M	33	42	32	33	42	29
	L	19	36	58	9	29	59

turn up on a scale measuring pessimistic outlook toward the world's future (not shown on this table), with isolationists scoring strongly pessimistic (in comparison with internationalists) by a ratio of approximately 5 to 1. The results on these scales are consistent for both parties and all education levels.

Whether the relationship between these personality measures and isolationism is causal or epiphenomenal is difficult to say. Like isolationism, they are all measures of dissatisfaction and fear. All refer to some imagined hostile force that prevents happiness and the realization of one's desires. That they express concern about the world or the society rather than about oneself is really beside the point. Most people who score high on these measures are implicitly complaining about their own disappointments and frustrations, their feelings of being left out, and their sense of impotence and futility. They and the world have somehow diverged.

For many people, therefore, a preference for isolationism may be largely an expression of protest and resentment. I am not suggesting that no isolationist genuinely believes in the specific recommendations of the isolationist philosophy; among the political influentials, in fact, only a minority of the isolationists (approximately one-fourth) score high on the marginality measures. Nevertheless, one of the attributes of the isolationist persuasion is its association with a network of responses that bespeak frustration and disappointment.

The results on the Anomy and Bewilderment scales (and on the political alienation scales to be presented below) signify that isolationism is also related to divorcement from one's own society. Despite their jingoism and their ardently professed love of country, many isolationists are in important respects disappointed in it—even to the point of repudiating some of its most fundamental values. Possibly, therefore, the antagonism they evince toward other nations is a displacement of their dissatisfaction with their own society. Since they cannot bring themselves to reject openly a nation with which they seek so urgently to identify, their dislike of it is masked even from themselves. The same mechanisms of psychological defense (described earlier) by which an individual conceals from consciousness certain unpleasant facts about himself, also prevent him from admitting to himself his true feelings about his country. Every bit of evidence we have turned up in our research on this question confirms that isolationists, chauvinists, jingoists, or any combination of the three harbor a disproportionate share of resentment and anger against the quality of contemporary American life, against many of its fundamental values, and against the nature and performance of its institutions.

Cognitive Capacity and Function

Isolationism, as we noted in Table 2, is found less frequently among the educated than the uneducated, still less frequently among the political influentials, and least frequently of all among politically active intellectuals. On this evidence, isolationism appears to be a deviant rather than a popular orientation among articulate Americans. This inference, of course, is also congruent with what can readily be observed in the thrust of American foreign policy since World War II. Membership in the United Nations, participation in NATO and other defense alliances, the Marshall Plan, extensive foreign aid programs, and numerous other instances of intervention in world affairs support the conclusion that the American norm is now one of international collaboration and involvement. This, in turn, suggests that support for isolationist sentiments at this time (and perhaps in some past periods as well) is a function of articulateness as such, and of one's ability to learn and take cognizance of the norms. If so, we may have come upon an additional reason for the powerful correlations shown between isolationism on the one side and the several forms of anxiety, low self-esteem, and marginality on the other.[26] These psychological states have a crippling effect on political socialization and the learning of community norms. They tend to impede effective social interaction and to impair the internalization of a society's implicit values. We find evidence throughout our data that persons who are in command of themselves, who are not exhausted by anxiety or incapacitated by guilt, disappointments, and frustrations, who are self-assured, personally effective, and secure in their relationships with others are somewhat more likely to be aware of, and to accept, the norms of the articulate culture. While socialization, of course, is strongly influenced by education and status, the findings on this matter hold for the leader samples as well as the masses, for the educated as well as the uneducated, and for those in the upper status categories as well as those in the lower.[27]

The data presented in Table 8 bear on this matter to some degree. In addition to the findings on education, the table shows the relationship between isolationism and three other measures of articulateness. The outcome is in every instance consistent with the hypothesis: an elevation in awareness or cognitive function decreases the frequency of isolationism. Even among the political leaders, differences in orientation toward intellectual activities and the life of the mind correspond closely with outlook on foreign policy questions: 78 per cent of the nonisolationists in this sample score high on Intellectuality, compared with only 30 per cent of the isolationists. The differences are also large on the Awareness scale, an achievement measure that assesses each respondent's level of information about political and social affairs. The internationalists are, to a significant degree, better informed about public affairs than are the isolationists. Other measures employed in the study, such as Mysticism and Acquiescence, furnish an indirect indication of intellectual capacity, an ability to reason from evidence, cognitive consistency, and the like. These scales also yield the same basic conclusion. From whatever direction one approaches this question, then, the influentials, the educated, the informed, and what Rosenau[28]

[26] For other research on the relationship of anxiety and self-image to social attitudes, see Farris, *op. cit.;* A. Brodbeck and H. Perlmutter, "Self-Dislike as an Indicator of Marked Ingroup-Outgroup Preferences," *Journal of Psychology,* Vol. 38 (1954), pp. 271–80; and H. Perlmutter, "Relations between the Self-Image, the Image of the Foreigner, and the Desire to Live Abroad," *Journal of Psychology,* Vol. 38 (1954), pp. 131–37.

[27] I have not included in this paper data on the relationship between social background and isolationism. On the relationship between various foreign policy attitudes and socioeconomic status, variously defined, see Key, *op. cit.,* pp. 130–34, 140, 150; Almond, *op. cit.,* Garrison, *op. cit.,* MacKinnon and Centers, "Social Psychological Factors in Public Orientation toward an Outgroup," *op. cit.;* P. Blau, "Orientation of College Students toward International Relations," *American Journal of Sociology,* Vol. 59 (1953), pp. 205–14; and W. Miller, "Socioeconomic Analysis of Political Behavior," *Midwest Journal of Political Science,* Vol. 2 (1958), pp. 239–55.

[28] See J. Rosenau, *Public Opinion and Foreign Policy* (New York: Random House, 1961).

Table 8
Isolationism and Cognitive Functioning
(Percentages Down)

		Isolationism								
		National Leader Sample *(n = 3,020)*			*General Population Sample* *(n = 1,484)*					
					High Education			*Low Education*		
		H	*M*	*L*	*H*	*M*	*L*	*H*	*M*	*L*
		(643)	*(1,150)*	*(1,227)*	*(199)*	*(359)*	*(229)*	*(358)*	*(260)*	*(79)*
Scales										
	H	66	74	85						
Education*	M	27	23	12						
	L	7	3	3						
	H	30	51	78	23	45	72	15	29	43
Intellectuality	M	42	35	18	44	38	23	39	40	43
	L	28	14	4	33	17	5	46	31	14
	H	37	15	6	42	19	3	67	32	11
Acquiescence	M	41	47	29	40	43	35	25	37	32
	L	22	38	65	18	38	61	8	30	57

		Minnesota Sample Only *(n = 1,082)*					
		High Education *(n = 643)*			*Low Education* *(n = 431)*		
		H	*M*	*L*	*H*	*M*	*L*
		(147)	*(272)*	*(224)*	*(203)*	*(177)*	*(51)*
	H	24	35	54	8	7	25
Awareness	M	33	39	34	24	44	43
	L	43	26	12	68	49	31

* High Education = some college, college graduate.
  Middle Education = some high school, high-school graduate.
  Low education = grade school.

has called the "attentive public" are significantly less isolationist than the less informed and less educated members of the population.

These findings are consistent with certain inferences that can be drawn from other parts of the data. From our examination of numerous personality and other types of variables, it appears that whatever impairs cognitive function or limits cognitive capacity tends to increase isolationist sentiments. Hence, social or cultural deprivation, remoteness from the centers of political culture, ignorance of facts, psychological disorders that have a deleterious effect on cognitive performance, or any other impediments to effective social learning tend to diminish support for the prevailing values of the society. (It does not follow, of course, that all who criticize the society are unaware.)

Some people who score as isolationists are simply unmindful of the full meaning of their responses.[29] Their support for isolationism is, in part, a preference for the simpler and more easily grasped view. To favor isolationism requires only one uncomplicated intellectual operation: One simply withdraws or disengages oneself. In this way, one can avoid having to face up to the complexities associated with international cooperation, such as the appropriate amount of autonomy to be yielded, the mutual obligations imposed upon the participating nations, the proper interpretation of treaties, and so forth. Conceivably, then, articulates, and especially intellectuals, may show more favor toward internationalism than others do because, in part, they are more conversant with the substance and implications of foreign policy questions and have a greater capacity to ponder them. This superiority in awareness both contributes to and results from the greater saliency that foreign affairs possess for such people. By training, self-image, knowledge, skills, mobility, and associations, they are simply more "cosmopolitan." By intellectual capacity—or at least by functioning intellectual capacity—they are better prepared to assess information and draw conclusions about thorny international questions. Then, too, they are usually far more exposed to the intellectual products of foreign nations, which tends, on the whole, to break down stereotypes and reduce fears of what is foreign and unfamiliar.[30]

That isolationist opinions are for many people an expression of parochialism is suggested by various other findings in the study. For example, persons who come from rural areas, even including political leaders, are significantly more isolationist than persons from metropolitan areas.[31] Internationalist sentiments are stronger among those in both the leader and

---

[29] P. Converse, "The Nature of Belief Systems in Mass Publics," in D. Apter (ed.), *Ideology and Discontent* (New York: The Free Press, 1964), pp. 206–61; also S. A. Stouffer, *Communism, Conformity, and Civil Liberties* (New York: Doubleday, 1955); S. M. Lipset, *Political Man* (New York: Doubleday, 1960); J. W. Prothro and C. Grigg, "Fundamental Principles of Democracy: Bases of Agreement and Disagreement," *Journal of Politics,* Vol. 22 (1960), pp. 276–94; R. Dahl, *Who Governs?* (New Haven: Yale University Press, 1961); and H. McClosky "Consensus and Ideology in American Politics," *American Political Science Review,* Vol. 58 (1964), pp. 361–82.

[30] There is abundant data on the relationship between foreign policy orientation and the amount of information about foriegn affairs. In general, those with a high degree of information are more likely to hold an internationalist orientation. In addition to the references cited in footnote 17, see Christiansen *op. cit.;* A. Campbell, P. Converse, W. Miller, and D. Stokes, *The American Voter* (New York: John Wiley and Sons, 1960); W. A. Scott, "Correlates of International Attitudes," *Public Opinion Quarterly,* Vol. 22 (1958), pp. 464–72; R. Schonbar, "Students' Attitudes toward Communists: I, The Relation between Intensity of Attitude and Amount of Information," *Journal of Psychology,* Vol. 27 (1949), pp. 55–72; and B. Shimberg, "Information and Attitudes toward World Affairs," *Journal of Educational Psychology,* Vol. 40 (1949), pp. 206–22. See also the summary of the literature in J. Robinson, *Public Information about World Affairs* (Ann Arbor: Survey Research Center of the University of Michigan, 1965).

[31] On the role of region and residence, see Key, *op. cit.,* pp. 99–120; Almond, *op. cit.;* and Fensterwald, *op. cit.* Also G. Belknap and A. Campbell, "Political Party Identification and Atiitudes toward a Foreign Policy," *Public Opinion Quarterly,* Vol. 15 (Winter, 1951–52), pp. 601–23. For roll-call analyses of congressional behavior, see C. Lerche, "Southern Congressmen

general population samples who belong to a larger number of organizations, among leaders who have held office at the national (as contrasted with local) levels of government, and among political actives who want the parties to be controlled nationally rather than locally. It may also be worth noting, though the interpretation is open to argument, that a significantly larger number of isolationists in the leader sample would prefer their party to control Congress rather than the Presidency. The explanation, presumably, lies in their greater provincialism and their conviction that Congress offers a firmer brake on international spending and involvement. There are no differences on this question among the general population. In any event, it is characteristic of "provincials" to respond less favorably to the unfamiliar and foreign, and this antipathy may find a natural outlet in isolationism.

Dichotomous Thinking

Not only the capacity, but the style of cognitive performance has a bearing upon the acceptance or rejection of isolationist views. The isolationist persuasion is one of a number of political orientations that are strongly characterized by a tendency to draw sharp we-they distinctions—to separate, in one writer's phrase, "the brother and the other."[32] This propensity is apparent in ethnocentrism, chauvinism, xenophobia, xenophilia (an inverted form of xenophobia), and the numerous caste distinctions that men have invented from the beginning of time.[33] In their extreme form, these divisions are usually accompanied by rituals that protect against impurity or the dilution of the ethnic or cultural strain. The sources of this propensity are now better understood than they once were, but it remains, nevertheless, a baffling and controversial phenomenon. It seems evident that the tendency to distinguish dichotomous categories is an aspect of the inflexibility syndrome, and that isolationism, like ethnocentrism, is a phenotypic expression of the inflexibility genotype. But this is obviously not the entire story.

Certain aspects of the attachment to one's nation are easy enough to understand: the nation is the definitive, norm-giving association, in which

and the New Isolationism," *Political Science Quarterly*, Vol. 75 (1960), pp. 321-37; and L. Rieselbach, "The Basis of Isolationist Behavior," *Public Opinion Quarterly*, Vol. 24 (1960), pp. 645-57; and "The Demography of the Congressional Vote on Foreign Aid, 1939-1958," *American Political Science Review*, Vol. 58 (1964), pp. 557-88.

[32] The phrase is that of B. Nelson, *The Idea of Usury, From Tribal Brotherhood to Universal Otherhood* (Princeton: Princeton University Press, 1949).

[33] For research employing these variables, see Brodbeck and Perlmutter, *op. cit.;* H. Perlmutter, "Correlates of Two Types of Xenophilic Orientation," *Journal of Abnormal and Social Psychology*, Vol. 52 (1956), pp. 130-35; and "Some Characteristics of the Xenophilic Personality," *Journal of Psychology*, Vol. 38 (1954), pp. 291-300; D. Campbell and B. McCandless, "Ethnocentrism Xenophobia and Personality," *Human Relations*, Vol. 4 (1951), pp. 185-92; T. Adorno et al., *The Authoritarian Personality;* E. Shils, *The Torment of Secrecy* (New York: Free Press, 1956); and T. Lentz, "The Attitudes of World Citizenship," *Journal of Social Psychology*, Vol. 32 (1950), pp. 207-14. For data on anti-Semitism and foreign policy orientation, see S. Crown, "Some Personality Correlates of War-Mindedness and Anti-Semitism," *Journal of Social Psychology*, Vol. 31 (1950), pp. 131-40.

there is a confluence of blood ties, law-making, defense and security functions, a common history and tradition, and a set of myths and symbols that together furnish an extraordinary impetus to unity. What is more difficult to explain is the tendency to exclude, by force, custom, law, or ritualistic practices those who have not previously qualified for admission. The unifying side of this behavioral phenomenon can be explained without recourse to esoteric assumptions or exotic variables. The tendency to dichotomize, however, and to reject as ineradicably tainted all those who fall on the other side of the line, is a more inscrutable form of human behavior, one that originates in the innermost reaches of the human personality. Certainly it is too formidable a question to be addressed in the context of our present inquiry.

Suffice it to recognize that we have given this tendency a name, but that we have not adequately explained it. Whatever its sources, its relationship to isolationist tendencies is overwhelmingly plain. As Table 9 clearly confirms, isolationists differ markedly from nonisolationists on measures that directly or indirectly reflect dichotomous thinking (chauvinism, ethnocentrism, anti-Semitism, and so on). Even among the political influentials, the probability of scoring high on, for example, ethnocentrism is almost ten times as great if one is an isolationist than if one is an internationalist. Similar results are found for all of the measures in the table.

Two of the scales—the We-They General and the We-They Specific—are likely to be unfamiliar, and deserve separate comment. These measures were constructed through item-rating procedures utilizing graduate students and research personnel. The We-They General scale was designed to measure the tendency to make dichotomous distinctions, without regard to any particular group or any specific set of characteristics. The We-They Specific scale was designed to assess the same trait, except that the stimuli were fairly specific and referred to particular groups or types of people. The results on both scales show an unmistakable—indeed, an overwhelming—disposition among isolationists to think in dichotomous terms. On item after item, no matter what the target group, the isolationists were significantly more disposed to set them apart or to identify them, implicitly or explicitly, as "different."

Further evidence of this inclination is provided by the responses to questions asking which of the groups listed has "too much power." The results for the leader sample are extremely impressive: the isolationists gave the "too much power" answer more often than the nonisolationists on nine of the ten groups listed. The only group toward which they showed hostility less frequently were the businessmen. The differences in the frequency with which the two groups expressed hostility were especially large in their responses to the foreign born (34 per cent versus 8 per cent), intellectuals (34 per cent versus 8 per cent), Negroes (34 per cent versus 10 per cent), and Jews (32 per cent versus 11 per cent). There were small differences in

Table 9
Isolationism and Dichotomous Thinking
(Percentages Down)

		Isolationism								
		National Leader Sample (n = 3,020)			General Population Sample (n = 1,484)					
					High Education			Low Education		
		H (643)	M (1,150)	L (1,227)	H (199)	M (359)	L (229)	H (358)	M (260)	L (79)
Scales										
We-They General	H	47	25	8	43	21	11	52	38	26
	M	2	5	5	31	33	22	33	33	27
	L	52	70	87	26	47	67	16	28	46
We-They Specific	H	36	10	1	49	23	4	64	37	19
	M	54	53	22	40	47	34	29	43	45
	L	11	37	77	11	30	62	7	20	36
Chauvinism	H	40	10	1	43	10	1	70	27	5
	M	37	31	10	39	40	17	25	46	39
	L	23	59	90	18	50	83	4	27	56
Ethno-centrism	H	39	19	4	50	17	6	55	27	9
	M	46	46	22	39	47	26	37	53	41
	L	15	35	75	11	36	69	8	20	51
Anti-Semitism	H	50	33	11	58	37	16	65	48	24
	M	12	13	7	17	17	15	15	15	24
	L	36	53	80	27	46	68	19	34	52
Segregation-Integration	H	53	33	12	48	27	12	60	41	24
	M	29	40	35	27	33	29	28	31	32
	L	17	28	54	26	38	59	22	28	45

their responses to farmers, and large differences (87 per cent versus 56 per cent) in their responses to labor unions. Part of this difference reflects the greater conservatism of the isolationists (see below), but much of it expresses their tendency to resent any group other than their own. In the general population, the responses on this question do not hold as consistently. Even in this sample, however, the isolationists were more likely than the nonisolationists to name foreigners, intellectuals, Negroes, and Jews as having too much power. There are smaller but significant differences for the responses to Catholics as well. The largest differences occur in the responses to foreigners: 49 per cent of the educated isolationists, compared with 10 per cent of the educated internationalists, name foreigners as having too much power. These and the findings reported earlier point not only to the greater xenophobia of the isolationists, but to their stronger disposition to regard all out-groups with aversion.

The Foreign-Domestic Attitude Cluster

In the hypothesis section, we raised the question of the relation between foreign policy attitudes and other political attitudes. It was suggested there that attitudes that spring from the same personality genotypes or cognitive styles might well belong to the same attitude cluster, and might therefore be understood partly in that light, rather than as unique stands arising out of political realities. In this section we will explore the connection between isolationism and a number of political attitudes ordinarily identified with domestic politics, specifically liberalism-conservatism, attitudes toward democracy and politics, and radical attitudes on the extreme left and right.

Liberalism-Conservatism

Despite the finding reported by other investigators that the correlation is low between the orientation of voters toward domestic and foreign policy issues (a finding we will consider in the section on issues), we expected to find a strong positive relationship between conservatism and isolationism. We had no reason to believe that the connection between them, if one should turn out, was causal (and we should in any event have had difficulty deciding the direction of the causal arrows), but we did believe that the two orientations contain many elements in common, spring from similar psychological sources, and confront the human condition in similar ways and with similar values.

We have elsewhere in our research been exploring in detail the nature and correlates of the liberal-conservative dimension. This inquiry has reinforced our conviction that liberalism-conservatism is a multifaceted dimension whose facets are only imperfectly intercorrelated. One can readily identify those elements that go with classical conservatism: resistance to change, veneration of the past, emphasis on tradition, order, status hierarchy, duty, obligation, obedience, and authority, and so on. One can also identify the elements of liberalism-conservatism that have to do with social and economic welfare, the promotion of economic equality, the protection of property, and government intervention to redress grievances, equalize opportunity, assist the unfortunate, and, more recently, regulate the economy. Other aspects of the liberal-conservative dimension concern basic assumptions about the nature of man, belief in human perfectability, the boundaries of social regulation, the rational planning of human progress, and so forth. While conservative (or liberal) orientations toward each of these subjects do not spring with equal force from the same motives, they do reflect underlying psychological and value dimensions and are more closely related than one might suppose.

Most conservatives hold what is sometimes characterized as a pessimistic view of man. Whereas liberals tend to profess the inherent goodness and perfectability of man, conservatives typically consider him a creature of appetite and impulse, easily tempted, often weak, and strongly in need of firm and strictly enforced rules of conduct. A man's afflictions, therefore, must in the conservative view be traced to his own character faults, to his indulgence of personal weaknesses, and to his failure to make sufficiently severe demands upon himself. Liberals are likely to trace human misfortune to social institutions and the vicissitudes of human existence, but conservatives are more given to blame the individual himself. It follows from this that liberals are ordinarily more willing to use the collective resources for repairing wrongs and relieving unhappiness. To the conservative, poverty, ignorance, and adversity are signs of the failure of character and furnish a correct estimate of the actual worth of the individual who is their victim. By the same token, achievement, wealth, and success are the marks of character, signifying a willingness to transcend one's limitations and to escape, insofar as it is possible, from the imperfection that brands all men. The liberal believes that human destiny can be vastly improved through rational or even planned approaches to the distribution of life's utilities, but the conservative regards such efforst as vain, and as an interference with the natural order, which differentiates men according to their worth.

By almost every criterion we have been able to examine, conservatives display less affection for man and less sympathy for his misfortunes. That some men have less access to life's chances must be accepted as an inevitable feature of the human condition. Inequality they believe, is not only endemic in human affairs, but may even be desirable. It places men in their proper stations, furnishes estimates of their merit, and distributes them into hierarchies that assist in maintaining order. A certain amount of charity toward those who have failed is appropriate, but a persistent and single-minded interest in alleviating their afflictions and elevating their status is mere sentimentality, corrupting both to the benefactor and the recipient.

This review of liberal and conservative beliefs could be extended, but enough has been said for our purposes. One can scarcely miss the resemblance between the conservative in this portrait and the isolationist who has been revealed in our data. They are differentiated not so much by what they believe about man and society, but by the questions to which they apply those beliefs. Conservatism says nothing about the relations between nations or the responsibility of one group of nationals for another. It has been an ideology principally of domestic politics. But little imagination is needed to appreciate the manner in which its doctrines can be applied to international relations.[34]

Some of the elements in the isolationist persuasion are nearly identical with those found in conservatism. Followers of both are reluctant to become involved with others or to assume responsibility for them. They oppose the

---

[34] Blau, *op. cit.,* discusses the relationship between conservatism and what he calls power orientation, and Lentz, *op. cit.,* the relationship between nationalism and conservatism.

rearranging of institutions for the purpose of correcting imbalances or promoting social and economic equality. They resist legislation that might interfere with a man's (or a nation's) autonomy and the disposition of his property, and they are, for the most part, inhospitable to social change. There is in both conservatism and most forms of isolationism the same emphasis upon frugality and the restricted use of resources, the same implicit belief that one's own good fortune—and, by extension, the nation's good fortune—is part of the natural order of things. Believers in both wish to be relieved of responsibility for the destiny of mankind and react with distaste to the "theorists" who wish to "save" the world.

The data in Table 10, and in subsequent tables, clearly confirm the strength of the connection between conservatism and isolationism. Observe that the relationship holds not only for classical conservatism (where it is very powerful), but for economic and "social-welfare" conservatism as well (especially in the leader sample). On the Liberal Issues scale, a measure composed of fourteen domestic issues reflecting attitudes toward humanitarianism and social welfare (e.g., social security, public housing, federal aid to education, minimum wages, and so on), only 7 per cent of the isolationists in the leader sample score high, compared with 40 per cent of the internationalists. Among Democratic leaders, the number of internationalists who hold strongly liberal views on these domestic issues is almost three times as great as the number of isolationists who do so.[35]

The strength of the relationship can also be seen in the results on the Business Attitudes scale. Despite their above-average cosmopolitanism, those most identified with typical business attitudes are far more likely to be isolationists. Apparently, the conservative features of this ideology are strong enough in many instances to overcome the forces that impel businessmen toward a more internationalist outlook. Among the political influentials, as broken down by occupation, the managers and proprietors of small businesses turn out to be the most isolationist of all groups, while both large and small businessmen are significantly more isolationist than persons coming from the professions. In the general population sample, the patterns are less clear, although isolationism is stronger among small businessmen, especially if they are Republicans.

Further evidence of the relationship between conservatism and isolationism can be gleaned from the responses to other questions in the study that indirectly reflect liberal-conservative preferences. These questions refer, for example, to self-characterizations as liberal or conservative, preferences for liberal or conservative leaders, the party faction (left or right of center) with which one identifies, reference groups from which one is likely to seek

[35] There are so few Republican leaders who score high on liberalism that one can appreciate the results for this sample only by examining the proportions scoring conservative. But 68 per cent of the isolationists in the Republican leader sample score conservative compared with 35 per cent of the internationalists.

Table 10
Isolationism and Liberal-Conservative Attitudes
(Percentages Down)

		Isolationism								
		National Leader Sample (n = 3,020)			General Population Sample (n = 1,484)					
					High Education			Low Education		
		H (643)	M (1,150)	L (1,227)	H (199)	M (359)	L (229)	H (358)	M (260)	L (79)
Scales										
Pro-Business Attitudes	H	80	58	27	53	43	24	50	37	19
	M	13	20	19	28	29	26	28	28	30
	L	7	22	54	19	28	50	22	34	51
Classical Conservatism	H	38	19	4	47	21	6	70	42	15
	M	35	32	17	28	39	21	24	32	42
	L	26	49	79	26	40	73	6	26	43
Economic Conservatism	H	62	48	27	26	23	21	15	17	15
	M	30	41	48	37	51	51	45	43	47
	L	8	10	25	37	27	28	40	40	38
Opposition to Government Welfare	H	71	59	48	39	43	39	25	25	25
	M	22	27	28	37	35	37	45	45	48
	L	7	13	24	24	22	24	30	30	27
Support for Liberal Issues	H	7	17	40	18	23	28	19	27	19
	M	20	30	32	59	58	54	61	56	63
	L	69	52	27	24	18	18	20	17	13

advice, party preference itself, and the response to views that characteristically differentiate Republican from Democratic leaders. On every one of these measures, those who respond in the conservative direction are significantly more isolationist than those who give liberal responses.

From whichever direction we approach the matter, then, the conclusion is plain that the conservative and isolationist orientations are highly interrelated, draw upon the same values, and—though we have not, for reasons of space, presented the data here—derive in substantial measure from similar personality configurations. It should also be noted that the correlations are stronger and more meaningful among the political influentials than among the general population— a reflection, no doubt, of their greater ideological consistency. Moreover, the nature and strength of the relationship is such as to suggest that it does not describe a fortuitous or temporary connection. Liberal and conservative groups will no doubt shift about on foreign policy questions from time to time, and may even on occasion reverse roles, but the pattern described in our data appears to be the dominant one.

Attitudes Toward Democracy and Politics

Many of the observations made in connection with the liberal-conservative distinction are equally relevant for the discussion of isolationism and democratic attitudes. Little, therefore, will need to be said at this point about the findings presented in Table 11. Mainly, we need to call attention to the fact that on every measure on which we have assessed democratic convictions, the isolationists turn out significantly less democratic than the nonisolationists. When we combine items from several of these scales into a compound measure we have called the Democratic Commitment Index, the strength of the relationship is increased even further. Among the leaders, for example, only 16 per cent of the isolationists score high on the Demo-

Table 11

Isolationism and Democratic Attitudes

(Percentages Down)

		Isolationism							
		National Leader Sample (n = 3,020)			General Population Sample (n = 1,484)				
					High Education			Low Education		
		H (643)	M (1,150)	L (1,227)	H (199)	M (359)	L (229)	H (358)	M (260)	L (79)
Scales										
Democratic	H	17	38	76	14	31	62	7	16	34
Commitment	M	44	93	20	43	43	30	29	44	45
Index	L	39	19	4	44	26	9	64	40	21
Elitism-	H	39	27	11	48	31	17	56	42	25
Inequali-	M	40	40	30	35	44	45	33	36	43
tarianism	L	21	33	59	17	25	38	11	22	32
Faith in	H	22	35	55	10	23	37	6	17	28
Democracy	M	53	49	39	52	53	47	53	51	54
	L	26	17	6	39	23	16	41	32	18
Faith in	H	51	30	10	55	32	13	70	42	16
Direct Action	M	26	26	20	24	26	21	18	28	20
	L	23	44	71	21	41	66	11	30	63
Faith in	H	56	59	71	50	53	55	45	43	35
Freedom	M	31	43	47	29	21	21	25	22	20
	L	54	40	39	22	26	24	30	35	44
Faith in	H	34	51	78	14	32	48	10	18	25
Procedural	M	41	35	26	47	44	37	43	50	54
Rights	L	25	15	4	39	24	15	47	32	20
	H	40	59	74	38	56	67	24	34	47
Tolerance	M	30	23	18	24	21	22	24	28	25
	L	30	18	8	38	23	11	53	38	28

Table 12

Isolationism and Political Alienation

(Percentages Down)

		National Leader Sample (n = 3,020)			General Population Sample (n = 1,484)					
					High Education			Low Education		
		H (643)	M (1,150)	L (1,227)	H (199)	M (359)	L (229)	H (358)	M (260)	L (79)
Scales Political Cynicism	H	25	10	3	44	20	8	61	22	13
	M	44	42	23	46	50	34	34	49	34
	L	31	48	74	11	30	58	6	28	53
Sense of Political Futility	H	10	3	1	40	21	8	55	24	15
	M	28	17	10	39	43	35	31	40	30
	L	62	79	89	21	36	57	13	36	54
Political Suspiciousness	H	21	8	3	41	17	7	50	19	10
	M	37	29	18	41	44	29	42	50	38
	L	42	62	79	18	39	64	8	30	52

(The header "Isolationism" spans the full table above the sample columns.)

cratic Commitment Index, compared to 76 per cent of the internationalists.

The isolationists, it is plain, have less faith in equality and popular democracy, are less committed to individual rights, and are less tolerant of people whose opinions differ from theirs. In the leader sample, modest differences show up even on Faith in Freedom, although the items in this scale are of an abstract nature and, as such, are widely subscribed to by nearly every group in the population. (In the general population the differences on this scale are not significant.) The magnitude of the differences on Faith in Direct Action are also noteworthy. This scale, which registers impatience with the democratic process, glorifies action "above all," and applauds the willingness to "take the law into one's own hands," suggests the same bullying attitude toward the rights of others that is embodied in isolationism, especially of the jingoist type.

The isolationists not only reject democratic beliefs more frequently than the internationalists do, but they are much more cynical about politics and more impatient with politicians and the political process (Table 12). Although Americans as a people (like the nationals of other countries) are fond of complaining about "politics," the isolationists among them are far above average in this respect. They also express, as they do in their responses to international affairs, a strong sense of futility and frustration about domestic affairs. Paradoxical though it appears, they perceive their own political system in much the same way they view international organizations: both are controlled by men who are opportunistic, deceitful, self-serving, and indifferent to the people's needs.

The rejection of politics and politicians is a characteristic feature of the attack on democracy—as can readily be discerned from the criticisms leveled against parliamentary government by various totalitarian movements. The line is by now familiar: politics in a democracy is characterized by talk without action, by the opportunism and self-serving of elected officials, by the wastefulness and duplicity of the competitive party system, and by a preference for negotiation, trial and error, and compromise at the expense of principle.

The similarities between these criticisms and the isolationist's opinions of international politics can scarcely be missed. As the data confirm, he finds both the domestic and international realms marked by disorder, uncertainty, "conniving," the usurpation of authority, the impotence of ordinary citizens against giant forces, and the manipulation of the masses by unscrupulous leaders. Thus, though he protests against the entanglements of world politics, he is scarcely more sanguine about the political entrapments within his own country. Here again we find evidence that isolationism is for many people an expression of disengagement and aversion that manifests itself repeatedly at many levels of interaction.

Extreme Belief

The tendency among isolationists to reject the institutions and practices of their own society can also be discerned in their responses to the doctrines of the radical right and radical left. In our brief discussion of populist movements we remarked on the persistent connection between their isolationism and their radical objections to the prevailing system of power and the forms of American life. The evidence indicates that the two forms of protest tend to go together even today. The more one resents one's own institutions, the more one tends to dislike other nations and to resist becoming involved with them. By rational standards this may not appear to make much sense, but by psychological criteria it is entirely plausible. The needs of an aversive personality can frequently be satisfied by a variety of stimulus objects.

Table 13 contains data on the relationship between isolationism and several scales that express radical or extreme political views. The items in the Left Wing, Right Wing, and Populist scales were initially drawn from the writings and programs of political movements organized to promote these doctrines. The Totalitarian scale contains the values that typically identify various modern totalitarian movements, e.g., the "politicalization" of culture, desire for a "closed society," an apocalyptic and messianic visionary flavor, glorification of a single belief system, and preference for social uniformity. The Fascist scale contains statements that are drawn from or favor political regimes of the Hitler and Mussolini type. All are strongly related to isolationism.

The most powerful and, of course, least surprising of the correlations is

Table 13
Isolationism and Extreme Belief
(Percentages Down)

		Isolationism								
		National Leader Sample (n = 3,020)			General Population Sample (n = 1,484)					
					High Education*			Low Education*		
		H (643)	M (1,150)	L (1,227)	H (199)	M (359)	L (229)	H (358)	M (260)	L (79)
Scales										
Left Wing	H	14	6	4	37	12	4	59	26	11
	M	31	24	22	38	33	26	29	38	37
	L	56	70	74	25	54	70	12	36	52
Right Wing	H	51	15	2	57	16	2	67	29	3
	M	42	51	22	38	45	21	29	52	52
	L	6	34	77	5	40	78	4	19	46
Populism	H	26	13	5	52	21	3	72	31	11
	M	55	49	36	40	41	27	25	51	39
	L	18	38	59	8	38	70	3	18	49
Totali-tarianism	H	24	11	1	45	20	4	63	35	16
	M	43	37	17	38	43	31	29	46	44
	L	33	53	81	18	36	65	7	19	39

		Minnesota Sample Only (n = 1,082)					
		High Education			Low Education		
		H (147)	M (272)	L (224)	H (203)	M (177)	L (51)
Fascist	H	22	10	8	38	18	4
Political	M	46	40	23	43	46	35
Sympathies	L	31	50	69	19	36	61

that between isolationism and right-wing beliefs. Organizations of the radical right have usually been among the most vociferous critics of the United Nations, foreign aid, and other overseas involvements, and have led the protests against what they claimed to be American defeats in the Cold War struggle against communism. Isolationist values correspond more closely with the values of right-wing movements than with those of any other group. Both are inspired by chauvinism; both conceive themselves the nation's defenders against its enemies. Both are impatient with or suspicious of the political process, and both regard themselves as dispossessed, pushed aside by men of doubtful patriotism and questionable objectives. The supporters of both political orientations are nostalgic for an era no longer possible; they continue to yearn for a return to the simplicity of an earlier period

when the nation was invincible and its own master. Xenophobia has characterized both, and their portraits of foreigners and foreign nations have been
remarkably alike. Both have been given to jingoism and heroic postures,
and both have repudiated the artificial, corrupt, and declining cultures of
the old world.[36] Both are attracted to conspiratorial explanations of human
affairs and both are inclined to attribute American reverses to softness,
duplicity, or even treason.

That these similarities have a pay-off in the realities of political action was
borne out in a study we conducted in Minnesota in 1954–55 on the nature
and sources of "extreme belief and affiliation," including support for
McCarthyism. Whereas those who were neither left-wing nor right-wing in
their political sympathies had a mean score of 2.62 on isolationism (a 9-point
scale), the right-wing sample—selected for their actual participation in right-
wing activities—had a mean score of 5.97. Isolationism seems also to have
been an element in support for McCarthy. Whereas the opponents of
McCarthyism had a mean score of 3.00 on isolationism, McCarthy's supporters in the general population had a score of 4.22, while the "hard-core"
McCarthyites—those who had attended meetings in his behalf, circulated
petitions in his defense, or promoted his presidential candidacy—had a score
of 6.10. Although Senator McCarthy himself might not be classified as an
isolationist (all who hold right-wing beliefs are not isolationist), the right-
wing policies he advocated and the criticisms he leveled against the conduct of American foreign policy were apparently attractive to people of
isolationist persuasion.[37]

The figures in Table 13, as well as our Minnesota data on left-wing sympathizers, also reveal a marked correlation between isolationism and support
for left-wing values. The connection is weaker than that shown for right-wing
supporters (and would doubtless be weaker still for a sample of Marxist
intellectuals), but it is strong enough to be significant. It may appear to some
that there is a discrepancy in the positive correlation of isolationism with *both*
left-wing and right-wing doctrines. This belief, however, assumes that there
is an inherent incongruity or antagonism between left-wing and right-wing
movements. We cannot at this point enter upon a discussion of the many
similarities between totalitarian ideologies of the left and right or of the similarities in the style and quality of political life instituted by such movements
upon coming to power. Nor can we elaborate on the obvious cohabitation of
left-wing and right-wing elements in American populist movements or on the
remarkable process by which numerous midwestern politicians of left-wing
isolationist persuasion were transformed into politicians of right-wing isolationist persuasion during the 1930s. Exploration of these matters would turn

---

[36] See Shils, *op. cit.*, especially pp. 78–86.
[37] On the McCarthy supporters, see N. Polsby, "Toward an Explanation of McCarthyism,"
in N. Polsby, L. Dexter, and P. Smith, *Politics and Social Life: an Introduction to Political
Behavior* (Boston: Houghton Mifflin, 1963), pp. 809–24.

up many parallels between the extreme left and right that lead them, on various occasions, to similar foreign policy orientations.

Our findings also reveal likenesses between left-wing sympathizers and isolationists. Both are dissatisfied with the state of American life. Both are deviant in American society today, and both draw on the psychological and attitude sources that give rise to deviancy. Both carry heavy loadings of hostility and psychological inflexibility and both tend to avoid, or to be excluded from, the reference groups of the society that bear the greatest responsibility for maintaining the prevailing norms. There is a strong element of paranoia in both isolationism and left-wing attitudes, a shared suspicion of politicians, newspapers, the two major parties, and other features that are alleged to constitute the "establishment." Both points of view reflect an unusual degree of frustration and hostility. Both are given to intemperate responses, and both betray an above-average tendency to distort or misread realities. Apart from such similarities, left-wing radicals tend to portray American foreign policy as inherently imperialist and expansionist, driven by the capitalist need for markets and investment opportunities. As a result, they tend to perceive many types of international activity (though not all) as manifestations of the drive for American hegemony at the expense of smaller, weaker, or more "progressive" nations.

Isolationism and Issue Orientation

One of the hypotheses set out at the beginning of the chapter predicted that personality variables would have less influence on orientation toward foreign policy *issues* than on foreign policy *attitudes,* but that the stands taken on these issues would nevertheless be affected by personality and attitude factors. It was further predicted that these relationships would be stronger among the political elite than among the general population, as the elite has greater interest in these questions and is more concerned to achieve a coherent, consistent set of political opinions.

The reasoning behind these predictions was as follows: Attitudes on foreign policy differ from opinions on foreign policy issues in that the former represent a disposition to respond in a consistent way to certain classes of stimuli, while the latter are specific to particular stimuli, are more bound by time and circumstance, and are more likely to reflect group associations and interests. One's opinions about NATO or defense spending or military intervention in the Dominican uprising are not likely to be as strongly motivated by affect or the need to "act out" as are one's attitudes about, say, foreigners or the loss of national sovereignty. Being more specific, these issues do not ordinarily furnish as much opportunity for private motives to be engaged and are less likely to awaken the visceral types of response that attitudes so often awaken.

Opinions on issues, as compared with attitudes, are usually (though not always) more concrete, less symbolic, and more dependent upon factual evidence. They are more heavily influenced than attitudes by party, social class, religion, or education. Many of them are technical and require knowledge of the stimulus object before an opinion can be formed.

While attitudes, of course, are also subject to reference group and situational influences, they are less labile than issue outlooks, more deeply rooted in the respondent's value system, and more likely to be independent of the usual external influences that so often affect opinions on issues. Most of the research available on these matters[38] suggests strongly that opinions on foreign policy questions are highly unstable, and may be pushed in one direction or another by events or by other short-term influences. This happens less often to an attitude, for it is more deeply integrated into an elaborate network of needs, motives, values, and other attitude dispositions. Hence, personality is likely to have less influence on the determination of opinions on issues than in the determination of attitudes.

There are, of course, exceptions to these generalizations, for issues can doubtless arise that are as heavily invested with affect and symbolism as attitudes are. Moreover, most foreign policy issues that have come to popular attention and that have awakened controversy (such as foreign aid or support for the United Nations) are bound to acquire significance beyond the question of their intrinsic merits—they are bound, in short, to have acquired a degree of *psychological* meaning. Often these opinions represent applications of an underlying attitude to a particular international question, and the feeling associated with the attitude is carried over in the response to the issue. In general, however, we expect personality factors to play a smaller role in the adoption of opinions than in the adoption of attitudes.

Some of the findings on the relation between isolationism and a number of foreign policy and domestic issues are contained in Tables 14 and 15. As Table 14 shows, isolationists and nonisolationists respond very differently to such foreign policy issues as immigration, foreign aid, level of tariffs, participation in NATO, and even defense spending. All the results are in the predicted direction, and the differences are in most instances fairly large. Among political leaders, for example, 55 per cent of the nonisolationists favor increased support for the UN, compared to 17 per cent of the isolationist group. The differences, it should be observed, are significantly larger for the leaders than for the general population (as predicted), and somewhat larger for the educated than the uneducated. Clearly, isolationist or internationalist general orientations tend to be carried over into the responses on specific issues,[39] especially among those who are politically participant and aware, for whom foreign policy attitudes and opinions are especially salient.

---

[38] See Converse, *op. cit.,* and Almond, *op. cit.*

[39] For an excellent study of public and congressional attitudes on a particular issue—the 1962 Reciprocal Trade Act—see R. Bauer, I. Pool, and L. Dexter, *American Business and Foreign Policy* (New York: The Atherton Press, 1963).

Table 14

Isolationism and Foreign Policy Issues
(In Percentages)*

	National Leader Sample (n = 3,020)						General Population Sample (n = 1,484)							
	Democrats (1,788)		Republicans (1,232)		Total (3,020)		Democrats (821)		Republicans (623)		High Education (787)		Low Education (697)	
	Inc.	Dec.**	Inc.	Dec.	Inc.	Dec.	Inc.	Dec.	Inc.	Dec.	Inc.	Dec.	Inc.	Dec.
Isolationism														
Immigration														
H	10	58	6	48	7	52	4	68	4	61	4	65	4	65
M	23	36	15	31	19	34	10	49	8	43	11	45	7	48
L	55	11	36	11	49	11	22	28	16	19	21	17	13	46
Tariffs														
H	27	23	32	14	30	17	21	22	18	16	24	18	17	20
M	18	31	17	21	17	27	18	21	15	21	19	25	14	16
L	5	59	9	46	6	55	6	39	10	33	7	40	11	25
Foreign Aid														
H	0	88	1	90	1	89	5	72	3	78	6	77	3	72
M	9	68	4	65	7	67	9	60	9	53	10	56	8	57
L	30	27	19	28	27	27	22	32	25	29	25	27	19	42
Reliance on the UN														
H	29	41	9	67	17	57	20	24	21	33	18	35	22	23
M	41	22	26	28	34	24	39	15	36	13	39	14	36	13
L	61	7	39	10	55	8	53	10	50	10	52	10	49	8
American Participation in International Military Alliances														
H	20	46	7	57	12	52	27	24	23	27	25	32	25	21
M	36	20	23	18	30	19	44	9	37	10	39	10	42	10
L	53	7	38	4	48	8	51	6	40	6	45	7	46	6
Defense Spending														
H	14	55	10	52	12	54	39	22	36	23	42	26	35	22
M	21	36	13	31	17	34	57	13	46	11	53	11	50	14
L	23	27	19	18	21	24	16	14	61	11	60	14	57	10

* Observe that the percentages in these tables are computed across for each sample, with the middle group, those who responded "same," omitted to conserve space.
** In these and subsequent tables, Inc. signifies a desire to increase support for the issue named; Dec. signifies a desire to decrease support for the issue.

Table 15

Isolationism and Selected Domestic Issues
(In Percentages)*

| | National Leader Sample (n = 3,020) | | | | | | General Population Sample (n = 1,484) | | | | | | | |
| | Democrats (1,788) | | Republicans (1,232) | | Total (3,020) | | Democrats (821) | | Republicans (623) | | High Education (787) | | Low Education (697) | |
	Inc.	Dec.**	Inc.	Dec.	Inc.	Dec.	Inc.	Dec.	Inc.	Dec.	Inc.	Dec.	Inc.	Dec.
Isolationism														
Government Control of Business														
H	9	62	1	89	4	78	17	37	10	47	12	50	16	36
M	14	49	0	85	8	64	17	33	7	47	9	45	17	31
L	28	24	1	78	20	40	24	29	5	44	16	38	18	25
Social Security														
H	49	8	15	22	29	16	68	4	64	4	63	7	67	2
M	51	5	22	9	38	6	69	2	54	4	60	4	66	3
L	71	2	31	9	59	4	72	3	51	2	59	3	75	4
Trade Union Regulation														
H	63	11	87	6	77	8	39	8	45	16	49	11	37	11
M	67	11	87	4	75	8	46	12	62	8	62	8	42	13
L	52	14	86	4	62	11	62	5	71	6	70	4	52	10
Federal Aid to Education														
H	50	26	14	55	29	43	68	8	60	12	65	16	65	6
M	59	16	22	42	43	27	79	4	65	6	75	5	69	5
L	77	7	32	32	63	14	80	5	71	7	74	7	85	1
Minimum Wage														
H	36	11	9	22	20	18	61	4	44	6	50	5	57	4
M	43	6	14	10	30	8	59	2	43	5	50	4	54	3
L	60	2	24	5	49	3	56	3	44	3	49	3	59	3
Slum Clearance and Public Housing														
H	63	12	33	32	45	24	73	7	68	14	75	10	68	11
M	75	7	39	19	60	12	84	4	73	6	79	5	77	5
L	86	3	49	13	75	6	83	6	81	2	82	3	82	8

* Percentages computed across for each sample, with those scoring same omitted to conserve space.

** Inc. signifies desire to increase support for the issue named; Dec. to decrease it.

In Table 15, isolationists and nonisolationists are compared in their responses to a set of domestic issues. Some observers have assumed that there
is little connection between the beliefs people hold on domestic questions and
their outlooks on foreign affairs.[40] The data in Table 15 show that this assumption is, on the whole, correct for the general population. A few connections can be discerned, but they are rather weak. Some of the relationships
among the general population, in fact, are actually reversals of the predicted
results: isolationists, for example, are more opposed to trade union regulation
than nonisolationists are. And there is slightly more support among isolationists than nonisolationists for increasing social security. On the other hand,
the internationalists show a slightly stronger preference for federal aid to
education and slum clearance. The results on this side of the table, in short,
are spotty, inconclusive, and inconsistent.

The results are different, however, when we turn to the data on the leaders.
Here the relationships are strong, consistent, and in the predicted direction.
The correlation reported earlier between isolationism and conservatism is
unequivocally borne out in these figures. Thus, whereas 59 per cent of the
internationalists favor increased support for social security, only 29 per cent
of the isolationists favor it. Similar differences can be discerned on all of the
other domestic issues in the table, except for the trade union issue, on which
the differences are too small to be of significance.

We turn, finally, to consider whether the attitude and personality factors
that give rise to general isolationist orientations have a similar influence on
the responses to specific issues. This question is dealt with in Tables 16–21,
and the answer is unequivocally in the affirmative. On all six issues in the
tables, the same basic correlation patterns observed in the analysis of the Isolationism scale can again be found. On the foreign aid issue (Table 18), for
example, 60 per cent of those who wish to decrease foreign aid score conservative on the Liberal Issues scale, compared with only 14 per cent conservative among those who wish to increase foreign aid. Those who are
opposed to foreign aid turn out to be more chauvinistic, more ethnocentric,
more hostile, more politically cynical, less socially responsible, more inflexible, and so on. The pattern is repeated on the immigration, tariff, NATO,
and UN issues. Only on the defense spending issue are the results equivocal.
This issue, it would appear, cuts across the divisions we have been dis-
cussing; and people with similar personality characteristics can be found
with equal frequency on either side of the question.

Not only, then, does the isolationist–internationalist division reflect itself
in actual stands on issues, but the forces that underlie these dispositions also
underlie the corresponding issue orientations. The correlations between personality and issues, of course, are usually not as large as they are between
personality and the Isolationism scale, but we did not expect them to be. As

---

[40] See the discussions in Key, *op. cit.,* pp. 163–68 and *The American Voter.*

Table 16

Support for Immigration and Selected Personality and Attitude Scales
(In Percentages)*

National Leader Sample Only
(n = 3,020)

Immigration	Liberal Issues		Pro-Business Attitudes		Calvinism		Chauvinism		Economic Conservatism	
	L	H	L	H	L	H	L	H	L	H
Increase	21	50	53	29	44	20	87	3	25	27
Decrease	61	11	17	64	19	33	40	27	13	49

	Elitism		Ethnocentrism		Faith in Democracy		Need Inviolacy		Hostility		Obsessive	
	L	H	L	H	L	H	L	H	L	H	L	H
Increase	58	12	75	4	9	55	67	14	52	12	37	37
Decrease	27	33	24	33	23	25	51	26	23	27	22	55

	Paranoid		Pessimism		Political Cynicism		Responsibility		Right Wing		Rigidity	
	L	H	L	H	L	H	L	H	L	H	L	H
Increase	62	12	48	6	65	5	11	49	73	5	58	18
Decrease	37	27	20	21	39	17	21	30	21	33	33	39

* Percentages computed horizontally for each scale. Those scoring in the middle range of the scale named have been omitted. The percentages therefore add up to less than 100.

Increase: n = 973.
Decrease: n = 851.

Table 17

Support for Tariffs and Selected Personality and Attitude Scales
(In Percentages)*

National Leader Sample Only
(n = 3,020)

Tariff	Liberal Issues		Pro-Business Attitudes		Faith in Democracy		Calvinism		Chauvinism		Economic Conservatism	
	L	H	L	H	L	H	L	H	L	H	L	H
Increase	57	16	19	62	18	28	21	33	42	26	13	50
Decrease	35	38	46	37	12	48	40	20	81	5	23	34

Tariff	Elitism		Ethnocentrism		Political Cynicism		Need Inviolacy		Hostility		Obsessive	
	L	H	L	H	L	H	L	H	L	H	L	H
Increase	30	29	31	23	44	14	54	24	27	28	25	51
Decrease	50	17	63	10	61	8	65	15	47	14	34	42

Tariff	Paranoid		Pessimism		Responsibility		Right Wing		Rigidity	
	L	H	L	H	L	H	L	H	L	H
Increase	40	23	23	19	23	33	22	32	34	38
Decrease	58	14	40	11	11	47	64	10	56	21

* Percentages computed horizontally for each scale. Those scoring in the middle range of the scale named have been omitted. The percentages therefore add up to less than 100.

Increase: n = 469.
Decrease: n = 1,094.

115

Table 18

Support for Foreign Aid and Selected Personality and Attitude Scales

(In Percentages)*

National Leader Sample Only
(n = 3,020)

Foreign Aid	Liberal Issues		Pro-Business Attitudes		Calvinism		Chauvinism		Economic Conservatism	
	L	H	L	H	L	H	L	H	L	H
Increase	14	64	71	14	53	16	87	3	38	16
Decrease	60	14	17	64	22	31	51	19	10	51

Foreign Aid	Elitism		Ethnocentrism		Faith in Democracy		Need Inviolacy		Obsessive	
	L	H	L	H	L	H	L	H	L	H
Increase	60	12	79	4	8	53	68	14	40	38
Decrease	33	28	32	25	18	32	55	22	26	52

Foreign Aid	Paranoid		Pessimism		Political Cynicism		Responsibility		Right Wing		Rigidity	
	L	H	L	H	L	H	L	H	L	H	L	H
Increase	63	13	49	8	68	6	10	52	80	4	60	18
Decrease	46	21	38	16	47	14	19	35	29	26	39	34

* Percentages computed horizontally for each scale. Those scoring in the middle range of the scale named have been omitted. The percentages therefore add up to less than 100.

Increase: n = 413.
Decrease: n = 1,673.

Table 19

Support for United Nations and Selected Personality and Attitude Scales
(In Percentages)*

National Leader Sample Only
(n = 3,020)

United Nations	Liberal Issues		Pro-Business Attitudes		Chauvinism		Economic Conservatism	
	L	H	L	H	L	H	L	H
Increase	25	44	48	33	74	7	26	28
Decrease	70	88	12	72	46	22	8	59

	Elitism		Ethnocentrism		Faith in Democracy		Calvinism		Hostility		Obsessive	
	L	H	L	H	L	H	L	H	L	H	L	H
Increase	49	19	59	12	12	45	37	23	43	17	31	45
Decrease	29	31	29	26	18	33	20	33	27	24	28	49

	Paranoid		Pessimism		Political Cynicism		Need Inviolacy		Responsibility		Right Wing		Rigidity	
	L	H	L	H	L	H	L	H	L	H	L	H	L	H
Increase	52	18	40	9	60	7	66	15	13	45	63	8	49	27
Decrease	44	22	21	22	43	16	53	25	21	32	19	38	38	31

* Percentages computed horizontally for each scale. Those scoring in the middle range of the scale named have been omitted. The percentages therefore add up to less than 100.

Increase: n = 1,176.
Decrease: n = 743.

Table 20

Support for Defense Spending and Selected Personality and Attitude Scales
(In Percentages)*

National Leader Sample Only
(n = 3,020)

Defense Spending	Liberal Issues		Pro-Business Attitudes		Faith in Democracy		Calvinism		Chauvinism		Economic Conservatism	
	L	H	L	H	L	H	L	H	L	H	L	H
Increase	30	33	42	37	15	43	31	25	62	12	19	33
Decrease	53	23	25	59	16	35	28	39	58	17	16	44

Defense Spending	Elitism		Ethnocentrism		Political Cynicism		Need Inviolacy		Hostility		Obsessive	
	L	H	L	H	L	H	L	H	L	H	L	H
Increase	43	21	51	15	58	10	60	18	36	18	31	47
Decrease	38	25	41	21	49	13	57	21	34	22	28	50

Defense Spending	Paranoid		Pessimism		Responsibility		Right Wing		Rigidity	
	L	H	L	H	L	H	L	H	L	H
Increase	49	17	37	11	15	40	47	15	46	31
Decrease	47	20	30	16	26	36	39	24	41	30

* Percentages computed horizontally for each scale. Those scoring in the middle range of the scale named have been omitted. The percentages therefore add up to less than 100.

Increase: n = 538.
Decrease: n = 1,030.

Table 21

Support for NATO and Selected Personality and Attitude Scales
(In Percentages)*

National Leader Sample Only
(n = 3,020)

NATO	Liberal Issues		Pro-Business Attitudes		Calvinism		Chauvinism		Economic Conservatism	
	L	H	L	H	L	H	L	H	L	H
Increase	27	39	47	33	34	24	74	8	22	30
Decrease	64	13	17	67	22	31	41	27	12	55

	Elitism		Ethnocentrism		Need Inviolacy		Hostility		Obsessive	
	L	H	L	H	L	H	L	H	L	H
Increase	50	19	59	11	66	16	43	16	33	45
Decrease	27	32	29	28	50	26	28	28	25	52

	Paranoid		Pessimism		Political Cynicism		Responsibility		Right Wing		Rigidity	
	L	H	L	H	L	H	L	H	L	H	L	H
Increase	55	16	43	9	61	8	12	45	59	10	48	28
Decrease	41	26	22	22	39	18	23	31	25	36	39	25

* Percentages computed horizontally for each scale. Those scoring in the middle range of the scale named have been omitted. The percentages therefore add up to less than 100.

Increase: n = 1,022.
Decrease: n = 631.

issues, they are more affected by competing influences and by some of the other factors indicated in our introductory remarks to this section.

The results in these tables do not tell us anything about the stability of issue orientations. Conceivably, there is some shifting about on these issues as circumstances change. The trends in the correlations, however, are so strong as to suggest that even these opinions are part of the personality and attitude network to which we referred earlier, and that the pattern of responses revealed in these tables is the characteristic one.

Pacific Versus Jingoist Isolationism

We began our analysis of isolationism on the assumption that, within the terms of our general definition, two basic sub-types could usefully be distinguished: the pacific and the aggressive (or jingoist) isolationists. While both, we believed, would seek to disengage themselves from the outside world, the pacific isolationist would prefer to have the nation withdraw into its own shell, safeguarding itself by having as little to do as possible with other nations and by avoiding the threat or use of force, while the jingoist isolationist would display a more bullying, sabre-rattling attitude toward other nations, and would rely for protection on superior military force and the threat of using it unilaterally. We expected to find that while both types would differ significantly from nonisolationists in their rejection of other nations, and while neither would exhibit an above-average concern for the maintenance (or achievement) of peace, the pacific isolationists would more closely resemble nonisolationists in their personality and attitude characteristics. Their isolationism, we thought, would be less motivated by aversive psychological needs, and would not to the same degree be associated with other attitudes that reflect intolerance and obduracy toward other men, political and economic conservatism, or disillusionment with the forms and quality of American institutions.

To test these notions an attempt was made to construct a jingoism scale from items already in the questionnaire pool. A number of possible items were submitted to a group of judges (graduate students and research workers at the University of California, Berkeley) to be rated according to the degree to which they expressed a jingoistic stance in the conduct of foreign policy. Six items that were most frequently and consistently rated as highly jingoistic were selected for initial inclusion in the scale. Of these, we eventually selected only the two that contained on their face the content of the jingoist concept.[41] The three isolationist categories (isolationist, middle, and nonisolationist) were then subdivided high, middle, and low on jingoism, and the resulting nine

---

[41] The two items retained were: "A nation faced with a bunch of really dangerous enemies might be better off to 'shoot first and ask questions afterward'"; and "Let's face it, the only way to bring peace and order back to the world is to make America the one powerful nation on earth."

groups were compared on various personality and attitude characteristics. The results on a selected group of representative scales are presented (in the form of percentages high only) in Table 22.

A word of caution is appropriate concerning the interpretation of this table. The use of so short a measure for so major a classification contains some risks both for validity and reliability. That the two items discriminate and are in some instances very powerful can readily be observed from the table. But the number of misclassifications and the danger of picking up spurious influences on the correlations is of course greatly increased as the number of items in a scale diminishes. A more serious difficulty, however, is the absence of an adequate measure of the pacific or conciliatory spirit in international relations. There were unfortunately no items in the item pool that could be used to measure this orientation, and we have therefore classified a respondent as pacific not by what he asserts or *affirms* about this matter (as we would have preferred) but by what he *repudiates.* Hence, a pacific isolationist (or a pacific nonisolationist) is one who rejects both items in the jingoist measure; an aggressive isolationist or nonisolationist is one who embraces both items.

These qualifications aside, the data in Table 22 tend on the whole to bear out our general expectations: Both pacific and jingoist isolationists differ from their nonisolationist counterparts in precisely the ways that isolationists and nonisolationists were shown to differ in the earlier sections of this chapter. In comparison with pacific nonisolationists, pacific isolationists are significantly more inflexible, hostile, and alienated in their personality characteristics, and significantly more ethnocentric, conservative, business oriented, undemocratic, and politically cynical in what they believe. With a few exceptions (the results on the Alienation and Business Ideology scales are exceptions in the leader sample), jingoist isolationists show up as even more extreme on these measures than the pacific isolationists do. Both types of isolationists, however, would have to be classified as comparatively aggressive in their international orientations—an inference buttressed by the correlations between Isolationism and Jingoism of .41 for the leader sample and .46 for the general population.[42] This is consistent with the strong indications in the data reported earlier that present-day isolationism represents, as stated in our hypothesis, a posture of belligerency rather than pacifism in international affairs, and that it "has more to do with hostility against foreign nations and disavowal of responsibility for the well-being of others than with the considered assessment of the risks arising from international 'entanglements.'" There appears to be little spirit of reciprocity in the isolationist orientation— in any of the forms in which we, at least, have observed it.

All this, of course, does not abrogate the fact that there are differences between the pacific and jingoist isolationists, and that there are reasons for the

---

[42] These correlations, it should be noted, do not appear to be spuriously influenced by the tone or flavor of the items in the isolationism scale, for most of these items were adjudged by our raters as free of belligerency—in fact, as falling on the pacific side of the distinction.

Table 22

Percentages High on Selected Personality
and Attitude Scales, by Isolationism and Jingoism*

Isolationism	National Leader Sample (n = 3,020)			General Population Sample (n = 1,484)		
	Jingoism				Jingoism	
	H (356)	M (959)	L (1,705)	H (295)	M (556)	L (633)
Alienation						
H	25	25	26	60	44	33
M	22	16	16	42	32	22
L	7	16	11	0	19	19
Intolerance of Ambiguity						
H	70	65	53	75	55	44
M	61	44	36	51	33	24
L	31	39	20	0	25	15
Pro-Business Attitudes						
H	84	79	78	52	51	50
M	59	61	55	40	37	44
L	48	39	23	0	20	24
Ethnocentrism						
H	53	41	24	67	49	39
M	33	23	11	43	21	13
L	10	8	2	0	13	4
Faith in Democracy						
H	10	23	29	6	5	13
M	18	34	41	11	17	27
L	28	44	58	0	34	35
Classical Conservatism						
H	57	37	25	75	58	46
M	36	22	12	44	35	21
L	14	9	2	0	19	4
Hostility						
H	49	39	23	60	41	24
M	38	26	15	46	26	15
L	28	16	5	0	9	7
Political Cynicism						
H	38	24	15	64	53	43
M	20	11	6	37	20	17
L	17	5	2	0	5	11

* Percentages middle and low have been omitted from this table to conserve space. All the figures in the table represent the proportion of each of the nine types of jingoists-isolationists who score high on the personality and attitude scales named.

difference. We have not yet been able to carry the analysis far enough to account adequately for the distinction, although we do know that the two groups differ somewhat in certain social characteristics (the jingoist isolationists, for example, are somewhat older than the pacific isolationists, and less educated) and in the personality and attitude characteristics suggested by the scales in Table 22. At the moment, however, we do not know which, if any, of these factors is most critical, and our uncertainty about the quality of the jingoist-pacifist measure has discouraged the more sophisticated analysis that would be required to answer the question. The question, however, will be explored in future research.

Summary

This paper has focused upon the personality and attitude correlates of foreign policy orientation, with special attention to the isolationist-nonisolationist orientation. Isolationists and nonisolationists were compared on a large battery of personality and attitude scales, as well as on other measures. The samples employed in the surveys from which the data were taken included a national sample of 3,020 political leaders, a cross-section national sample of 1,484 adults, and a cross-section statewide sample of 1,082 Minnesota adults. A number of hypotheses were tested and the results evaluated.

It was found, among other things, that isolationism is a complex attitude that can be arrived at by different routes and understood in different ways. While it is obviously a political attitude influenced by political circumstances, reference groups, demographic factors, and other such determinants, it is also shaped to a considerable extent by a complex set of personality variables, primarily of an aversive nature. Such personality states as misanthropy, psychological inflexibility, manifest anxiety, and low self-esteem have a powerful influence on the attitudes one adopts toward other nations and toward foreign policy. Such personality factors, together with social opportunity and intellectual endowment, affect cognitive capacity and function, and these, in turn, further influence one's disposition to favor withdrawal from, or entrance into, international involvements.

Isolationism was also found to be part of a network of attitudes that are related to common underlying personality dispositions. Among these are classical and welfare conservatism, radical doctrines of the extreme right and extreme left, and attitudes critical of democratic beliefs and practices. Despite its strong chauvinistic overtones, isolationism is frequently associated with feelings of disappointment in one's own society and disaffection from the political institutions of one's country. The isolationist orientation parallels closely other forms of belief that rely heavily upon dichotomous thought processes, that lack breadth of perspective, and that seek to exclude whatever is different, distant or unfamiliar. It also parallels other attitudes that are marginal or deviant in relation to the society. Like other deviant orientations, it signifies for some of its proponents a failure of socialization and an inadequate internalization of the norms. It is more common among those who are, by any criterion and for any reason, parochial and less common among those who are open to experience and who are cosmopolitan in their perspective.

Although isolationism manifestly appears as a peaceful withdrawal from international entanglements and frequently has been interpreted as a simple desire to keep one's country from becoming militarily embroiled, it is characteristically xenophobic and belligerent in its posture toward foreign affairs. It represents, for the most part, a rejection of other men rather than a concern for them, a disavowal of responsibility and a strong urge to disengage oneself from obligations toward others. One can scarcely begin to understand the phenomenon, therefore, if one confines his analysis to the familiar political categories.

A subgroup of so-called pacific isolationists was located and analyzed. While this group possesses characteristics closer to those of the non-isolationists and displays less of the bullying militancy that marks the jingoist isolationist, its members possess many of the same personality and attitude characteristics found among the jingoist isolationists, though in lesser degree.

The responses of isolationists and nonisolationists to a number of foreign policy and domestic issues were also examined. It was found that one's attitude toward isolationism has a marked effect on one's opinions on issues, particularly among the political influentials, for whom issues are more salient and ideological consistency is more valued than for ordinary citizens. The influence of personality and attitude variables on specific foreign policy issues was also examined. The results closely paralleled those found for the isolationist-internationalist dimension: those personality and attitude variables that correlated strongly with isolationist sentiments were likewise found to be correlated with opinions on specific foreign policy questions. The paper furnishes evidence for believing that our understanding of both foreign policy attitudes and issues can be significantly enhanced through the examination of psychological variables.

The findings reported in this paper are drawn, with only a few exceptions, from our two national surveys of political leaders and the general population. However, most of the personality and attitude scales included here were also used in the surveys we conducted several years earlier on Minnesota samples. Owing to space limitations and a desire to keep from inundating the reader with more data and discussion, we have omitted from the foregoing the presentation of the Minnesota findings. We have, nevertheless, computed the Minnesota results, and find that in every instance in which the same measures were employed in both the national and Minnesota surveys, the outcome is the same. The findings reported here, in short, have been independently and closely confirmed in an entirely separate study conducted at a different time on an entirely different sample.

Appendix: The Effects of "Acquiescent" Response Set

Since all nine items in the Isolationism scale have an "agree" scoring direction, a number of operations were carried out to check for the possibility of bias arising from the "acquiescent" tendency. In one of these operations, a sample of isolationists and nonisolationists were, by a random procedure, exactly matched on acquiescence, and each of the matched samples was then compared on a selected set of variables. An illustration of the results is contained in Table 23. The results make it plain that the differences reported in the body of the paper are not the spurious products of acquiescent response set. This procedure, it should be noted, imposes a much more severe restriction on the data than is necessary or justified. Nevertheless, differences reported in the paper remain substantial and statistically significant when acquiescence is controlled in this way.

Table 23

Isolationists and Nonisolationists Matched on Acquiescence and Compared on Selected Scales

(Percentages Down)

	Isolationism			
	National Leader Sample		*National General Population Sample*	
	H (444)	L (444)	H (186)	L (186)
Intolerance of Ambiguity				
H	54	34	42	18
M	28	27	39	37
L	18	39	19	45
Pro-Business Attitudes				
H	78	37	48	23
M	15	20	27	39
L	8	44	25	48
Ethnocentrism				
H	29	7	41	10
M	51	30	43	31
L	20	63	16	59
Hostility				
H	29	14	22	9
M	52	45	52	40
L	20	40	26	52
Responsibility				
H	37	43	22	46
M	32	44	42	44
L	31	14	36	10
Tolerance				
H	45	73	40	62
M	29	18	23	21
L	26	9	37	17

CHAPTER 3

Psychological Dimensions of Anomy

Since Merton's seminal contribution of 1938, around 35 scientific papers have appeared on the subject of anomy,[1] most of them since 1950. In addition, the concept has been used in a large number of books and essays and applied to discussions of an astonishing variety of topics, ranging from delinquency among the young to apathy among the old, and including along the way such matters as political participation, status aspirations, the behavior of men in prisons, narcotics addiction, urbanization, race relations, social change, and suicide.

Virtually all of this work has employed a single explanatory model for the analysis of anomy: a specified social-cultural condition gives rise to specified feelings in individuals which in turn result in specified behaviors. Different writers have worked variations on this scheme, but nobody has challenged the scheme itself or attempted a fundamental revision of it. Since it is our purpose in this paper to offer such a revision, we shall begin by showing the main ways in which the model is used in the recent literature. Even a brief review will demonstrate that while the variations have been many, the theme remains the same, with the result that the literature of anomy is much more heterogeneous in appearance than it is in fact.

Most of the variations have taken place in the first component of the sequence, the social condition that triggers the subsequent responses. To Durkheim, anomy meant a condition of de-regulation or relative normlessness in a social group. In his view, anomy was endemic in modern societies, and especially virulent in the economic sector where all the customary restraints and moral limits on men's aspirations were being undermined by the capitalist ethic of greed and gain. This weakening of restraints gave men a feeling of wandering through an empty space with no landmarks from which to take a bearing and set a course. Society imposed no limit on man's

Co-authored with John H. Schaar and reprinted, with permission, from the *American Sociological Review*, Vol 30, No 1, Feb. 1965, 14–40.

This is publication A34 of the Survey Research Center, University of California, Berkeley. The data presented in the paper have been prepared and analyzed under grants from the Rockefeller Foundation and the Social Science Research Council. A fellowship to the senior author by the Center for Advanced Studies in the Behaviorial Sciences was of great value in processing the Minnesota study. This investigation was supported in part by Public Health Service Research Grant MH-05837, from the National Institutes of Health.

[1] The word is Greek in origin. It was transliterated into Latin as *anomia* and into English as anomy. In that spelling the word was frequently used by 17th century writers. Durkheim transliterated the word into French as anomie, and recent American writers have adopted his usage. Since the concept now enjoys full recognition in the vocabulary of American social science, we thought it appropriate to restore the word in its English spelling.

"insatiable and bottomless" cravings for wealth, prestige, and power, and when a man's goals are infinite, his strivings are futile. "Those who have only empty space above them are almost inevitably lost in it, if no force restrains them."[2] Each step upward only discloses to the climber the infinite reaches beyond; each success turns into another failure. In the end, "reality seems valueless by comparison with the dreams of fevered imagination; reality is therefore abandoned. . . ."[3] Finding no fixed reference points by which to locate itself, the soul tires of its wanderings through a social landscape desolate of norms. The struggle seems futile, life itself loses value, and the result for many is anomic self-destruction.

Except for his passionate rhetoric, all the elements of Durkheim's treatment still remain in the recent literature, albeit in different proportions and vocabularies. Most importantly, the categories of his explanatory model are unchanged.

Merton's work illustrates this.[4] Discarding Durkheim's concept of man as a bundle of passions which can be tamed only by social restraints, he examines the actual social pressures upon persons to violate the accepted codes. He retains Durkheim's definition of anomy as a condition of relative normlessness in a society, but offers a revised statement of its causes. Whereas Durkheim held specifically that anomy was produced by an economic ethic that removed all limits from greed, Merton sees anomy as the result of "a breakdown in the cultural structure, occurring particularly when there is an acute disjunction between the cultural norms and goals and the socially structured capacities of members of the group to act in accord with them. . . . When the cultural and the social structure are malintegrated, the first calling for behavior and attitudes which the second precludes, there is a strain toward the breakdown of the norms, toward normlessness."[5]

But when Merton applies this general conception to a specific social setting, the results are quite similar to Durkheim's. Merton believes that modern American society has placed a tremendous emphasis on the goal of success, which means "accumulated wealth," without a corresponding insistence on pursuing that goal by legitimate means. Where Durkheim says greed, Merton says success. But do the two really mean different things?[6] For both writers, the basic point is that in some societies certain goals, which are in their nature unlimited, have been pursued so fervently that the appropriate normative restraints have virtually collapsed. The result is "a strain toward anomie and deviant behavior."[7]

[2] Emile Durkheim, *Suicide* (1897), trans. John A. Spaulding and George Simpson, Glencoe, Ill.: Free Press, 1951, p. 257.

[3] *Ibid.*, p. 256.

[4] Robert K. Merton, *Social Theory and Social Structure* (rev. ed.), Glencoe, Ill.: Free Press, 1957, pp. 121–194.

[5] *Ibid.*, pp. 162–163.

[6] See *ibid.*, esp. pp. 136–139.

[7] *Ibid.*, p. 157.

Merton's analysis of the behavioral consequences of anomy is more complex than Durkheim's. Merton does not deal with a single action, such as suicide. Rather, noting that the malintegration of cultural goals and institutionalized means falls with different impact upon persons located at different points in the social structure, he constructs a typology of modes of adaptation and offers some arguments and evidence to suggest which of the modes will typically be followed in given social groups. In Merton's scheme, then, while anomy produces a strain toward deviant behavior, the content as well as the incidence of that behavior varies among groups differently located in the social system. In other words, deviant behavior, which takes a number of forms, is the final indicator of anomy—although Merton concedes that not all deviant behavior is produced by malintegration and anomy.[8] He offers no tests, however, for telling which is and which is not.

In sum, Merton's fundamental logic is Durkheim's: social condition → psychological state → deviant behavior. The content of each category is different, but the categories themselves and the relations between them are the same. Moreover, both writers focus on the two outside links of the causal chain and have little to say about the link in the middle. In this sense, their orientation is sociological rather than psychological.

In addition to the manifestly sociological work, there is a large body of writing that appears to be psychologically oriented. It focuses on the middle link in the same causal chain: anomy is conceptualized as a state of mind rather than as a state of society. MacIver, for example, defines anomy as "the state of mind of one who has been pulled up by his moral roots. . . . The anomic man has become spiritually sterile, responsive only to himself, responsible to no one. He lives on the thin line of sensation between no future and no past."[9]

The most important work here is that of Leo J. Srole.[10] Srole conceptualized anomy as a psychological state which refers to "the individual's generalized, pervasive sense of 'self-to-others belongingness' at one extreme compared with 'self-to-others distance' and 'self-to-others alienation' at the other pole of the continuum."[11] He then postulated five attitudinal-ideational components of the anomic state of mind, and devised a five-item scale to

---

[8] See *ibid.*, p. 177.

[9] Robert M. MacIver, *The Ramparts We Guard,* New York: Macmillan, 1950, p. 84.

[10] Srole's work on anomy, to our knowledge, consists of these items: "Anomie, Authoritarianism and Prejudice," *American Journal of Sociology,* 62 (July, 1956), pp. 63–67; "Social Dysfunction, Personality and Social Distance Attitudes," unpublished paper read before the American Sociological Society, Chicago, 1951; "Social Integration and Certain Corollaries: An Exploratory Study," *American Sociological Review,* 21 (December, 1956), pp. 709–716; and "Interdisciplinary Conceptualization and Research in Social Psychiatry," unpublished paper read before the American Sociological Society, Detroit, 1956. A few pages in Srole, *et al., Mental Health in the Metropolis,* New York: McGraw-Hill, 1962, touch on anomy but do not add to his previous published work on this subject.

[11] Srole, "Social Integration . . . ," *op. cit.,* p. 711.

measure them.[12] The scale has been employed in a large number of investigations. Srole's scale and Merton's typology of modes of adaptation are the two most widely used research instruments in the study of anomy.

In his earliest work, Srole used the standard explanatory model in which social malintegration stands as the independent variable and the mental state of anomy as the dependent variable. He theorized that "to a large degree the state of anomia in an individual is dependent upon and determined by the condition of sociological integration at the points of the social system concurrently occupied by him."[13] In his later work, however, Srole broadened this formulation to include the possibility that anomy might be a function not only of social conditions but also of personality factors. In Srole's words, "the original emphasis on the sociogenesis of the anomic state has been refined to include psychogenic personality factors in an interactive relationship with elements of dysfunction and malintegration in the social system."[14]

However plausible this broadened formulation may seem, it appears in Srole's paper only as an assertion, not as a proposition grounded in psychological theory. Nor has this broader conception yet given birth to much research on the psychogenesis of anomy. In a recent exploration of the relations between anomy and various degrees of mental disturbance, Srole tested the general proposition that anomy is positively correlated with mental disturbance and found that the relation held only between anomy and "severe" disturbance.[15] He also found (as all other investigators have) that anomy is inversely related to social and economic status independently of the mental disturbance factor. Therefore, he concluded, social dysfunction, by which he meant low status, was the independent variable: "Both anomia with psychopathology and anomia without psychopathology are postulated as consequences of social dysfunction. Both combinations stand in a strong inverse linear relationship with socio-economic status. This fact would indicate that our social class system is a major axis of differential concentrations of dysfunctional elements in the moving social settings of people's life histories."[16]

As this account shows, Srole has not gone beyond the basic theoretical framework established by Durkheim and Merton. For him as for them, the psychological state of anomy reflects economic and social conditions. This is true not only of Srole's own work, but also of the many other studies in which his scale has been used. Virtually all of these studies have examined

---

[12] Both the components of anomy and the scale items are in *ibid.,* pp. 712–713.

[13] Srole, "Interdisciplinary Conceptualization and Research . . . ," *op. cit.,* p. 3.

[14] *Ibid.,* pp. 4–5.

[15] *Ibid.* The study rested on a probability sample of 1660 individuals, aged 20–59, and living in "Midtown." These persons were given a questionnaire of some 400 items, about one-third of which related to psychological and social role functioning. Psychiatrists on a hospital staff made the "mental disturbance" ratings on the basis of these data.

[16] *Ibid.,* p. 15.

the sociostructural foundations of anomy. They have, in the main, tried to find out where the anomic individuals are located in the social structure, though a few have investigated the relations between anomy and such other attitudes as authoritarianism and prejudice.

No writer known to us has specifically explored the relations between anomy and various dimensions of personality. Nor has anyone tried to assess the contributions various psychic states may make to anomy *independently* of the person's social status. No study has attempted to revise even in a modest way the thesis that certain objective social conditions cause anomy and that, conversely, individuals' anomic feelings may be taken as evidence that those objective social conditions exist. We hope to take a few steps toward these ends. Before that, however, there are still some preliminary questions.

One who reads the modern literature of anomy senses, beneath the dispassionate scientific method and vocabulary, passions no less intense than Durkheim's, and moral concerns not too different from his. Its authors are interested in something more than the advancement of science. They are involved in a question that troubles everyone who gives serious thought to the quality of modern life: the question of community and purpose. Does our society show signs of moral breakdown? Are we adrift, wandering without clear goals, out of touch with the cherished values that make up our heritage? Are the ties that bind us together in networks of mutual care and sympathy dangerously strained and weakened?

These are fashionable themes today, the *leitmotifs* of social and political criticism. They appear in the discussion of a thousand questions—juvenile delinquency, family relations, unemployment, economic growth, education, political reform, foreign policy—and in a variety of forums, including professional journals of social science. We do not mean to dismiss these themes nor to belittle this literature, but we do suggest that these discussions are embarrassed by problems that resist scientific analysis and by assumptions that are hard to defend in scientific terms.

Sometimes the assumptions are explicit, as they are when a writer states that "man is a creature who must avoid competing loyalties."[17] Usually, however, they are implicit. There is an assumption in much of the literature, for example, that men find it extremely difficult to function under conditions of normative uncertainty and conflict. But how much uncertainty and what kinds of conflict, and whether the limits are the same for all men—these decisive questions are nowhere squarely confronted. Instead, one encounters only vague warnings that men need secure moral codes, and cannot function effectively unless their society is "well integrated." What Americans once considered their greatest challenge to the past and promise to the future—the

---

[17] Sebastian de Grazia, *The Political Community: A Study of Anomie,* Chicago: University of Chicago Press, 1948, p. 154.

affirmation that men could freely assume responsibility for their own lives, that they would flourish in the open spaces cleared of the walls and towers of dogmatic codes, fixed statuses, and entrenched authorities—appears in this literature as our greatest vulnerability. Perhaps this is as much a manifestation of a failure of nerve as an exercise in scientific analysis.

All these writers assume, and many of them state explicitly, that anomy is a "problem" in our society, that our society suffers to a substantial degree from disintegration of the norms. But by what standard can this be judged? On the crucial questions of the "anomicity" of this society as compared with others, and of how much anomy can be safely tolerated, we can say little that is scientifically grounded without evidence from cross-cultural studies of great depth and scope. Lacking such evidence, we can only worry and argue. On *a priori* grounds one can argue that modern society, with its intricate division of labor, pluralism, rapid change, high mobility, weakening of traditional institutions, and so forth, is highly susceptible to normative uncertainty, conflict among men, and strain between cultural goals and institutionalized means. But whether these things in fact produce anomy, or whether anomy is more pervasive today than in previous societies, cannot be said with much confidence. Many forces that appear on *a priori* grounds to produce anomy may be effectively counteracted by, for example, the prodigious advances in communication, education, literacy, and economic well-being. In short, we must acknowledge complexity, and concede that many of the social conditions that are loosely thought to be destroying norms may simultaneously be welding the population into a stronger and more coherent value community than existed in the past. There may be a "selective fallacy" at work in much of the literature of anomy, as suggested by the fact that while normlessness is one of the *leitmotifs* of contemporary American social criticism, conformity is another. We are simultaneously said to be plagued by lack of shared norms and threatened by too much agreement on norms. Something has been left out of each picture.

Two kinds of evidence are currently offered to support the thesis that ours is an anomic society. Critics of modern society frequently cite rates of crime, delinquency, divorce, and so on as evidence of moral breakdown. But these and other presumed signs of anomy are very complex phenomena which may or may not reflect anomy, and which may themselves be produced by factors that have little to do with the general state of the norms.

Similar considerations apply to the other type of evidence. Many investigators who have administered the Srole scale to various samples report that a large proportion of respondents score "high" on the scale,[18] and this finding is then sometimes said to indicate a high degree of anomy in the society

---

[18] "High" is usually defined as responding in an anomic direction to three or more of the items in Srole's five-item scale. The percentage of "highs" in eight studies that have used the scale ranged from 28 to 39.

itself. Srole, for example, writes that his scale, along with other techniques, permits us to gain knowledge of "one of the most pervasive and potentially dangerous aspects of Western society, namely, the deterioration in the social and moral ties that bind, sustain and free us."[19]

The logic of psychological scale construction, however, will not support inferences from scale scores to the state of the society, because the distribution of scores is a function of the difficulty of the scale items themselves. One could construct an anomy scale composed of such "easy" items that almost everyone would score "anomic;" one could also construct a scale consisting of such "difficult" items that almost nobody would score "anomic." From the findings yielded by the easy scale we might infer that the society is highly anomic, whereas we might infer from the difficult scale that the society is happily free of anomy. Obviously, the procedure is fallacious. An ordinal scale permits many kinds of comparison among the people who respond to it, but it permits no statements about the absolute magnitude of the property it purports to measure.

Moreover, the leap from the subjective feelings expressed by individuals to statements about objective social conditions is a perilous one. What people believe about a society may or may not be an accurate reflection of its nature: perceptions and feelings are never a literal copy of what is "out there" but are always powerfully shaped by the needs, motives, attitudes, and abilities of the observer. Hence, we can never confidently assume that because some people feel anomic the society is anomic. Moreover, even if one could establish that some members of a society report strong anomic sentiments, one could label the society anomic only after systematically comparing that society with others. No one, including Durkheim, who came closest, has done this.

More than that, the findings already available concerning the location of anomic individuals in the social structure raise some difficult questions both for the standard explanatory scheme and for the notion of the anomic society. Investigators who have administered the Srole scale to various samples have uniformly reported that anomy is highest among certain sectors of the population: old people, the widowed, the divorced and separated, persons of low education, those with low incomes and low prestige occupations, people experiencing downward social mobility, Negroes, the foreign-born, farmers and other rural residents.[20] The tendency to perceive the society as anomic depends very much on one's location in the social structure.

All the groups just mentioned have one thing in common: they are outside the articulate, prosperous, and successful sectors of the population. Anomic feelings appear most frequently and most strongly among those who, for

[19] "Social Integration and Certain Corollaries . . . ," *op. cit.,* p. 716.

[20] Our own findings, based on broader samples and employing a different measure of anomy than any other study of the topic to date, follow the same pattern. These findings will be reported in subsequent publications.

whatever reason, are stranded in the backwaters of the symbolic and material mainstream, those whose lives are circumscribed by isolation, deprivation, and ignorance. Persons who do not share in the life of the articulate and active community are prone to confusion about the norms. In comparison, the relatively successful, well-educated, articulate and aware groups show little difficulty in finding order and meaning in society. Although their society is undergoing rapid change, contains competing value systems, and is increasingly urban and secular, they do not seem especially perplexed and uncertain. They do not report strong feelings of aimlessness, drift, and confusion, and they score low on measures of anomy. It appears, then, that anomy in part reflects patterns of communication and interaction that reduce opportunities to see and understand how the society works, and what its goals and values are.

We have tried to clear the ground. Hopefully, we have established two modest conclusions: virtually all studies of anomy have employed the same explanatory model; and it is extremely difficult at present to say anything scientifically persuasive about the question of the anomic society. It should be clear that we are not addressing the substantive question of whether or not our society is predominantly "healthy" or anomic. We merely suggest that the standard explanatory model is both oversimplified and over elaborate: many of the empirical findings concerning anomy cannot be understood within the terms of the model; and many of the findings can be explained without recourse to the elaborate notions of dysfunction and malintegration employed in the model. Given these considerations, we propose to revise the model so as to approach anomy as a set of learned attitudes and to make more adequate provision for the contribution of psychological factors independently of social structure.

Personal Factors in Anomy

We propose to conceptualize anomy as a state of mind, a cluster of attitudes, beliefs, and feelings in the minds of individuals. Specifically, it is the feeling that the world and oneself are adrift, wandering, lacking in clear rules and stable moorings. The anomic feels literally *de*-moralized; for him, the norms governing behavior are weak, ambiguous, and remote. He lives in a normative "low pressure" area, a turbulent region of weak and fitful currents of moral meaning. The core of the concept is the feeling of moral emptiness.

The norms of a society are, of course, learned; so too are the anomic feelings that there are no norms. What is learned is a function of many things: what is actually "out there" to be learned; the nature and quality of the teaching process; the learner's own ability and motivation; the strength and frequency of reinforcement; the amounts and kinds of impediments to learning, and so forth.

From the basic proposition that anomic feelings are learned, there follows a more specific proposition that applies with special force to the theory of anomy: whatever interferes with learning the norms of a society tends to increase anomic feelings among its members. This proposition is also supported by empirical findings, some of which were mentioned above. First of all, persons who are in an effective social position to learn the norms do not report a high incidence of anomic feelings. This suggests that the norms are in fact "out there" and can be "seen" by those who are in a position to see them. The conclusion is fortified by a small number of studies dealing with the question of "consensus" in American society. These studies have uniformly found that the values usually considered fundamental to our way of life (e.g., belief in freedom, domocracy, constitutional and procedural rights, tolerance, human dignity) are shared more widely and held more strongly among people in positions of leadership, influence, and high status than among the less favored classes.[21] Conversely, those who occupy social positions remote from the mainstream exhibit a high incidence and intensity of anomic feelings. Because of poverty, or little education, or the conditions of their employment or residence, these people are relatively isolated from the cultural mainstream. This conditon reduces communication and impairs their ability to learn the norms of the larger community which, in turn, gives rise to feelings of normlessness. In short, whatever interferes with one's ability to learn a community's norms, or weakens one's socialization into its central patterns of belief, must be considered among the determinants of anomy.

Some of these determinants are obviously sociological in the sense that certain roles, statuses, and social settings impede the learning process. Others, however, are psychological and personal; if this were not the case, we would expect all persons in a given role or social setting to be anomic. But this is clearly not the fact.

The two sets of determinants sometimes act together, and sometimes independently of each other. People who share the same social circumstances within a given society do not all react to the society in the same way. The same holds for those who have similar psychological and intellectual characteristics. We would suppose, however, that certain personality types (say, highly anxious persons) in certain social circumstances (say, low status and education) in certain societies (say, pluralistic and rapidly changing) would be highly susceptible to anomy, while self-confident persons of high status in a relatively simple and stable society might be virtually immune. The

---

[21] See, for example, Samuel A. Stouffer, *Communism, Conformity, and Civil Liberties,* New York: Doubleday, 1955; James W. Prothro and Charles M. Grigg, "Fundamental Principles of Democracy: Bases of Agreement and Disagreement," *Journal of Politics,* 21 (1960), pp. 276–294; Seymour Martin Lipset, *Political Man,* New York: Doubleday, 1960, Ch. 4; and Herbert McClosky, "Consensus and Ideology in American Politics," *American Political Science Review,* 58 (June, 1964), pp. 361–382.

important point is that anomic feelings are not necessarily produced by a single cause or factor, or even by a cluster of factors all of which are on the same level of analysis, but are likely to appear whenever learning of the norms is severely impeded. Impediments may arise from an individual's social setting, from his personality characteristics, or from both.

The theory of anomy on which we shall proceed can be summarized by the following diagram:

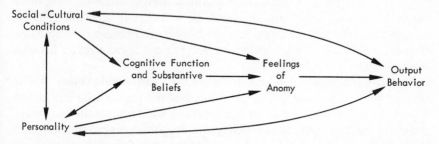

In the present paper we are not concerned with all the elements in this causal pattern. Our primary intention is to identify and to explain some of the personality and cognitive factors that contribute to anomy. We also offer some suggestions concerning the interrelations between personality factors, social-cultural conditions, and anomy. Examination of the other links in the model will be left for subsequent publications. Hopefully, this exploration of the psychological dimensions of the anomic state of mind will direct attention to some important but neglected factors in the study of anomy.

The personal factors that impair learning and socialization may be divided into three categories: (1) *Cognitive factors* that influence one's ability to learn and understand; (2) *Emotional factors* that tend to lower one's ability to perceive reality correctly; (3) *Substantive beliefs and attitudes* that interfere with successful communication and interaction. There might well be other such categories; and surely these three are not as independent of each other in reality as they are in our list. Still, the list provides a satisfactory base from which to open an exploration of the psychological dimensions of anomy.

Cognitive factors

The maxim has it that ignorance is bliss. A host of considerations suggest that the contrary is more likely the case. Those whose intellectual or cognitive equipment lacks power and efficiency find it difficult to organize and understand the events and ideas they encounter, and this difficulty apparently produces, not security and confidence, but bewilderment and anxiety. Those who cannot think clearly or relate events to each other, or organize their observations and experiences into meaningful structures, are most prone to be confused about their society's values and to see the society itself as lacking in order and meaning. In modern, rapidly changing, complex societies, such incapacities may be especially important determinants of anomic feelings. An individual with relatively poor cognitive capacities may manage to comprehend events within a small, stable, and simple life space, but he will find it more difficult to comprehend the apparent confusion and ambiguity of very complex ideas and of events performed by actors personally unknown to him, acting in a space far removed from him, and talking in a language frequently unfamiliar to him. Having only a meager sense of what these events, ideas, and actors are all about, he will readily conclude that his society lacks order and meaning, that its values are incoherent, contradictory, or even nonexistent. Such conclusions will register themselves in his own mind as feelings of anomy.

Cognitive incapacity may be a matter of poor native endowment. It may likewise be socially induced, in the sense that the person who has lacked opportunities for education and communication is left without the knowledge and skills needed to understand society. Poor cognitive functioning may also result from various psychological disorders that interfere with rational and realistic thought. Whatever its origin, we expect persons with low cognitive capacity to be more susceptible to anomy than persons with high cognitive capacity. This hypothesis will be tested below.

Emotional Factors

What we have in mind here are a variety of psychological states that warp perception, interfere with cognitive functioning, or render one very uncomfortable in the face of ambivalence and ambiguity. These mental states may produce a tendency toward anomy in a number of ways. Some psychic states directly distort perception. Others so impair cognitive functioning that the person is unable to structure the world realistically. Still others so reduce his ability to interact successfully with his fellows that he fails to learn what they believe and value. This failure of learning may be especially important in the growth of anomy. One does not learn values and norms in precisely the way one learns facts: one is "socialized" into them through numerous interactions—living, working, and talking with others—repeated over time and in a variety of contexts. Some psychic states (e.g., extreme hostility toward others) reduce one's ability to interact, and therefore prevent one from becoming well-acquainted with society's norms and values, leading one to see the society as anomic. This proposition, which will be refined and tested below, is also relevant to the third cluster of personal factors that encourage anomy.

Substantive Beliefs and Opinions

A person's opinions and values have a considerable effect on the way he is received by a community or group. Newcomb showed in the Bennington study that persons who had acquired the "proper" values and beliefs were more readily accepted by the members of a group and more easily attained prestige positions within the group.[22] Moreover, once a person has learned and accepted a group's values to the extent necessary to secure acceptance, his very participation will reinforce its values in his mind. Many studies of small groups have shown that group leaders, who, of course, participate most fully in the group life, are more devoted than the average member to the group's values.[23] Partial acceptance of the rules will get one into the club; once inside, the processes of indoctrination and absorption can be carried much farther.

On the other hand, persons who fail to learn the dominant values of a group, or who hold beliefs and opinions not widely shared, are not likely to be well received by group members. This in turn reduces communication and makes socialization into the group even more difficult. A deviant lacks the intimate, vital experience of participation which is essential to full appreciation of the group's norms and values. His knowledge of those norms may be abstract and "theoretical," insensitive to subtle shadings of mood and meaning—a caricature rather than an accurate portrait. In addition, since the deviant sees a group that has rejected him only from the outside, he may also see its activities as senseless and incoherent.

The connection between the holding of deviant beliefs and the feeling that society is anomic is in some instances dependent on certain personality states. A substantial body of evidence indicates that many persons who hold extreme views on political, economic, and social questions feel an unusually keen need for order and certainty in their lives.[24] This need is served by passionate attachment to a belief system. Because these people cannot gain the psychological security they crave unless they see their own beliefs embodied in the world outside, they easily come to feel that a social order not arranged along the lines of their own belief systems is really no order at all.

We shall formulate some of the general hypotheses just proposed more specifically and submit them to tests of verification after we have described the samples, questionnaires, and attitude scales employed in the present study.

Procedures

The data were collected from two general population samples: one, a cross section of the population of Minnesota (N = 1082), and the other a cross

---

[22] Theodore M. Newcomb, *Personality and Social Change,* New York: Holt, Rinehart and Winston, 1943, esp. Ch. 8.

[23] See George C. Homans, *The Human Group,* New York: Harcourt, Brace, 1950.

[24] See, e.g., T. W. Adorno, *et al., The Authoritarian Personality,* New York: Harper, 1950; and Milton Rokeach, *The Open and Closed Mind,* New York: Basic Books, 1960. Our own data, to be published subsequently, provide further support for this observation.

section of the national population (N = 1484). The Minnesota survey, done in 1955, was conducted with the cooperation of the Minnesota Poll, which designed the sample and selected the respondents. The sample for the national survey, carried out in 1958, was drawn by the Gallup Poll, which also administered the questionnaire. In both surveys, the interviewers explained how the questionnaire should be filled out and then left it with the respondent, who completed and returned it by mail. Although this departs from the more standard methods—a departure dictated by the great length and unusual content of the questionnaires—the characteristics of the samples are very close to those of the populations sampled.[25] The Minnesota survey, which was designed primarily to investigate various forms of extreme or "marginal belief," is called the Marginal Believer (MB) study, while the national survey, which focused on political affiliation, activity, and belief, is called the Political Activities and Beliefs (PAB) study.

The questionnaires for both studies, though different in some respects, had similar basic formats. Both were of the self-administering type. Both contained questions about the respondent's personal and social characteristics, group memberships and identifications, and political attitudes, interests, and activities. Both also contained a large number of attitude and personality scales, each typically composed of nine agree-disagree items. The MB questionnaire had 512 such items, randomly presented but in reality divided into 63 scales. The PAB questionnaire contained 390 items composing 47 scales, many of which had also been used in the MB study. These extensive questionnaires provide a vast amount of information on large samples drawn from different populations at different times. With this base, not only can one assess the relations between anomy and many other attitudes and personal characteristics, but one can also replicate the inquiry by comparing the results of the two studies.

The construction and testing of the large inventory of scales in these questionnaires took about two years and required the preliminary sampling of 1200 residents of the Minneapolis-St. Paul community.[26] The responses of this sample were scored and analyzed by face inspection and modified Guttman procedures to ascertain their internal consistency, their face relation to the attribute being measured, and their unidimensionality. For some scales, empirical validation was achieved through the use of criterion groups; for others, a panel of judges was used to ascertain validity; for still others more emphasis was placed on internal consistency and reproducibility. One or more procedures for estimating validity were carried out for each scale in both studies.

[25] For the details, see McClosky, *op. cit.,* pp. 380–382.
[26] Twenty of the scales were developed by McClosky alone. The Dominance and the Social Responsibility scales were constructed in collaboration with Harrison Gough and Paul E. Meehl. All the others were developed in collaboration with Kenneth E. Clark and Paul E. Meehl. Arnold Rose was a member of the research team at an early stage.

The Anomy scale was one of a set designed to measure response to the social and political community. Other measures in this set included bewilderment, pessimism, alienation, and sense of political futility. The definition of anomy employed in the construction of the scale is consistent with the definition already indicated, placing primary emphasis on feelings of normlessness and de-regulation.

Like the other scales, the Anomy scale began as a large pool of items, each of which was designed to assess one or another facet of the anomic state of mind. Through preliminary screening and pre-testing, the initial pool was cut to 11 items, which were then submitted to a sample of 273 Minnesota adults. Their responses were scrutinized for internal consistency, subjected to a Guttman reproducibility procedure, and finally reduced to the nine items presented in order of item difficulty in Table 1.

The validity of the scale can be assessed by several different criteria. One criterion is face validity: Do the scale items appear to express the sentiments and beliefs that constitute the anomic state of mind? This is an important test in this case, because the people we designate as anomic are those who say precisely the sorts of things and display precisely the sorts of feelings that these items express. In short, the items define, by their content, our conception of anomy.

We are satisfied that the scale passes this test. With the possible exception of number 7, each item manifestly expresses one or another dimension of the anomic mentality. The items express the feelings that people today lack firm convictions and standards, that it is difficult to tell right from wrong in our complex and disorderly world, that the traditional values which gave meaning to the individual and order to the society have lost their force, and that the social ties which once bound men together have dissolved.

Do the items express what other students mean by anomy? To answer this question we submitted the items to several groups of graduate students in political science and psychology, and to some 40 Fellows at the Center for Advanced Study in the Behavioral Sciences. In every instance, the proportion who judged the statements as expressing some aspect of anomy was high enough to satisfy us that the scale items do in fact embody the feelings and beliefs associated with the concept.

A second method of assessing the scale's validity is to observe its relation to other attitudes that one would expect, on theoretical grounds, to find associated with feelings of anomy. One would expect an anomic person to feel lonely and distant from his fellows, to be confused and bewildered by events in his society, to report a strong sense of political futility, to feel pessimistic about himself and the future, and to display cynical attitudes toward the men and practices governing society and the state. All these expectations are clearly born out by the correlations between Anomy and the variables just mentioned, as can be seen from Table 2. The magnitude

Table 1

The Anomy Scale: Items and Level of
Item Difficulty (PAB Sample—N = 1484)*

	Per Cent Who Agree	Per Cent Who Disagree
1. With everything so uncertain these days, it almost seems as though anything could happen.	82.3	17.7
2. What is lacking in the world today is the old kind of friendship that lasted for a lifetime.	69.3	30.7
3. With everything in such a state of disorder, it's hard for a person to know where he stands from one day to the next.	50.0	50.0
4. Everything changes so quickly these days that I often have trouble deciding which are the right rules to follow.	48.5	51.5
5. I often feel that many things our parents stood for are just going to ruin before our very eyes.	47.6	52.4
6. The trouble with the world today is that most people really don't believe in anything.	44.1	55.9
7. I often feel awkward and out of place.	37.3	62.7
8. People were better off in the old days when everyone knew just how he was expected to act.	27.4	72.6
9. It seems to me that other people find it easier to decide what is right than I do.	27.1	72.9

* Since the logic of this type of scale construction forces the respondent to agree or disagree, the proportion of "No Answers" is very small—about 1 per cent on the average. These have been omitted from the tabulation.

and direction of these correlations assured us that the Anomy scale is located in the proper attitude domain.

A third way to assess scale validity is to apply the usual technical tests for unidimensionality. Although this test matters, it is less important than the validity measures already discussed. Indeed, no one can be certain that anomy should be thought of as a unidimensional attitude: much evidence suggests, as we will show, that it is only one facet of a many-sided sense of malaise or distress.

These demurrers made, we can still report that the scale exhibits a fair degree of unidimensionality. Reproducibility procedures carried out on both

Table 2

Correlations Between the Anomy Scale and Selected "Validating" Scales*

	Alienation	Bewilder-ment	Pessi mism	Feelings of Political Impotence	Political Cynicism	Life Satis-faction
Sample:						
PAB: N = 1484	+.60	NA	+.50	+.54	+.59	−.41
MB: N = 1082	+.58	+.62	+.43	+.55	+.62	−.39

NA = Not Available.

* All figures are Pearson product-moment correlations and all are significant beyond the .01 level.

the PAB general population sample and on a national sample of 3020 political influentials produced coefficients of reproducibility of .80 and .83, respectively. Observe also that all the items but one fall into the second and third quartiles of item difficulty: hence, the reproducibility coefficients are not factitiously increased by the use of items of very high or very low difficulty. The scale, then, achieves a satisfactory degree of internal cohesion and unidimensionality.

Although a nine-item scale cannot be expected to produce an extremely high reliability score, the split-half reliability coefficient as corrected by the Spearman-Brown formula is a satisfactory .76. An alternative computation utilizing a formula presented by L. J. Cronbach[27] yields a reliability coefficient of .77. Additional evidence of the stability (if not, technically speaking, the reliability) of the scale can be gleaned from a comparison of the Anomy correlations in the MB and PAB studies. The relation of Anomy to a subset of 41 variables was tested in the MB study and, in effect, retested in the PAB study. Although to correlate the two sets of correlations may in some quarters be considered unorthodox, it is nevertheless worth noting that the correlation in this case was an astonishingly high .98. Thus, people in the PAB sample who possess certain social, attitudinal, or personality characteristics register scores on the Anomy scale that are very similar to the scores made by their counterparts in the MB sample.

The criteria of face validity, correlation with related scales, reproducibility, and reliability, are the appropriate tests by which to judge the quality of the Anomy scale. Other tests might be proposed, but they are not appropriate in this case. For instance, one common validation procedure is to check respondents' scale scores against some independent and external criterion (preferably behavioral) which assesses the same dimension that the scale seeks to measure. But for anomy, no feasible criterion is available. Obviously, there is no recognizable group of anomics to whom one might turn to

[27] *Essentials of Psychological Testing* (2nd ed.), New York: Harper and Row, p. 141.

validate an anomy scale, as one can turn to groups of liberals or right-wing extremists to validate a liberalism or fascism scale. Rates of divorce, crime, delinquency, alcoholism, suicide, and so on, are also inappropriate criteria; for it is by no means certain that anomy typically produces these consequences or that a large proportion of them are caused by anomy. When a particular attitude has known, measurable behavioral consequences, as is the case, for example, with ethnocentrism, these consequences can serve as indicators that the attitude is present. When the consequences of an attitude are not really known, the best indicators of the presence of the attitude are the scale items themselves.

Another external criterion suggested by the literature is the observed level of agreement on basic norms. Although this mode of validation flows logically from the standard sociological theory of anomy, we doubt its utility. For one thing, which values should be used to measure the level of agreement? Americans, for example, agree more about liberty than about equality. They agree more about freedom in the abstract than about freedoms in the particular. For another thing, disagreement with norms is known to be a function of social position. In the face of such facts, how can agreement on values be used to assess anomy?

There are still other difficulties. Men might agree about what they actually believe and still feel a strong sense of anomy. Conversely, men might disagree sharply and not feel anomic. Plainly, what matters in conceptualizing anomy is not the actual state of agreement on norms but the feelings men have about the state of the norms. Otherwise, any society pervaded by sharp disagreement over basic values would have to be considered an anomic society, and a society with few such differences would have to be considered non-anomic. But that conception appears nonsensical when one recognizes that even in the "consensual" society many people feel aimless and adrift.

A word about analysis procedures before turning to the findings. For convenience, we have broken all the scale distributions into approximate thirds, which meant in the case of Anomy that those who scored 6–9 were considered highly anomic, those who scored 3–5 were designated as the middle group, and those who scored 0–2 were classified as low or non-anomic. We shall report the data principally in percentage form, comparing the high, middle, and low anomics on a number of dimensions. Wherever parallel sets of data exist for both the MB and PAB samples, they will be presented.

We have also carried out a number of procedures to control for possible "contaminating" factors. Thus, we have run the Anomy scale against the other scales with education, socio-economic status, and acquiescence controlled, among others. In addition, we have analyzed the relations between anomy and certain personality and attitude dimensions in samples matched for seven social and demographic characteristics.

Findings

In this section we shall test the general hypotheses stated above, as well as some specific hypotheses derived from them.

Cognitive Factors

A society's norms must be learned, and one of the factors determining ability to learn them is cognitive capacity. A person who finds it extremely difficult to grasp the relations among ideas and events, to reason from effects to causes, and to organize his thoughts and perceptions into coherent wholes, is likely to see the social world as confusing and confused. Thus, our hypothesis is that level of cognitive functioning and anomy are inversely related.[28]

The most widely used measure of level of cognitive functioning is, of course, a standard intelligence test, but it was impossible to administer such a test in the present study. This, however, does not jeopardize our purposes. There is a great deal of "slippage" between cognitive capacity, as measured solely by intelligence test scores alone, and the level of cognitive functioning at which an individual actually conducts his life. Cognitive functioning is a composite made up of a number of dimensions, and to get at these, other measures than a standard intelligence test are needed. Our questionnaires contained a number of measures that tap various recognizable dimensions of cognitive behavior. Taken together, they provide a fairly accurate profile of a respondent's level of cognitive functioning. Specifically, we have five such measures:

1. The usual data on years of formal schooling completed were collected. While education is primarily a "social" variable, it has also repeatedly been

[28] This is not the place to enter the nature-nurture debate. Suffice it to say that both hereditary and environmental factors affect the level of cognitive functioning. Social scientists are familiar enough with the findings on the impact of sociological factors on intelligence test performance. Perhaps they are less familiar with the findings on the relations between genotypic similarities and similarity of performance on intelligence tests. A recent survey of 52 studies conducted over the past 50 years concluded that "a marked trend is seen toward an increasing degree of intellectual resemblance in direct proportion to an increasing degree of genetic relationship, regardless of environmental communality. Furthermore, for most relationship categories [e.g.: parent-child; one-egg twins] the *median* of the empirical correlations [between genetic relation and performance on mental tests] closely approaches the theoretical value predicted on the basis of genetic relationship alone." L. Erlenmeyer-Kimling and Lissy F. Jarvik, "Genetics and Intelligence: A Review," *Science*, 142 (December 13, 1963).

We cite these findings because they suggest how important it is in social science inquiry to acknowledge, in both theory and method, the existence of factors operating at the genetic-psychological level. The standard theory of anomy incorporates a "uniformitarian" perspective: it takes no systematic account of individual differences. Any full explanation must give due consideration to both sets of factors. This is basic to the present paper. In principle, this inquiry into personality factors should be pushed back to genotypic differences, on the premise that they produce differences in behavior potentials, while environmental differences produce different performances. Work on the genetic bases of psychological variations has barely begun, however, so we cannot push the inquiry back that far. But we can insist that an appreciation of the causal role of personal factors is essential to a comprehensive theory of anomy.

shown to provide an indirect measure of the knowledge-and-skills aspect of cognition. Plainly, persons with little or no education are likely to lack much of the knowledge and many of the tools necessary for effective cognitive functioning and for coping with the social world.

2. The "Intellectuality" scale measures one's orientation toward and participation in intellectual and cultural activities.

3. The "Awareness" scale is a rather simple information test. It provides a useful brief measure of the respondent's knowledge of some basic features of the political and social system. A person who scores poorly on this test will scarcely be able to perform effectively as a citizen, for he lacks even an elementary knowledge of how the system works.

4. The "Mysticism" scale measures belief in such things as spiritualism, necromancy, astrology, and the prophetic portent of various kinds of signs and wonders. Essentially, an individual's score reflects his conviction that strange and supernatural forces move among men and hover over their affairs. It therefore measures the degree to which one is attracted by magical rather than rational and scientific explanations. Note that the scale gets at something different from mere feelings of ignorance or inability to comprehend complex phenomena. It taps the feeling that many events are inherently inexplicable by the ordinary methods of reason and proof because the events themselves are the products of extraordinary and mysterious forces beyond the understanding of mere men. The person who holds such beliefs has largely abandoned the rules of logic and evidence in the search for meaning.

5. An "Acquiescence" measure, consisting of 19 pairs of contradictory items, was included for the usual purpose of gauging and controlling for response set. This measure, however, does more than improve the analyst's confidence that the relationships he has discovered among a number of variables are not merely artifacts of the tendency to acquiesce; it also discloses something about the quality of the respondent's intellectual life. Specifically, the tendency to acquiesce reflects an undiscriminating and illogical mind, one that works carelessly and makes few and superficial intellectual demands on perceptions and cognitions within a stimulus field. The Acquiescence scale measures the consistency-logicality dimension of cognitive functioning.

Table 3 provides the material for testing the hypothesis that level of cognitive functioning is inversely related to anomy, and it shows that the hypothesis is overwhelmingly confirmed. For example, a person who scores high on the Mysticism scale is nearly seven times as likely to score high on Anomy as a person who is low on Mysticism. Similar ratios obtain in the comparisons between persons who score high and low on Intellectuality, Awareness, Education, and Acquiescence. In both samples and on all five dimensions of cognitive functioning the results run uniformly and powerfully in the predicted direction.

Table 3
Level of Cognitive Functioning and Anomy

(*In Percentages*)

	National Sample Anomy				Minnesota Sample Anomy			
	High	*Middle*	*Low*	*(N)*[a]	*High*	*Middle*	*Low*	*(N)*[b]
Education								
High	13.9	41.5	44.5	(402)	8.2	34.6	57.2	(292)
Middle	35.5	40.4	24.0	(757)	26.7	34.1	39.2	(498)
Low	60.6	30.3	9.1	(320)	49.7	32.1	18.2	(280)
Intellectuality								
High	15.0	38.5	46.4	(532)	8.4	31.2	60.4	(369)
Middle	40.5	40.9	18.6	(555)	26.6	36.3	37.1	(388)
Low	54.6	35.2	10.2	(392)	51.7	33.2	15.1	(325)
Awareness[c]								
High					8.1	30.9	61.0	(295)
Middle					23.6	33.6	42.8	(381)
Low					46.3	35.7	18.0	(406)
Mysticism[c]								
High					47.2	33.7	19.1	(413)
Middle					21.9	39.9	38.2	(406)
Low					6.8	24.0	69.2	(263)
Acquiescence								
High	64.6	29.9	5.5	(492)	57.5	32.6	9.9	(334)
Middle	28.1	48.1	23.8	(530)	22.8	40.7	36.5	(359)
Low	11.7	36.8	51.5	(462)	7.2	28.0	64.8	(389)

[a] In this and most subsequent tables, the National Sample N is 1479 instead of the 1484 actually in the original sample because five persons did not report education.
[b] Of the 1082 persons in the Minnesota Sample, 12 did not report education.
[c] Not available for the Minnesota Sample.

Additional evidence for the hypothesis was obtained from a procedure designed to measure the consistency with which a person reasons from a general principle to a particular application. Fourteen pairs of items were constructed, each pair composed of a general statement of an idea and a particular application of that idea. In both samples, and for almost every pair of items, the highly anomic were less consistent than the non-anomic.

Emotional Factors

We have suggested that the ability to comprehend a society's norms depends in considerable degree on the individual's personality. Certain personality states can lower the level of cognitive functioning, distort perception, interfere with social interaction and communication, and generally impair the ability to sort out and make coherent connections among the diverse elements of the social world. We shall examine four interrelated personality clusters which produce a tendency toward anomy: psychological inflexibility, anxiety, low ego strength, and generalized anger and aggression.

1. Inflexibility. The line of reasoning followed so far suggests that one of the personality states most conducive to anomy is psychological inflexibility. This condition is characterized by unusual rigidity in the employment of defense mechanisms. Highly inflexible persons tend toward premature cognitive closure and are inclined to restrict the range of alternatives they consider relevant to the handling of a problem. They hang tightly to their established perceptual and cognitive structures and resist changes in their set ways of thought and action: trial-and-error behavior, for example, is difficult for them. The psychologically inflexible also have a low tolerance for ambiguity. They crave order, fixed patterns, clear and simple alternatives.

The contingencies and diversities of a complex and changing society are highly unsettling to such people, and they tend to extend their need for order and predictability to the society at large. Their urge to assert rigid control over the forces affecting their personal lives registers itself in the wish to bring the community itself under firm control. Only then can they feel at home in the world. Furthermore, persons in the grip of a powerful need for certainty are likely to see the world around them as less orderly than it may in fact be. Blind to the continuities and stabilites, and hypersensitive to the novelties and instabilities, such persons cannot perceive what many observers have reported, namely that beneath the changes in the face of America, a remarkably stable core of values and beliefs has endured.[29]

To test the hypothesis that inflexibility produces a tendency toward anomy, we included three measures of inflexibility in the study design. The three were also combined into a summary measure, which we have called the "Inflexibility Index." Table 4, in which the relations between these measures and anomy are presented, shows a very strong connection between inflexibility and anomy. For example, 67 per cent of those in the national sample who score high on the Inflexibility Index also score high on Anomy, whereas only 13 per cent of low scorers on the Index are high on Anomy. The disproportion is almost equally large for the Minnesota sample, running from 48 to 12 per cent. Similar results obtain for each of the component measures. Thus, in the national sample, one who scores high on Intolerance of Ambiguity is almost five times as likely to score high on Anomy as one who scores low on Intolerance of Ambiguity; in the Minnesota sample the ratio is four to one.

These powerful correlations are all the more impressive and theoretically meaningful when one considers that the three inflexibility variables represent

---

[29]See, e.g., Clyde Kluckhohn, "Have There Been Discernible Shifts in American Values During the Past Generation?" in Elting E. Morison (ed.), *The American Style: Essays in Value and Perspective,* New York: Harper, 1958, pp. 145–217.

Table 4
Psychological Inflexibility and Anomy

| | *(In Percentages)* | | | | | | | |
| | National Sample Anomy | | | | Minnesota Sample Anomy | | | |
	High	*Middle*	*Low*	*(N)*	*High*	*Middle*	*Low*	*(N)*
Intolerance of Ambiguity								
High	55.5	35.3	9.2	(578)	45.3	34.8	19.9	(417)
Middle	31.4	42.4	26.2	(474)	22.0	37.2	40.8	(341)
Low	11.5	38.6	49.9	(427)	11.7	28.4	59.9	(324)
Rigidity								
High	51.9	34.2	13.9	(632)	39.5	35.9	24.6	(418)
Middle	28.0	43.7	28.3	(375)	21.7	39.7	38.6	(290)
Low	18.2	40.3	41.5	(472)	19.8	26.5	53.7	(374)
Obsessiveness								
High	46.0	36.0	18.0	(594)	34.1	36.3	29.6	(419)
Middle	31.9	42.1	26.0	(373)	25.9	33.6	40.5	(301)
Low	24.8	38.9	36.3	(512)	22.4	30.7	46.9	(362)
Inflexibility Index								
High	67	27	6	(250)	48	41	11	(157)
Mid-High	43	39	18	(466)	34	35	31	(325)
Mid-Low	26	45	29	(417)	23	35	42	(346)
Low	13	38	49	(346)	12	27	61	(242)

genotypic psychological states. The scales tapping them draw on personality material exclusively and are free of social or political content. A typical item from the Intolerance of Ambiguity scale: "I am the sort of person who likes to know just where he stands on everything." From the Obsessiveness scale: "I honestly believe I have more persistence than most people." From the Rigidity scale: "It bothers me when something unexpected interrupts my daily routine." Clearly, there is no connection between the face content of the items in these scales and that of the Anomy items. Hence, Table 4 shows two sets of variables distinct in nature and content, yet highly correlated with each other. Inflexibility reduces one's capacity to accommodate to diversity and contingency, and limits one's ability to perceive the uniformities that may underlie diversity. Faced by complex stimuli from the social world, inflexible persons are easily overwhelmed. Their anxiety is aroused, they become confused, and they register intense feelings of anomy.

2. Anxiety. Persons who suffer from a high degree of anxiety are also likely to exhibit anomic feelings. The chain between these two states has a number of links. Since an inverse relationship exists between level of cognitive functioning and anomy, anything that impairs the quality of cognitive

functioning thereby heightens the tendency toward anomy. That anxiety has a crippling effect on the cognitive process is not only established in numerous experiments but is apparent as well from everyday observation. Second, persons who feel generally anxious about themselves—about their health, their achievements, their strength and worth—also typically feel anxious about the external world. Their inner anxiety spills over onto the outer world, and they tend to project upon the external world the doubts and fears that dominate their own mental life. They see the society as uncertain, confused, lacking in clear standards and direction—in short, as anomic. Third, intense anxiety sometimes leads its victims to withdraw from reality, or at least to retreat from contacts with the outside. Obviously, this reduces socialization and learning, and thus indirectly increases the tendency toward anomy.

The MB study offers three scales for testing the hypothesis that anxiety increases anomy. The Manifest Anxiety scale measures generalized or "constitutional" anxiety. Its items refer to restlessness, high state of excitation, hysteria, susceptibility to loss of consciousness, and the like. The Stability-Disorganization scale assesses such characteristics as inability to concentrate, proneness to debilitating worry, and indecisiveness. A Bewilderment scale gauges a respondent's tendencies to regard the external world as unfathomable, complicated, and upsetting. Although some of the items in the Bewilderment scale express sentiments similar to some of those in the Anomy scale, the first two are close to being pure, clinical-type measures, and thus are especially useful for testing the hypothesis.

Table 5 shows that the hypothesis is strongly confirmed. For example, the probability of being anomic is over four times as great when one scores high on Manifest Anxiety as when one scores low. Similar results appear for the other two scales.

3. Low Ego Strength. This label refers to generalized feelings of personal inadequacy and self-contempt. We have in mind here people who feel psychologically maimed, crippled, and therefore unsightly in their own and others' eyes. Typically a person with low ego strength lacks self-confidence, gains little satisfaction from life, and is pessimistic about the future. He often bears a heavy burden of guilt, oppressive for its very vagueness and pervasiveness. Haunted by the fear that others will discover his unwholesome thoughts and acts, he urgently tries to keep his inner self inviolate. For him, the conviction that the society is anomic may be psychologically functional; his anomic feelings serve as a part of his system of self-defense and self-justification. One who feels inadequate, guilty, unhappy with the way he has managed his life, and uncertain of his worth may find it important to blame his malaise on the system rather than on himself. Not he, but the society is confused, chaotic, and sullied; being itself disordered, society has made him its victim. Thus we hypothesize that persons who possess low ego strength are likely to score high on anomy.

Both studies included a number of measures designed to assess particular dimensions of ego strength. Compared to "pure" personality variables, such

Table 5

Anxiety and Anomy

| | (*In Percentages*) Minnesota Sample Anomy | | | |
	High	Middle	Low	(*N*)
Manifest Anxiety				
High	52.4	35.1	12.5	(248)
Middle	26.4	35.5	38.1	(533)
Low	10.3	29.2	60.5	(301)
Stability-Disorganization				
High	51.8	32.6	15.6	(365)
Middle	21.6	36.7	41.7	(393)
Low	8.6	31.2	60.2	(324)
Bewilderment				
High	61.0	26.9	12.1	(331)
Middle	22.9	43.0	34.1	(393)
Low	2.8	29.6	67.6	(358)

as hostility or paranoia, some of the variables in this cluster contain a larger component of "social" influences. One scale measures psychological guilt, another self-confidence. A third, Need Inviolacy, probes the depth of the respondent's fear of being unmasked, having his wishes and thoughts disclosed. An Alienation scale taps the feeling of loneliness and the yearning for supportive primary relationships. Two scales, Life Satisfaction and Status Frustration, assess the respondent's feeling that he has managed his life satisfactorily and has achieved the success he had hoped for and thought he deserved. Two others, Pessimism and Political Futility, measure respectively one's hopes and fears for the future, and the degree to which one feels capable of directing future events toward satisfactory outcomes. The Dominance scale gauges the subject's security in social relationships, his self-assurance, and his forcefulness and ability to influence others. Finally, a Social Responsibility scale measures adequacy of social adjustment and personality integration. This battery of instruments permits a broad appraisal of the main components of ego-strength. Table 6 shows their relations with anomy.

Each of the ego-strength variables is related to Anomy in the direction predicted by the hypothesis. Furthermore, the connections are in each case linear and very powerful. Although a few of the correlations are slightly inflated by the similarities in content between several of the Anomy items and several items in the ego-strength scales, the correlations remain so large and consistent for all scales and individual items in this group as to leave no doubt that the weaker the self-image, the stronger the feelings of anomy.

4. Generalized Aggression. Both controlled experiments and daily observation indicate that persons in the grip of powerful, generalized emotions of

Table 6
Ego Strength and Anomy

	National Sample Anomy				Minnesota Sample Anomy			
	High	*Middle*	*Low*	*(N)*	*High*	*Middle*	*Low*	*(N)*
Guilt								
High	64.0	30.4	5.6	(431)	51.7	35.1	13.2	(296)
Middle	34.5	46.9	18.6	(467)	30.3	39.2	30.5	(370)
Low	14.1	37.9	48.0	(581)	8.9	27.6	63.5	(416)
Self-Confidence								
High					13.4	33.9	52.7	(336)
Middle					28.1	34.7	37.2	(449)
Low					44.1	31.7	24.2	(297)
Need Inviolacy								
High	62.1	30.8	7.1	(491)	50.1	32.7	17.2	(355)
Middle	36.3	45.0	18.7	(380)	25.8	42.1	32.1	(252)
Low	12.5	40.8	46.7	(608)	12.4	29.9	57.7	(475)
Life-Statisfaction								
High	18.3	37.7	44.0	(459)	13.0	30.6	56.4	(369)
Middle	33.3	42.3	24.4	(496)	27.5	37.2	35.3	(374)
Low	51.5	35.7	12.8	(524)	44.6	33.0	22.4	(339)
Alienation								
High	62.0	32.6	5.4	(497)	59.2	26.4	14.4	(284)
Middle	32.5	46.6	21.0	(539)	28.7	41.0	30.3	(380)
Low	8.1	35.4	56.4	(443)	6.0	31.8	62.2	(418)
Status Frustration								
High	61.0	32.1	6.9	(305)	56.1	27.8	16.1	(180)
Middle	37.1	42.2	20.7	(593)	30.4	38.8	30.8	(418)
Low	19.5	38.2	42.3	(581)	15.3	31.4	53.3	(484)
Pessimism								
High	60.3	32.8	6.9	(436)	55.0	29.8	15.2	(198)
Middle	30.9	42.7	26.4	(709)	28.8	37.7	33.5	(539)
Low	11.1	37.1	51.8	(334)	11.0	29.6	59.4	(345)
Political Futility								
High	62.4	31.3	6.3	(447)	61.3	27.4	11.3	(266)
Middle	32.4	44.1	23.5	(549)	26.7	41.2	32.1	(408)
Low	12.8	38.9	48.2	(483)	7.4	30.1	62.5	(408)
Dominance								
High	18.0	37.8	44.3	(551)	7.6	30.6	61.8	(424)
Middle	32.8	44.0	23.2	(457)	31.7	35.2	33.1	(335)
Low	57.3	34.2	8.5	(471)	50.8	35.9	13.3	(323)
Social Responsibility								
High	12.0	40.3	47.6	(382)	5.0	28.7	66.3	(282)
Middle	29.5	44.4	26.1	(583)	21.4	37.8	40.8	(439)
Low	58.6	30.5	10.9	(514)	53.7	32.4	13.9	(361)

[a] Not available for the National Sample.

rage and fear are often unable to separate their internal feelings from objective reality. The storm within boils over and damages the world without. Such persons tend to see events as caught up in the same whirlwind that buffets them. They are inclined to blame their own misfortunes on forces outside themselves, and to wish to punish others for the injuries that have been worked on them. Attributing malevolent intentions to the forces pressing upon them from the outside, they are likely to hate society for what they believe it has done to them. To judge the society as anomic is a way to express anger at it and simultaneously to make it responsible for the wrath one feels within.

Rage can lead to anomy by still another route. Persons high in hostility tend to be judgmental and severe in their attitudes toward others, and deficient in the capacity for sympathetic and trusting responses; their personal relationships are often tense, insecure and unrewarding. Through feedback, the turmoil they stir up around themselves intensifies the needs and feelings that produced the turmoil in the first place. Under these conditions, the uncertainty and instability in one's personal relationships are easily equated with the presumed uncertainties of the larger social order. Such persons perceive the world as uncertain and unreliable—anomic.

Four measures were used to tap various dimensions of generalized aggression. The questionnaires included scales, basically clinical in nature, of Hostility and Paranoia. Two other scales assess the tendency to be judgmental and severe in one's orientation toward others, to be intolerant of their weaknesses, and unforgiving of any trait of behavior that does not seem "strong" or "tough." One of these scales was called "Intolerance of Human Frailty," and the other "Contempt for Weakness." The connections between these four variables and Anomy are presented in Table 7, and in every instance the results support the hypothesis. The two clinical variables, Hostility and Paranoia, show extremely powerful correlations with Anomy. The correlations on the other two are not quite as high, perhaps because they are really projections onto external objects of personal hostility and self-doubt, and there is always some slippage between a genotypic personality state and its manifestation in the social world.

Substantive Beliefs and Opinions

We have now seen that many psychological states, because they impair social interaction, and hence impede perception and learning, indirectly give rise to anomic feelings. A person's substantive views about what the world is like may produce the same results, especially if his values, beliefs about people, and opinions on public questions are so extreme as to be unsettling to others.

Individuals whose beliefs deviate widely from those commonly held are not likely to be wholly accepted into the community, for extreme views typically express, implicity or explicitly, rejection not only of the commonly held beliefs but also of those who hold them. Thus, deviant beliefs constitute

Table 7
Aggression and Anomy

| | (In Percentages) | | | | | | | |
| | National Sample Anomy | | | | Minnesota Sample Anomy | | | |
	High	Middle	Low	(N)	High	Middle	Low	(N)
Hostility								
High	62.0	32.5	5.6	(413)	53.3	33.3	13.4	(246)
Middle	32.9	46.2	20.9	(632)	29.1	38.0	32.9	(495)
Low	12.7	33.2	54.2	(434)	7.9	27.6	64.5	(341)
Paranoia								
High	63.1	32.5	4.4	(567)	56.8	31.2	12.0	(391)
Middle	27.8	48.5	23.7	(443)	19.0	44.1	36.9	(331)
Low	8.1	36.5	55.4	(469)	4.7	26.6	68.7	(361)
Intolerance of Human Frailty								
High	54.3	34.2	11.5	(582)	46.3	34.6	19.1	(272)
Middle	27.2	44.3	28.6	(637)	26.4	36.6	37.0	(546)
Low	11.5	34.2	54.2	(260)	12.1	26.5	61.4	(264)
Contempt for Weakness								
High	56.9	33.6	9.5	(390)	49.5	35.7	14.8	(305)
Middle	32.2	42.0	25.7	(735)	23.9	34.9	41.2	(478)
Low	17.0	36.7	46.3	(354)	12.4	29.4	58.2	(299)

barriers to effective interaction, and therefore to the kind of learning that requires close and repeated association with others.

An individual whose deviant and extreme opinions bar him from full participation in the larger society will very likely be imperfectly aware of what other members of that society believe and value, and he may easily confuse his ignorance of the norms with the conviction that no norms exist. Or, because his own strong beliefs deviate so radically from those held by others, the extreme believer may be inclined to think that other, more moderate persons really have no worthwhile values at all. What appears to the moderate as realistic good sense strikes the extremist as wishy-washy confusion masquerading as moderation.

Finally, our own data show that holding extreme views is associated with various psycho-pathological states, such as intense anxiety, hostility, and inflexibility. Here the extreme substantive views are really expressions— almost symptoms—of the underlying psychological state, and may be functionally important in satisfying the needs of the personality system. Often, these psychological disturbances themselves greatly impede interaction; when the disturbance expresses itself in radically deviant substantive views, the barriers to successful interaction grow even higher. Inability to surmount those barriers produces feelings that the society itself is disordered and confused.

For these reasons, we expected to find the holding of deviant beliefs positively associated with Anomy. A number of scales in our study tapped respondents' commitments to various deviant ideologies and attitudes. Data on these scales are presented in Table 8. The Totalitarianism scale measures the degree to which one is prepared to sacrifice human values to an overriding political objective. The Left Wing and Right Wing scales draw their items directly from the writings produced by political movements of the extreme left and right. The Fascism scale is not the familiar California F Scale, but a measure composed of items drawn mainly from the political texts of Fascism. Our general hypothesis predicts that persons who score high on these scales are likely to be anomic.

The findings in all cases run powerfully in the predicted direction. The high correlations between Anomy and extreme substantive beliefs strengthens our thesis that Anomy reflects a failure of socialization all along the line. Not only does the anomic feel confused and normless, but he also leans toward values and opinions that are rejected in his society. Both the feeling of emptiness and the leaning toward extreme opinions are two aspects of an underlying failure to assimilate the modal values of a society in a balanced, concrete, accurate way.

Table 8
Extreme Beliefs and Anomy

		National Sample Anomy				Minnesota Sample Anomy		
	High	*Middle*	*Low*	*(N)*	*High*	*Middle*	*Low*	*(N)*
Totalitarianism								
High	64.6	30.0	5.4	(500)	47.5	34.2	18.3	(480)
Middle	29.3	28.5	22.2	(559)	15.5	40.2	44.3	(368)
Low	7.6	35.5	56.9	(420)	7.3	22.2	70.5	(234)
Fascist[a]								
Values								
High					58.2	26.8	15.0	(194)
Middle					31.4	39.3	29.3	(417)
Low					12.3	31.4	56.3	(471)
Left Wing								
High	72.7	24.9	2.4	(410)	68.5	24.2	7.3	(232)
Middle	32.8	49.8	17.4	(488)	31.3	44.2	24.5	(310)
Low	10.5	38.7	50.8	(581)	8.5	31.7	59.8	(540)
Right Wing								
High	71.2	26.1	2.7	(490)	69.8	25.9	4.3	(212)
Middle	27.7	51.6	20.7	(560)	30.9	42.8	26.3	(434)
Low	3.5	35.7	60.8	(429)	4.6	28.2	67.2	(436)

(In Percentages)

[a] Not available for the National Sample.

So far, our data have referred to substantive beliefs and opinions about actual objects in the social environment, and about questions concerning the way social, economic, and political affairs are and ought to be handled. We now turn to a different kind of belief, namely, attitudes about people. Certain beliefs about people can have the same negative effects on interaction and learning as the substantive views just discussed. Here we refer to a cluster of attitudes which might for convenience be called misanthropy. Included under this heading are feelings of generalized mistrust and suspiciousness toward people, a readiness to find fault in others and to be harshly judgmental toward them, an unwillingness to extend sympathy, a conviction that if people are having trouble they probably deserve it, and a tendency to reject out of hand and under stereotyped slogans members of groups other than one's own.

The questionnaires contained a number of scales that tap these attitudes. The Calvinism scale, in setting forth the values of the Protestant Ethic,

Table 9
Misanthropy and Anomy

	National Sample Anomy				Minnesota Sample Anomy			
	High	Middle	Low	(N)	High	Middle	Low	(N)
Tolerance								
High	21.6	40.6	37.8	(638)	18.1	32.1	49.8	(414)
Middle	36.0	39.1	24.9	(350)	24.0	31.8	44.2	(267)
Low	51.9	35.4	12.6	(491)	40.7	36.4	22.9	(401)
Faith in People[a]								
High					6.3	29.7	64.0	(300)
Middle					26.0	39.4	34.6	(439)
Low					49.3	29.7	21.0	(343)
Calvinism[b]								
High	46.7	42.3	11.0	(437)				
Middle	35.8	38.7	25.5	(695)				
Low	19.0	33.4	47.6	(347)				
Elitism, Inequalitarianism								
High	50.2	36.4	13.5	(572)	46.4	34.0	19.6	(291)
Middle	32.2	41.7	26.1	(575)	28.6	39.7	31.7	(413)
Low	14.2	36.8	49.1	(332)	13.0	26.7	60.3	(378)
Ethnocentrism								
High	57.5	35.2	7.3	(640)	54.4	34.1	11.5	(261)
Middle	27.4	46.1	26.5	(412)	28.2	39.8	32.0	(462)
Low	8.9	36.3	54.8	(427)	8.4	25.4	66.2	(359)

(In Percentages)

[a] Not available for the National Sample.
[b] Not available for the Minnesota Sample.

measures the tendency toward judgmentalism and severity in one's demands upon others. The other labels, listed in Table 9, adequately convey the attitudes being measured.

The first two scales in Table 9 (Tolerance and Faith in People) measure a receptive orientation toward people, while the other three assess various dimensions of a rejective orientation. The relation between Anomy and each of the scales in both sets runs massively in the predicted direction. Persons who are highly tolerant of others and who have strong faith in the abilities and virtues of their fellow men are much less likely to score high on the Anomy scale than are persons who are not receptively oriented. On the three rejective variables, the direction is reversed: persons who score high on them are much more likely to score high on Anomy as well.

The Question of Spuriousness

To complete our presentation of the data, we must address one final question. Are the reported correlations between various personality states and anomy genuine and autonomous, or are they epiphenomenal, the secondary products of environmental forces that underlie the psychological states?

This is a critical question, for personality and culture are, after all, elaborately intertwined, and the possibility must be faced that we are attributing to the one a power that properly belongs to the other. If, as some students believe, personality expresses the social setting so closely as to be inseparable from it, it obviously cannot play the independent, and often decisive, role we have assigned to it in our explanatory model. That social learning is vital to the formation of personality and that different social settings give rise to different modal personality configurations, can scarcely be doubted.[30] But the matter, so far as it bears on the explanation of anomy, does not end there. For one thing, the social forces that have most to do with fashioning personality (e.g., primary influences in early childhood) are not necessarily the same forces that are alleged to induce anomy (e.g., status frustration, malintegration, conflict between social goals and means, etc.). For another, although persons from the same social settings resemble each other more closely on the average than they resemble persons from other social settings, they nevertheless vary widely in their personality patterns. They also vary in their response to the social norms—a variation that appears to follow closely the variations in their personalities.

We are convinced—and we believe the data will confirm it—that the principal source of anomic feeling resides for some people in their social settings; for others in their individual personalities; and for still others, in a combination of the two. This means that a person can express anomic

---

[30] See, for example, August B. Hollingshead and Frederick C. Redlich, *Social Class and Mental Illness,* New York: Wiley, 1958.

feelings without possessing the personality traits (or alternatively, the social characteristics) that are correlated with anomy. It also means that either of those major determinants may be sufficient to evoke anomic responses, regardless of the contribution of the other. Extremely inflexible persons, for example, are significantly more anomic than flexible persons in every sample (including our elite sample of political influentials), and in every social, economic, or educational setting in which we have compared them. But it also means that someone can possess the "appropriate" personality (or social) characteristic *without* being anomic. In other words, whether the personality genotype gives rise in every individual to identical phenotypic manifestations may in part depend on the environment (which can be taken to include not only the broad social conditions and the immediate life space of the individual, but also the salience of the norms, their clarity, complexity, and accessibility, and so forth). Some social conditions combine with personality to intensify the anomic response, while others combine to diminish it. Thus, the mean Anomy scores of persons with, say, extreme anxiety, will be higher among the poor than among the wealthy, among the uneducated than among the educated, among those in unskilled occupations than among those in the professions.

To satisfy ourselves that the correlations between assorted psychological states and Anomy are genuine, we carried out a number of procedures to control for such variables as education and occupation, both of which correlate significantly and negatively with Anomy (Anomy correlates —.43 with education, —.37 with occupational status). Since the responses to the Anomy items are also affected by acquiescent response set, controls for this factor were also introduced. Limitations of space prohibit a full presentation of these data, but Table 10 illustrates them by showing the effects of occupational status and acquiescence.

The correlations between Anomy and representative personality variables remain strong and significant when these variables are controlled; and the results are essentially the same when these controls are applied to the correlations between Anomy and all the other personality and attitude variables treated in this paper. Similar conclusions emerge when education is controlled.

These tests, however, still leave the possibility that the variations in Anomy were produced, not by a single social factor, but by a combination of several. To explore this possibility, the data were put to the more demanding test of controlling simultaneously for seven of the major sociological variables that were correlated with both Anomy and personality factors.

The national sample of 1484 adults was first broken into two groups: those who scored at the upper end (scores 6–9), and those who scored at the lower end (0–3) of the Anomy scale. Those who fell in the middle range were excluded from this procedure. We then drew randomly from these two groups every person whose particular combination of sociological charac-

Table 10

Mean Scores on Representative Personality Scales for High, Middle, and Low Anomics, with Occupational Status[b] and Acquiescence Controlled[a]

	Dominance	Hostility	Paranoid Tendencies	Intolerance of Ambiguity
High Occupation				
High Anomy	3.3	4.1	4.9	5.7
Middle Anomy	4.4	3.3	3.5	4.6
Low Anomy	5.7	2.2	1.8	3.1
Middle Occupation				
High Anomy	3.1	4.3	5.5	6.2
Middle Anomy	4.0	3.6	3.8	4.7
Low Anomy	4.8	2.3	2.0	3.4
Low Occupation				
High Anomy	2.4	4.3	5.5	6.0
Middle Anomy	3.3	3.3	3.6	4.8
Low Anomy	4.2	2.4	2.2	3.7

	Intolerance of Human Frailty	Rigidity	Responsibility	Sense of Political Futility
High Acquiescence				
High Anomy	5.2	4.0	4.7	4.6
Middle Anomy	4.6	3.5	5.8	3.8
Low Anomy	4.0	3.3	6.0	2.7
Middle Acquiescence				
High Anomy	4.3	3.4	5.6	4.2
Middle Anomy	3.8	2.8	6.5	3.3
Low Anomy	3.4	2.5	6.9	2.4
Low Acquiescence				
High Anomy	4.0	2.7	6.1	3.8
Middle Anomy	3.5	2.8	6.7	2.8
Low Anomy	2.9	2.2	7.4	2.0

[a] National Sample; N = 1484.
[b] The occupational breaks were as follows: High = professional, managerial and upper white collar; Middle = clerical, skilled, and lower white collar; Low = unskilled workers and farmers.

teristics was matched by a person from the other group. Our objective was to identify high and low anomics who possessed the same pattern of sociological characteristics. The seven sociological variables were education, age, size of community, occupational status, race, sex, and region.[31]

[31] Sub-classifications employed within each category were: Education—11th grade and below, 12th grade and above; Age—under 35, 35–54, 55 and over; Size of community—rural, urban; Occupational status—3 levels derived from an index combining occupation and income; Race—white, non-white; Sex—male, female; Region—north, south.

This procedure yielded a total of 275 matched pairs, i.e., 275 high anomics whose individual social characteristics were specifically matched by those of 275 low anomics. The responses of the two groups of matched pairs on all scales in the PAB questionnaire were then compared. The findings for the main personality variables treated in this paper appear in Table 11. For

Table 11
Matched Samples of Anomics and Non-Anomics Compared on Selected Variables[a]

(*In Percentages*)

	Alienation		Contempt for Weakness		Conventionality	
	High	Low	High	Low	High	Low
High Anomy	59	8	39	13	35	24
Low Anomy	8	56	15	31	8	48
	Dominance		Ethnocentrism		Guilt	
	High	Low	High	Low	High	Low
High Anomy	22	51	50	9	52	16
Low Anomy	48	17	13	42	7	64
	Hostility		Human Frailty		Intellectuality	
	High	Low	High	Low	High	Low
High Anomy	47	13	58	7	21	36
Low Anomy	9	46	24	31	46	18
	Intolerance of Ambiguity		Life Satisfaction		Need Inviolacy	
	High	Low	High	Low	High	Low
High Anomy	59	11	17	51	52	20
Low Anomy	23	44	48	22	14	65
	Need Status		Obsessiveness		Paranoid Tendency	
	High	Low	High	Low	High	Low
High Anomy	34	22	53	26	66	9
Low Anomy	9	56	27	45	13	57
	Pessimism-Optimism		Rigidity		Tolerance	
	High	Low	High	Low	High	Low
High Anomy	51	8	59	19	31	46
Low Anomy	11	41	28	44	50	22

[a] The N for each matched sample is 275. Persons who scored in the middle range of either the Anomy scales or the personality scale are omitted from this table. Percentages are computed horizontally and would sum to 100 if the middle group were included. Computing the percentages horizontally rather than vertically—reversing the direction of the computations shown in previous tables—was made necessary by the prohibitive cost of running 18 separate matched sample procedures, one for each of the independent variables. While the present table gives essentially the same results, it unfortunately makes comparison with previous tables difficult. Note that the 0–3 cutting point used here to identify non-anomics differs—for reasons of sample size—from the 0–2 classification used earlier.

the sake of brevity, those who scored at the "middle" level on the personality variables have been omitted from the table.

The overall result is clear: when high and low anomics are simultaneously matched on the seven social characteristics, high anomics continue to differ from low anomics on the same psychological variables we have been analyzing. Furthermore, the differences remain in every instance large enough to leave no doubt that personality factors determine Anomy independently of social influences. A person who scores high on the Anomy scale, for example, is five times as likely to score high on Hostility as his "sociological twin" among the low anomics. The ratio for Guilt is over seven to one, and for Paranoia almost five to one.[32]

These findings confirm the argument we presented at the outset. So powerful, and so clearly independent of social influences, are the correlations between certain personality states and anomy, that they cast much doubt on the adequacy of the standard sociological explanation of anomy.

The standard explanation raises another, related question of spuriousness. Basic to that explanation is the proposition that anomy results from "the conflict between culturally accepted values and the socially structured difficulties in living up to these values. . . ."[33] Our culture, according to Merton, prescribes success as a goal for all Americans, but the social system imposes barriers to the achievement of the goal, so that it is easier for some to follow the prescription than for others. When the social structure bars persons located at certain points within it from moving upward toward the goal of wealth and higher status, the result is "a strain toward . . . normlessness."[34]

This is the theoretical foundation of a large body of writing which has either implicitly assumed or explicitly asserted that persons who have lost out in the race for wealth and status show a high incidence of anomic feelings *because* they have lost the race. In this view, a felt discrepancy between status aspiration and actual achievement is the direct and most basic cause of the anomic mentality. This is probably the most widely accepted generalization in the sociological literature of anomy.

As usually presented, this explanation either ignores personality factors or plays them down. If it mentions them at all, it treats them merely as secondary variables that derive from status frustration or from similar forms of social disjunction. Hence, the observed relation between personality and

---

[32] We are aware that the matched-sample procedure does not include all the possible combinations in the same frequency with which they appear in the population. A sufficient number and variety of combinations are present, however, to warrant confidence in the results. This confidence is increased by the magnitude of the differences between the high and low groups, and by the fact that no matter which of the particular social variables we control, the results are essentially unchanged.

[33] Merton, *op. cit.,* p. 191.

[34] *Ibid.,* p. 163.

anomy is considered by many sociologists to be spurious, a mere artifact of their supposedly common ancestry.

We cannot hope, in a brief discussion, to resolve an issue of such magnitude and complexity. We can, however, present evidence directly relevant to it, based on three scales in our study. One is a scale of "Material Aspirations" which measures the hunger for wealth and for the coveted objects that wealth can purchase. A second, labelled "Aspiration-Ambition," assesses the strength of a person's actual commitment to the values of success and prestige, and his yearning for achievement and reputation. Neither of these measures is significantly correlated with the Anomy scale: the correlation for the first is .07, and for the second, .01.

The third measure, Status Frustration, has already been mentioned (see Table 6), and its correlation with Anomy is a significant .42. This scale, however, differs from the other two precisely in its stronger expression of "frustration"—it expresses envy of those "born into a higher position in life," deference (and resentment) toward those who enjoy good breeding, wealth, better education, or other marks of superiority, and a sense of shame and self-doubt because of low birth or failure to have risen higher. This scale, in short, reflects several of the key emotional elements that we have already shown to be major determinants of anomy. A genuine measure of status frustration, clearly, is bound to be as heavily infused with psychological elements as with sociological ones. It is equally plain that its relation to anomy is weaker than that of many of the personality variables we have considered. Nor is there any evidence that it is a more specific "cause" of anomy than the other factors we have observed.

Suppose, however, that for the moment we consider status frustration as a purely sociological measure and as a decisive influence upon anomy. If we were to remove status frustration from the phenomenal field, would personality continue to exert the influence we have attributed to it? In Table 12 we present the correlations between anomy and selected personality variables before and after status frustration has been partialed out. The zero-order correlations are, to be sure, diminished by this procedure, but so modestly as to have no substantial effect on either their magnitude or their statistical significance. Such reductions as do occur, furthermore, are doubtless related in part to the affective elements that the Status Frustration scale has in common with the personality scales.

Hence we conclude that the psychological variables operate independently. While status frustration is related to anomy, it is only one of many forces capable of producing anomic responses. Not only does it fail to eliminate the correlations between anomy and personality factors, but it may itself be an aspect, or product, of the sense of generalized malaise and dissatisfaction with oneself that is characteristic of the anomic state of mind.

Table 12

Correlations Between Anomy and Selected Personality Variables Before and After the Effects of Status Frustration are Removed

ANOMY	Dominance	Guilt	Hostility	Intolerance of Ambiguity	Intolerance of Human Frailty	Need Inviolacy	Paranoid	Rigidity
Original Zero-Order Correlations	−.47	.59	.53	.51	.45	.56	.66	.41
First-Order Partial Correlations with Status Frustration Held Constant	−.42	.51	.45	.43	.41	.48	.58	.34

Summary and Concluding Remarks

We have attempted in this paper to show that the tendency to perceive the society as normless, morally chaotic, and adrift—in a word, anomic—is governed not only by one's position and role in the society but also, in no small measure, by one's intellectual and personality characteristics. Anomic feelings, we have said, result when socialization and the learning of the norms are impeded. Some impediments to learning are social, but others are personal and psychological. Thus, persons whose cognitive capacity is for some reason deficient are more likely to view the society as disorderly and bewildering, and to deplore the incoherence of its value system. Similarly, persons strongly governed by anxiety, hostility, and other aversive motivational and affective states suffer not only from impaired cognitive functioning but also from a tendency to distort their perceptions of social "reality," to accommodate poorly to social change, complexity, and ambiguity, and—through the projection of their anxieties, fears, and uncertainties—to perceive the world as hostile and anxiety-ridden. These personality dispositions also reduce their chances for effective interaction and communication, hampering further their opportunity to learn the norms and to achieve a more coherent sense of how the society works. A further hindrance to effective interaction and socialization results from the holding of extreme or deviant views.

Contrary to Srole's claim that anomy reflects mental disturbance only when the latter is "severe," and that social dysfunction is the independent variable producing anomy both with and without psychopathology, we found that personality factors are correlated with anomy at all levels of mental disturbance, and that they function independently to produce anomy among people in all educational categories and in all sectors of society.

Although we have focused in this paper on individual and personality factors as determinants of anomy, we have never suggested that sociological factors play no part. We have claimed, rather, that the bulk of writing on anomy to date has, by its almost exclusive focus on sociological variables, failed to take account of the type of influences we have examined here, and by virtue of that failure has also failed to give a correct account of the sociological influences. By forcing all determinants into a single analytic category—by, so to speak, pouring everything into the same container— nothing can be seen clearly. Far from denying the existence of sociological factors, an attempt to assess the contribution of personality to anomy is a necessary step toward clarifying their real significance.

While recognizing that social influences are important in bringing about anomic feelings, we are inclined to question whether the standard explanatory concepts employed so far, such as social dysfunction, malintegration between culturally approved goals and institutionalized means, discrepancy between aspiration and achievement, the limitless nature of the success imperative, or the presumed human need for clear limits, are necessary or sufficient conditions for anomy, or even whether they are the most appropriate concepts for explaining it. Apart from the difficulty of operationalizing these notions, little convincing evidence—in the form of "hard" data—has been presented to show that they play the role commonly attributed to them. We have suggested that an alternative and possibly more useful approach might be to regard anomy as a by-product of the socialization process—as a sign of the failure of socialization and of the means by which socialization is achieved, namely, communication, interaction, and learning—and we have presented data that furnish at least indirect support for this view.

To avert misunderstanding, we also want to point out that we have not directly addressed the substantive question of the alleged anomic condition of modern society. Our society may be more or less anomic than it used to be, or than other, simpler societies are now. About that we know very little. We have suggested that much of the discussion of this topic rests on questionable assumptions and proceeds by dubious methods. Our main concern has been to show that within the same society some people are highly resistant to anomy while others are highly vulnerable, and that one's susceptibility may be determined by personality factors quite apart from the state of the society or one's position in it.

One final observation. In most of the scientific literature, anomy is conceptualized either as a particular kind of response arising from a particular state of society, or as a particular state of society itself. For the most part, we too have treated anomy as a particular moral-psychological state, but we have also intimated that it may not be a specific and isolable condition clearly distinguishable from other moral-psychological states. It may, rather, be one dimension of a many-sided malaise. We found, for example, that persons who score high on the Anomy scale also score high on scales measuring pessimism, bewilderment, alienation, anxiety, hostility, and sense of political futility. High anomics also express extreme attitudes on authoritarianism, totalitarianism, chauvinism, political cynicism, and the like. That these symptoms of distress are so often found together in the same persons suggests that those persons are afflicted by a complex and pervasive malaise.

This is not to say that anomy is identical with any one or all of these other components. Each component was individually defined, tested and validated, and each is conceptually different from the others. What it does suggest is that while it is defensible to approach anomy as a variable in its own right, and while it is possible to distinguish a state of normlessness from other states of moral-psychological disturbance, it may not be defensible to conceptualize anomy as a unique disease that afflicts men in certain kinds of societies. Anomy, in sum, may be only one of many symptoms expressing a negativistic, despairing outlook both on one's own life and on the community in which one lives. Whether these symptoms are reducible to a common core, whether they are mainly symptoms of underlying aversive personality states, or whether they truly reflect the condition of modern society and are themselves the "disease," are among the urgent questions to which future research might usefully be addressed.